# Quantitative Methods for Economics

Peter Holl

PITMAN 150 YEARS

PITMAN PUBLISHING
128 Long Acre, London WC2E 9AN

First published in Great Britain 1987

**British Library Cataloguing in Publication Data**

Holl, Peter
    Quantitative methods for economics.
    1. Economics — Statistical Methods
    I. Title
519.5′02433    HB137

    ISBN 0–273–02539–2

Printed in Great Britain by the Bath Press, Avon

To my parents — in love, honour and affection.

# Contents

# Acknowledgements

The author and publishers would like to thank each of the following listed below for giving permission to use copyright material. In each case the author alone bears responsibility for the analysis and interpretation of the material.

MacMillan Publishing, for material contained in *Strategy Structure and British Enterprise*, by D F Channon
Cambridge University Press for material contained in *Growth Profitability and Valuation* by A Singh and G Whittington
Controller of Her Majesty's Stationery Office for material taken from Family Expenditure Survey, UK National Accounts, Economic Trends, Annual Supplement and Annual Abstract of Statistics.
Times Books Limited, London.
*The Observer*
*The Financial Times*
*The Daily Telegraph*

Considerable effort and time have been spent tracing copyright holders. If any has been inadvertently overlooked the publisher will be pleased to correct this situation at the first available opportunity.

# Preface

This book has been written against the background of teaching introductory statistics over a number of years to students at various institutions in the UK and North America. These students have mainly been first year students taking courses in Economics, Economics and Accounting and Systems Science. Although it has been prepared with first year university students in mind the amount of mathematical background required by the reader is quite minimal and I hope that the resulting intuitive and applied approach followed in the book will make it appealing to the business person and practitioner whose main concern is the use of the methods discussed.

The first few chapters are of a descriptive nature. These are followed by a brief discussion of probability and probability distributions after which the reader is introduced to the main ideas of statistical inference which is at the heart of statistical analysis. Within each chapter sections are numbered consecutively as are tables, diagrams, examples and exercises. Table 4.2 is therefore the second table of Chapter 4 and Figure 5.1 is the first figure of Chapter 5. I have also introduced a distinction between examples and exercises; examples are introduced and worked out fully within each chapter while exercises are given at the end of each chapter for the readers to attempt themselves. As far as possible these examples are based on published data rather than hypothetical data in an attempt to make them more realistic and more meaningful.

Finally, I would like to express my gratitude to various people. To Mike Hauser who edited the manuscript and to Joanna Gomulka who read it through and made various helpful comments. But especially I would like to thank my wife, Jean, who spent many hours typing the manuscript quickly and very efficiently.

Peter Holl

The City University
London
February 1987

# Preface

# 1 Introduction

## 1.1 Theory and evidence

The relationship between theory and evidence is at the centre of any social scientific enquiry. Beginning with a given set of assumptions a theoretical framework is constructed which is then put to the test by relating it to the data available. This general approach is shown in Fig. 1.1. If the theory is not fully supported by the evidence there are various possible causes. The first, illustrated in part (a) of the diagram, involves conflict between theory and evidence caused by faulty data. The solution to the problem in this situation requires the collection of new, accurate data allowing the theory to be tested afresh.

The second possible cause of conflict is that the theory explains part of the data available but not all of it. This is shown in part (b). In this case it is probably necessary to go back to the theoretical framework with a view to refining it and then testing it again to see if its ability to explain the data has improved.

Finally, it may turn out that the theory and the evidence are totally unrelated as shown in part (c) of the diagram. If it is known that the evidence available is accurate the solution in this situation is to go back to the drawing board and construct a new theory based on a fresh set of assumptions.

This interplay between theory and evidence requires the use of various techniques and tools of analysis which collectively are referred to as *Statistical Methods* and it is the introduction and use of these methods which form the basis of this book.

## 1.2 Statistics

While the term Statistical Methods refers specifically to the techniques available for empirical analysis, *Statistics* as a discipline needs to be understood in a broader setting which involves data collection, data processing and the interpretation of results.

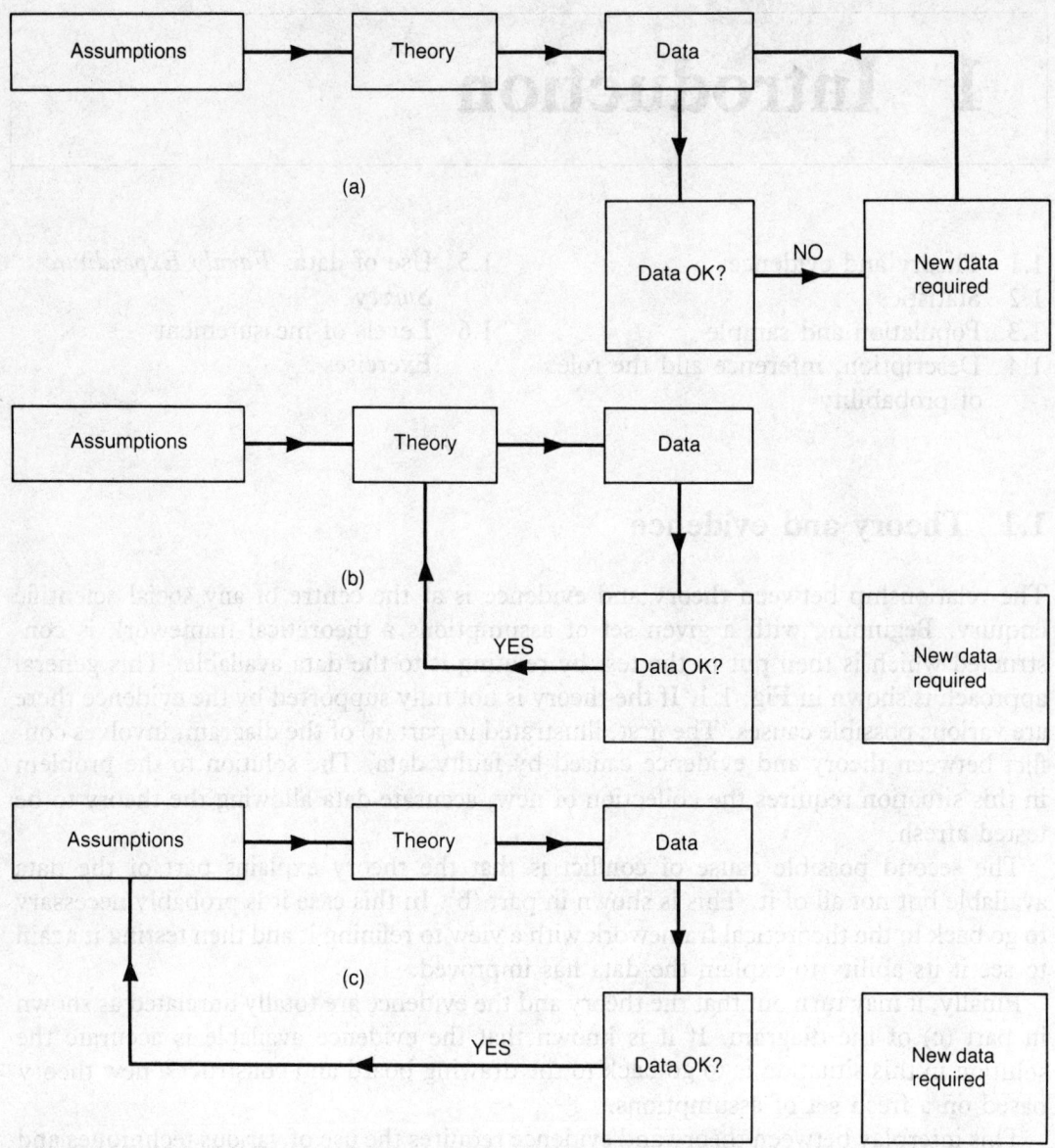

Figure 1.1  Interplay between theory and evidence

## Data collection

At the data collection stage it is necessary to decide which variables are being measured and the units in which measurement is made. For example the variables and units might be:

    *Variables*  income; profits; investment; GNP
    *Units*  households; firms; industry; country

Data therefore might consist of income per household (£), profits per firm (%), investment per industry (£m) or gross national product per country ($00m).

## Data processing

Once data have been collected they need to be processed and it is at this stage that the use of statistical techniques is required. If a large amount of data has been collected, the *preliminary* stage of processing involves standing back from the mass of detail in order to get an overall perspective. To this end the information is often summarised in groups and presented in tabular and graphic form.

The next stage of data processing is the *intermediate* stage where various formulae are introduced in order to provide mathematical descriptions of the data. For example, we may wish to calculate different kinds of average measures of a variable or the degree of association between two variables.

At the *final* stage of processing we attempt to test the statistical reliability of the results obtained. Because the data are non-experimental in nature there are difficulties in testing them and it is necessary to assess the amount of confidence we have in our results.

## Interpretation of results

When assessing the statistical reliability of the results the process of interpretation has already begun, but to the purely mechanical content of the testing procedure we need to add various other considerations which are of a less tangible nature. The quality of any research project cannot rise above the *quality of data* used. Even if the data used are the best available they will nevertheless contain errors to a greater or lesser extent, and in the light of this it may be necessary to adjust the confidence we have in the final conclusions drawn.

Moreover, it is necessary to take into account the effect of *omitted variables*. Because the data used in the social sciences are not generated under laboratory-controlled conditions we cannot easily remove the effects of other variables. At the theory stage we might argue that a variable $Y$ is affected by another variable $X$, assuming that all other variables are held constant. In practice, of course, $Y$ will be affected not only by $X$ but also by other variables as well, and when we come to interpreting the results obtained we need to be confident that the relationship being investigated is in fact that between $Y$ and $X$ rather than a relationship between, say, $Y$ and $Z$.

A further consideration when interpreting results concerns the *assumptions of the technique* used. Each technique and formula is usually based on assumptions governing the nature of information used or the way in which it has been generated. If these assumptions are not valid in any given practical situation the use of a particular technique may produce biased results leading to misleading conclusions.

# 1.3  Population and sample

Statistics as a discipline can be thought of as an area of scientific inquiry whose central concern is the investigation of the properties of populations, and in order to appreciate this approach to the subject it is necessary to define, and discuss the differences between, a sample and a population. A set of observations from a given source is called a *sample* while the source from which it comes is called the *population*. For example, the population might contain all first year university students in the UK and the sample might contain all first year students in a given university.

There are various aspects of this distinction which are important for our purposes. The first concerns accuracy. One way of investigating the properties of a population is to question every member of it. Such an approach, however, is often precluded because it is too expensive in terms of time and money. It is therefore necessary to select a sample which reflects the basic structure of the population as accurately as possible so that by studying the sample we are in fact studying the population in miniature.

The second aspect concerns the definition of a sample which in practice will vary from one situation to the next. Consider Fig. 1.2 which is an extension of the example concerning first year students. The figure shows three groups of observations: group A, group B and group C. If we wish to say something about all first year students in the country we could define group A as the population and group B as the sample. But if we wished to investigate all first year students at a given university we may decide to

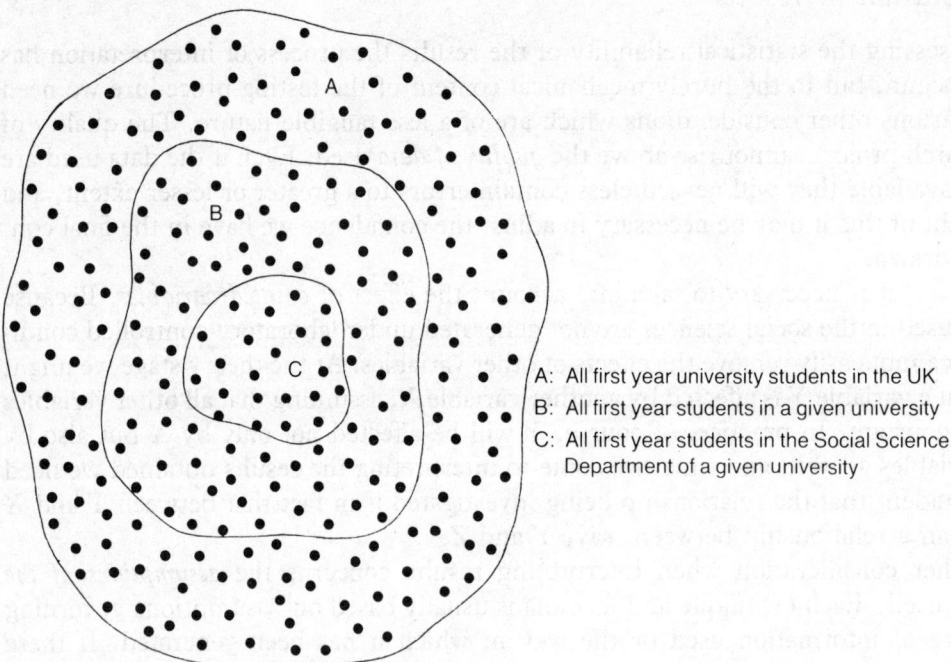

A:  All first year university students in the UK
B:  All first year students in a given university
C:  All first year students in the Social Science
     Department of a given university

Figure 1.2  Sample and population

do so by investigating all first year Social Science students, so that group B now becomes the population and group C the sample. From this example we can see that it is ultimately the questions and issues being investigated which in practice determine whether a given group of obervations form a sample or a population.

The third important aspect concerning the distinction between population and sample is implicit in our previous discussion. In any typical research situation information about the sample will be known while information about the population will be unknown. We might know, for example, that the average height of students in group B in Fig. 1.2 is 1.70 m, but by definition we do not know the average height of students in group A from which group B has been selected. The question that we then have to ask, which is examined in the next section, is this: Given the known information about the sample what can we infer about the population from which the sample comes?

## 1.4  Description, inference and the role of probability

Just as the distinction between sample and population is at the heart of statistical analysis so too is that between description and inference. *Descriptive* statistics are concerned with describing various features of interest of the sample. In the previous section, for example, we saw that the average height of the sample was 1.70 m. We might go further and calculate the ratio of average heights of the tallest 10% and the shortest 10%. In each case we are describing different features of the sample. But if we use this sample information to draw conclusions concerning the population we move into the area of *inferential* statistics.

Describing the features of a sample and making inferences about a population are two distinct and separate processes and some way has to be found whereby they can be linked together. This is done by reference to the theory of *probability* and a brief introduction to this area of analysis follows.

Consider the data given in Table 1.1 showing the result of an opinion poll designed to predict the outcome of the Glasgow Hillhead by-election on Thursday 25 March 1982 when Roy Jenkins the SDP candidate was elected to parliament. According to the poll, 26% of a sample consisting of 943 voters intended voting for the SDP party. From this descriptive measure of the sample we might be tempted to infer that on election day Mr

Table 1.1  Result of Gallup poll for Glasgow Hillhead by-election, 25 March 1982

| | Fieldwork dates | Size of sample | SDP vote (%) |
|---|---|---|---|
| Gallup poll | March 18–22 | 943 | 26 |
| Election figures | | 30 299 | 33 |

Jenkins could have expected 26% of all voters in the constituency to vote for him. In fact on election day he received 33% of the votes. Assuming that the aim of the poll was to predict the outcome of the election, we need to ask why it proved to be inaccurate. There are two possible explanations worth considering.

The first concerns the timing of the poll. The fieldwork for the poll was carried out at least three days before election day. Since the last few days leading up to an election often have a significant effect upon its outcome, it is possible that the difference between the poll result and the election result reflects a change in public opinion during this period.

A second explanation of the difference in the results emerges if we stop to consider the nature of the problem at hand. By using the result provided by the sample to draw a conclusion about a population we are making a generalisation on the basis of limited information. By taking a sample we necessarily exclude much of the information available in the population and this loss of information introduces the possibility of error into the analysis: to a greater or lesser extent the sample may not be an accurate representation of the population. With the possibility of such error we introduce uncertainty into the decision-making process, and we therefore are drawing inferences against a background of uncertainty.

Let us now return to our example. We have seen that there is a difference of seven percentage points between the sample (poll) figure and the population (election) figure, and we need to be able to say whether this difference is more likely to be the result of changed public opinion (in which case we conclude that the poll was an inaccurate measure of voting intentions) or the result of minor errors necessarily associated with the sampling process (in which case we conclude that the poll can be taken as a sufficiently accurate reflection of voting behaviour on election day). It is probability theory which allows us to decide between these two competing explanations, thereby providing the crucial link between statistical description and statistical inference.

## 1.5  Use of data: *Family Expenditure Survey*

For many of the practical examples in this book data have been taken from various government publications, most frequently from the *Family Expenditure Survey (FES)*. In the following description of the main features of *FES*, we will be providing a general background for the examples and we will also take the opportunity to illustrate ways in which errors can arise in the process of data collection.

The routine processing work for the survey is carried out each year by the Department of Employment. At the initial stage of the survey about 11 000 private householders are selected to take part and, where possible, every address is visited. The information collected from each household falls into three groups.

1   General household data such as number of members of household, number of adults and children, age of each person, working status, marriage status, payment of standing orders, rent, etc.

2 Details of income received from employment, social security benefits, amount of tax paid, nature of employment, etc.
3 Information provided by record books kept by each person over 16 years of age in the household. These record books are kept over a two-week period, and each person is asked to keep a daily record of expenditure noting both the amounts and items of expenditure.

The usual response rate is about 65%

The mass of information collected is processed and analysed by computer and a summary of the results is published annually by Her Majesty's Stationery Office (HMSO).

In such a large exercise as this it is inevitable that errors occur. In particular we can expect the presence of *sampling error*. If the sampling exercise were to be repeated with different households, while keeping the same sample size, the results would almost certainly be different. This chance variation from one sample to another is called sampling error and a measure of its extent is provided by a statistic called the *standard error*. In Chapter 7 it will be shown that we can be quite confident that the unknown population value being estimated by the sample will be within a range of values given by twice the standard error either side of the sample value (see Example 1.1).

A further source of error is to be found in the *incorrect recording* of data. Some items of information requested in the survey, such as income received from self-employment and amount of tax paid, are of a sensitive nature and the possibility of wrong information being given cannot be ruled out.

Finally, in any sampling exercise *sampling bias* may be present. Since it is not usually compulsory for individuals to take part in government surveys non response may be quite high and the non respondents cannot be ignored if they display common characteristics. For example, in the *FES* it is known that there is a high degree of non response amongst the self-employed. Although it may not be possible to rectify this source of bias, it is important to realise when interpreting the results obtained that the final sample of respondents fails to adequately reflect the self-employed sector of the population. The sample is therefore said to be a *biased representation* of the overall population.

# Example 1.1 _____

The data below, showing the percentage of 6944 households with certain durable goods, are taken from Table 4, *FES*, 1980.

|  | One car (%) | Telephone (%) |
|---|---|---|
| All households | 45.0 | 71.6 |
| Standard error | 0.6 | 0.5 |

If we are confident that the unknown population value falls within the values given by twice the standard error either side of the sample value, it follows that for all households with:

(a)  one car, the population value is somewhere between the values $45.0 - (2 \times 0.6)$ and $45.0 + (2 \times 0.6)$, i.e. between 43.8% and 46.2%

(b)  telephone, the population value falls between $71.6 - (2 \times 0.5)$ and $71.6 + (2 \times 0.5)$, i.e. between 70.6% and 72.6%

Sometimes the *FES* gives the percentage standard error in place of the standard error, i.e. the standard error expressed as a percentage of the sample statistic. For the information given above we can work out the percentage standard error as follows:

(a)  one car – percentage standard error $= \dfrac{0.6}{45.0} \times 100 = 1.33$

(b)  telephone – percentage standard error $= \dfrac{0.5}{71.6} \times 100 = 0.70$

## 1.6  Levels of measurement

In order to analyse any set of data the information it contains needs to be measurable. There are various ways in which measurement can be performed and the kind of measurement will often determine the nature and extent of quantitative investigation that is possible.

The lowest level of measurement is *nominal* measurement in which observations are classified into convenient and meaningful groups. In Table 1.2 the 256 individuals in the first income group have been arranged according to whether they are male or female, whether adult or child and whether working or not working. Sometimes it is useful to assign numbers to the groups: for example we could give the group of males the number 1 and the group of females the number 2. There would, however, be no mathematical relationship between the numbers chosen, and the application of the four basic arithmetic operations of addition, subtraction, multiplication and division would not apply to the numbers in the context in which they are to be understood.

The next level is *ordinal* measurement. Observations are once again arranged into groups but in such a way that an ordered relationship is established between them. Table 1.2 shows that all individuals have been arranged into groups according to the income of the household to which they belong. Group 1 contains households whose income is amongst the lowest 3% of all household incomes and group 2 contains households whose income falls between the lowest 3% and the lowest 8%. Given this information we can say that any household from group 1 will have an income level less than the income of any household in group 2, but we are unable to say by how much. Also, as with nominal measurement, we are not able to use the four basic arithmetic operations on the data.

The final level of measurement is *interval* measurement. When data are measured in

Table 1.2  Household characteristics and income

|  | Gross normal weekly income of household (£) | |
| --- | --- | --- |
|  | Group 1 | Group 2 |
| Total number of persons | 256 | 606 |
| Male | 77 | 146 |
| Female | 179 | 460 |
| Adults | 238 | 569 |
| Children | 18 | 37 |
| Persons working | 48 | 44 |
| Persons not working | 208 | 562 |
| Average age of head of household | 64 | 69 |

Adapted from Table 6, *FES*, 1980

this way it is possible to indicate not only the direction of differences between observations but also the degree of difference. For example Table 1.2 shows that the average age of the heads of households in groups 1 and 2 is 64 and 69 years respectively, and we can conclude not only that the average for group 2 is higher than for group 1, but also that it is higher by 5 years which is a difference of 7.8%. At this stage of measurement, all four of the basic arithmetic operations can be used.

## Exercises

**1.1**  Combine all three parts of Fig. 1.1 into a single diagram and use it to review your understanding of the interplay between theory and evidence.

**1.2**  The figures below show the percentages of smokers and ex-smokers in samples taken during 1960, 1970 and 1980.

|  | 1960 | 1970 | 1980 |
| --- | --- | --- | --- |
| Smokers | 72 | 63 | 56 |
| Standard error | 2 | 1 | 2 |
| Ex-smokers | 10 | 15 | 20 |
| Standard error | 3 | 2 | 1 |

(a)  If we are confident that the population percentage lies within the values given by twice the standard error either side of the sample percentage, calculate the population percentage for smokers in each of the three years. Do the same for ex-smokers.

(b)  On the basis of these calculations compare the trends in the percentage of smokers and ex-smokers over the entire period. Is there any conflict between the two trends? Discuss.

**1.3**  If we were confident that each of the population percentages in the previous question lies within the values given by *three* times the standard error either side of the sample percentage would your conclusions be affected?

**1.4**  The data below are taken from *FES*, 1980.

| Household group | Number of households | Households with telephone (%) | Standard error |
|---|---|---|---|
| (1)  1 man, 1 woman, non retired | 1376 | 78.4 | 1.1 |
| (2)  1 man, 1 woman, 1 child | 692 | 79.5 | 1.5 |
| (3)  1 man, 1 woman, 3 children | 330 | 75.2 | 2.4 |
| (4)  2 adults, 4 or more children | 122 | 58.2 | 4.5 |

Can you detect any relationship between the number of households in each group and the sizes of the standard error? If so how can you account for it?

**1.5**  The values in the table below have been calculated on the assumption that the population value for each item lies within twice the standard error either side of the sample value. For each item:

(a)  calculate the standard error;

(b)  obtain the sample value for average weekly household expenditure;

(c)  calculate the percentage standard error;

(d)  confirm your answers to (b) and (c) by making reference to *FES*, 1980, p. 30.

| Item | Upper and lower values of average weekly expenditure (£) for population | |
|---|---|---|
| | Lower | Upper |
| Housing | 5.42 | 6.78 |
| Food | 8.54 | 10.10 |
| Clothing and footwear | 1.45 | 2.57 |
| Services | 2.41 | 3.37 |

**1.6** Use the information given below to calculate the standard error for each type of income.

| Source of income | Average weekly household income (£) | Percentage standard error |
|---|---|---|
| Wages and salaries | 104.78 | 1.2 |
| Self-employment | 8.16 | 6.3 |
| Investments | 4.49 | 4.1 |
| Social Security | 17.60 | 1.3 |

*FES*, 1980, Appendix 3

**1.7** Express each of the variables given below in units designed to illustrate any one of the three levels of measurement.
(a) rainfall
(b) marks obtained in an examination
(c) shoe size
(d) intelligence quotient (IQ)
(e) political affiliation
Where possible show how each of these variables can also be expressed in different ways to illustrate two or three levels of measurement.

**1.8** Look through *FES*, 1980 and find at least two examples of variables for each of the different levels of measurement discussed in Section 1.6

# 2 Tables and diagrams

From our discussion of the *Family Expenditure Survey* in the previous chapter it is obvious that processing the data collected is a huge task. In 1980 the response of 67% meant that returns from over 7000 households had to be analysed with much data being provided by each adult member of the household. With such a vast amount of information it would be easy to get lost amidst the detail, and the first stage of data processing is to summarise the data in order to highlight some of its main features. To achieve this end data are often arranged in diagrammatic or tabular form. A variety of methods is available, each closely related to the others but presenting the same data from a different perspective. Some of the most common and useful methods are discussed in this chapter.

## 2.1 Frequency distributions and histograms

One way of presenting data in summary form is to arrange observations into a *frequency distribution*. With such a distribution it is necessary to select convenient class intervals and record the number of observations falling in each class. This can be explained further by considering the data in Table 2.1 showing changes in the *Financial Times* Industrial Index for the first 30 trading days in 1984. For these values we can select equal class intervals of width 10 units beginning at the value $-20$ and ending at the value $+20$. The number of observations for each class interval is recorded in Table 2.2 which presents the frequency distribution of the data contained in Table 2.1. The distribution tells us that there are 3 observations between the values $-20.0$ and $-10.0$, 12 between $-10.0$ and $0.0$, etc.

With the values now organised in a more manageable form certain features of the data are more readily apparent. We can see, for example, that more observations fall in the second class interval than in any other and that a substantial majority of the observations fall between the values $+10$ and $-10$.

When organising the data in this way it is inevitable, and indeed desirable, that some

Table 2.1  Changes in the level of the FT Index
for the first 30 trading days in 1984

| | | | | |
|---|---|---|---|---|
| $-3.9$ | $-6.8$ | $+2.7$ | $+4.4$ | $-16.9$ |
| $-1.5$ | $+6.0$ | $+3.0$ | $-7.3$ | $-15.8$ |
| $+13.3$ | $+12.1$ | $-12.0$ | $-0.8$ | $+5.3$ |
| $+10.7$ | $+5.6$ | $+10.0$ | $-2.2$ | $-3.7$ |
| $+5.7$ | $-6.6$ | $+15.6$ | $-5.1$ | $+4.1$ |
| $-3.2$ | $+14.1$ | $-5.4$ | $+8.3$ | $-2.4$ |

Table 2.2  Frequency distribution of changes in
FT Index (I)

| Class intervals ($X_i$) | Frequency ($f_i$) |
|---|---|
| $-20.0$ up to but less than $-10.0$ | 3 |
| $-10.0$ up to but less than  $0.0$ | 12 |
|   $0.0$ up to but less than   $10.0$ | 9 |
|  $10.0$ up to but less than   $20.0$ | 6 |
| | 30 |

of the original detail is lost. It is also possible to lose either too much detail or too little.
If we lose too little the resulting summary is not sharp enough and if we lose too much
the resulting summary is too vague. For example, if it is felt that more detail is required
than provided in Table 2.2 we could choose intervals 5 units wide instead of 10 units
wide. The result of doing this is shown in Table 2.3. From the new distribution it is
clear that more detail is given but it could be argued that this has resulted in a loss of

Table 2.3  Frequency distribution of changes in
FT Index (II)

| Class intervals ($X_i$) | Frequency ($f_i$) |
|---|---|
| $-20.0$ up to but less than $-15.0$ | 2 |
| $-15.0$ up to but less than $-10.0$ | 1 |
| $-10.0$ up to but less than  $-5.0$ | 4 |
|  $-5.0$ up to but less than   $0.0$ | 8 |
|   $0.0$ up to but less than   $5.0$ | 4 |
|   $5.0$ up to but less than  $10.0$ | 5 |
|  $10.0$ up to but less than  $15.0$ | 5 |
|  $15.0$ up to but less than  $20.0$ | 1 |
| | 30 |

clarity. In Table 2.2 the frequencies show a clear pattern, rising to a peak and then consistently declining. On the other hand no such pattern is discernible in Table 2.3 making it less easy to interpret the general behaviour of changes in the FT Index.

A frequency distribution can also be presented in graphic form. If we plot the variable $X_i$ along the horizontal axis and the frequency $f_i$ vertically, the resulting diagram, as shown in Fig. 2.1 for the frequency distribution in Table 2.2, is called a *histogram*. The area of the histogram consists of the sum of the areas of each of the four rectangles and the area of each rectangle is the product of its height and width. Since the width of the class intervals is fixed, the frequencies are proportional to the areas of the rectangles and can be represented directly on the vertical axis.

From the histogram we can also obtain the *frequency polygon* shown in Fig. 2.2. This can be obtained by drawing straight lines joining in series the midpoints of the tops of each rectangle. The midpoints of the first and last rectangles are joined to the horizontal axis as shown which ensures that the area contained in the frequency polygon equals the area of the histogram (see Exercise 2.2).

In Table 2.2 the class intervals are constant in width. In many situations, however, we have to deal with class intervals that are not constant in width and this makes the drawing of the histogram less straight forward. Suppose we had arranged the data in Table 2.1 into a distribution with unequal intervals as shown in Table 2.4. A comparison of Tables 2.2 and 2.4 shows that the only difference between the two distributions is that the last class in the former has been divided into two smaller classes in the latter. If now

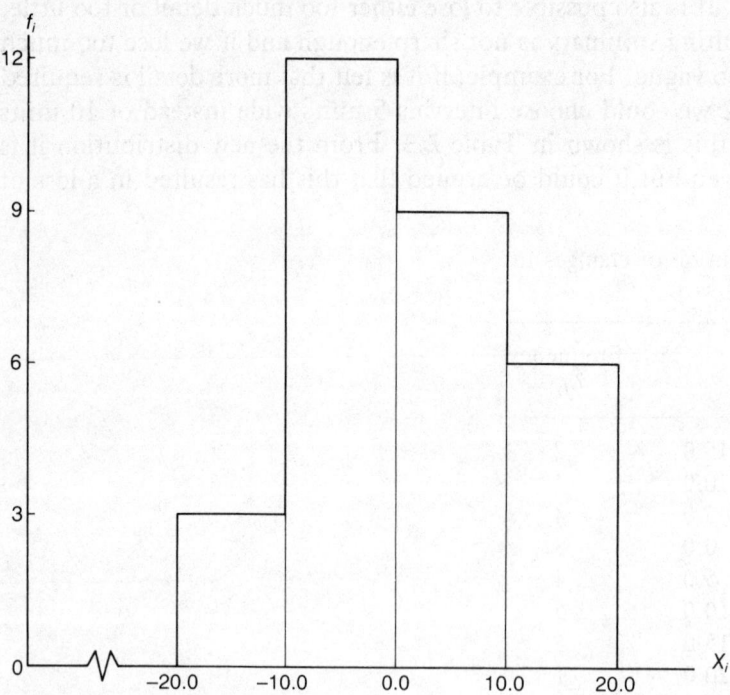

Figure 2.1   Histogram of changes in FT Index

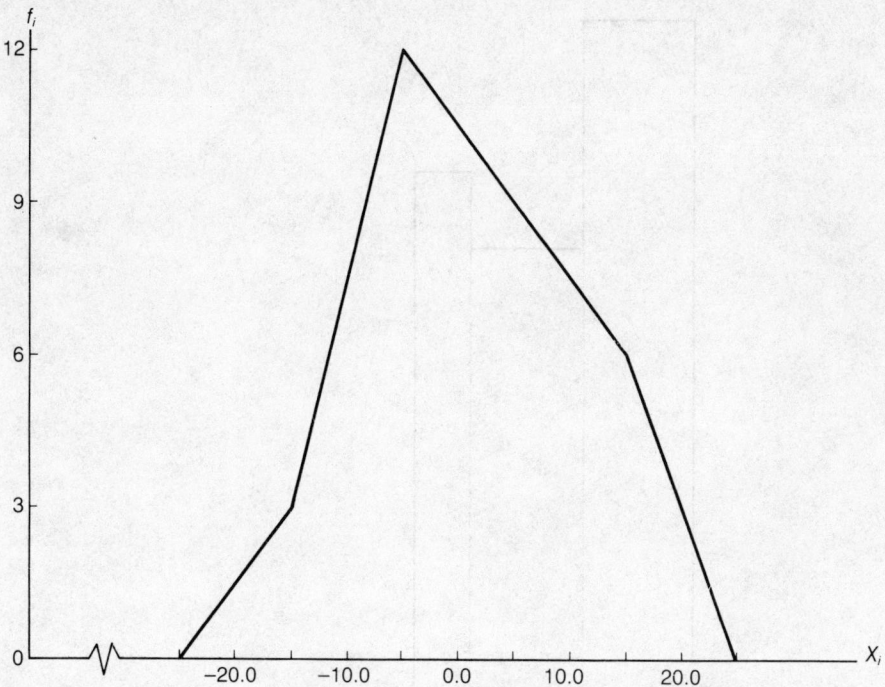

Figure 2.2   Frequency polygon of changes in FT Index

we draw the histogram for Table 2.4 in the manner previously described with frequencies measured on the vertical axis the result will be markedly different from Fig. 2.1 (see Exercise 2.10). This is so because the combined area of the last two classes in the new histogram is only half the area of the last class in Fig. 2.1. In order to accurately draw the histogram in this situation we need to adjust the frequencies to take into account the differing class intervals.

This is done by expressing the frequencies in proportion to the area of each rectangle rather than to the height as before. This is shown in Table 2.4. The last column gives the *frequency density*, calculated by dividing the frequency by the width of the class interval.

Table 2.4   Frequency distribution of changes in FT Index (III)

| Class intervals $(X_i)$ | | Frequency $(f_i)$ | Class width | Frequency density |
|---|---|---|---|---|
| −20.0 up to but less than | −10.0 | 3 | 10 | 0.3 |
| −10.0 up to but less than | 0.0 | 12 | 10 | 1.2 |
| 0.0 up to but less than | 10.0 | 9 | 10 | 0.9 |
| 10.0 up to but less than | 15.0 | 5 | 5 | 1.0 |
| 15.0 up to but less than | 20.0 | 1 | 5 | 0.2 |

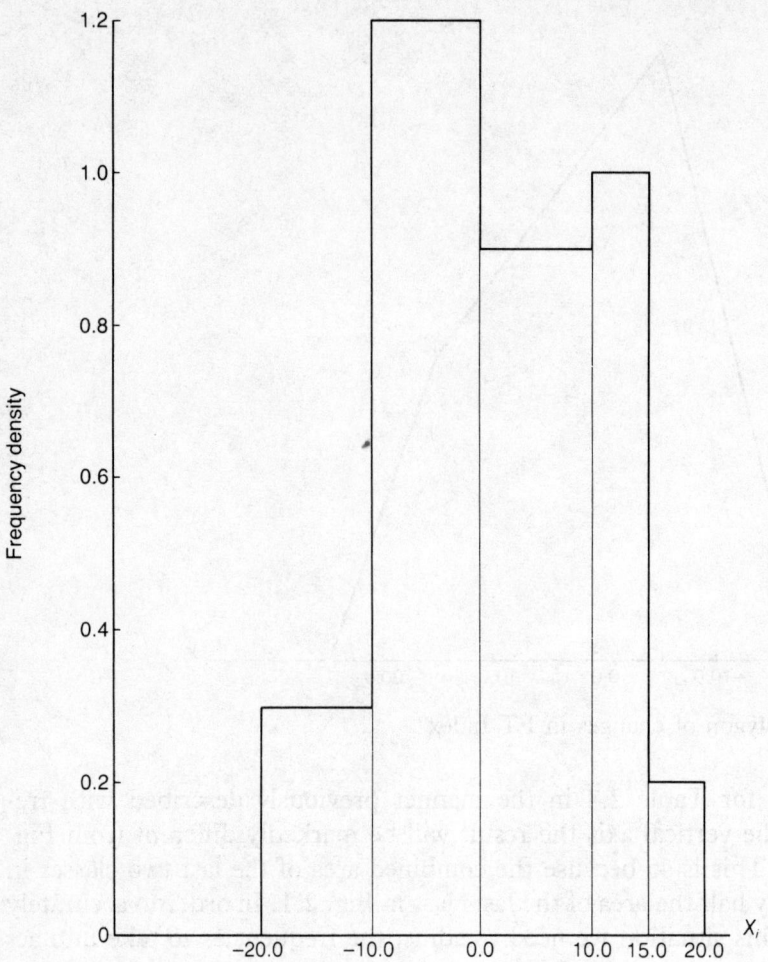

Figure 2.3  Correctly drawn histogram for Table 2.4

The histogram can now be drawn by plotting frequency density vertically against the unequal class intervals plotted horizontally. The histogram for the distribution given in Table 2.4 is shown in Fig. 2.3.

Note that when class intervals are constant the frequency is proportional to both the height and the area of each rectangle of the histogram and the frequencies therefore do not have to be adjusted (see Exercise 2.11).

## 2.2  Cumulative distributions and ogives

A frequency distribution shows how many observations there are in each of a number of class intervals. From here we may wish to proceed further and ask how many of the observations in the distribution are more than or less than a given value for the variable

*X*. We can answer these questions by obtaining a *cumulative frequency distribution* from the original frequency distribution and presenting the results in a diagram called an *ogive*.

Table 2.5 contains the frequency distribution of the size of 92 large British manufacturing enterprises. Size is measured in terms of the total sales of each firm, the original data being given in Exercise 2.3.

We may first wish to consider how many companies in the distribution are less than a certain size. For this we require a cumulative frequency distribution in which, beginning at the top of the frequency column and moving downwards, we add the number of observations in each class to the combined sums of the observations in all previous classes. This is shown in the third column of the table which shows that 74 of the 92 companies in the sample are less than £300m in size and 89 are less than £600m in size. The first value in the cumulated column is 23 and the final value must be equal to the total frequency of 92.

The fourth column in the table shows the upper value of each class interval corresponding to each value in the cumulative frequency column.

Columns 3 and 4 together constitute the cumulative frequency distribution where the cumulation begins at the top and ends at the bottom. If we now plot the cumulative frequencies ($Y1$) on the vertical axis against the upper values of the class intervals ($X1$) on the horizontal axis the resulting diagram is called an ogive. This is shown in Fig. 2.4 which tells us how many firms are less than the values of each upper class limit. This of course is obvious from inspection of the table but it is not obvious from the table how many firms are less than a given size when that size is different from the upper value of any of the class intervals.

To solve this problem we need to be able to interpolate the values of the cumulative

Table 2.5   Cumulative frequency distributions of size of 92 large British manufacturing enterprises (£m), 1969–70

| Class interval—£m ($X_i$) | Frequency ($f_i$) | Cumulative frequency ($Y1$) | Upper class limit ($X1$) | Cumulative frequency ($Y2$) | Lower class limit ($X2$) |
|---|---|---|---|---|---|
| 0–100 | 23 | 23 | 100 | 92 | 0 |
| 100–200 | 38 | 61 | 200 | 69 | 100 |
| 200–300 | 13 | 74 | 300 | 31 | 200 |
| 300–400 | 7 | 81 | 400 | 18 | 300 |
| 400–500 | 5 | 86 | 500 | 11 | 400 |
| 500–600 | 3 | 89 | 600 | 6 | 500 |
| 600–700 | 1 | 90 | 700 | 3 | 600 |
| 700–800 | 0 | 90 | 800 | 2 | 700 |
| 800–900 | 1 | 91 | 900 | 2 | 800 |
| 900–1000 | 1 | 92 | 1000 | 1 | 900 |

frequency distribution between class intervals. This can be done with the ogive. If we draw a vertical line through the value $X1 = 260$, it crosses the ogive at the point where $Y1 = 69$ which shows that 69 of the 92 companies are less than £260m in size.

Notice also that each value on the axis $Y1$ can be expressed as a percentage of the total number of observations in the sample. This is shown on the vertical axis at the right of the diagram. From this axis we can see that the 69 firms less than £260m in size represent 75% of the entire sample.

The part of Fig. 2.4 on this page shows the number of firms less than a given size and is therefore referred to as a 'less than' ogive. In a similar way we can construct a 'more than' ogive showing the number of firms more than a given size. In this case we construct a cumulative frequency distribution where the cumulation of the frequencies begins at the bottom and ends at the top. The values obtained are shown in columns 5 and 6 of Table 2.5. The resulting ogive therefore contains values of $Y2$ on the vertical axis and $X2$ on the horizontal axis as shown in the part of Fig. 2.4 on p. 19. From the diagram we see that only 3 firms are greater than £600m in size and that 54 firms are greater than £150m in size.

Finally, notice that since we are dealing with the same information in both cases the

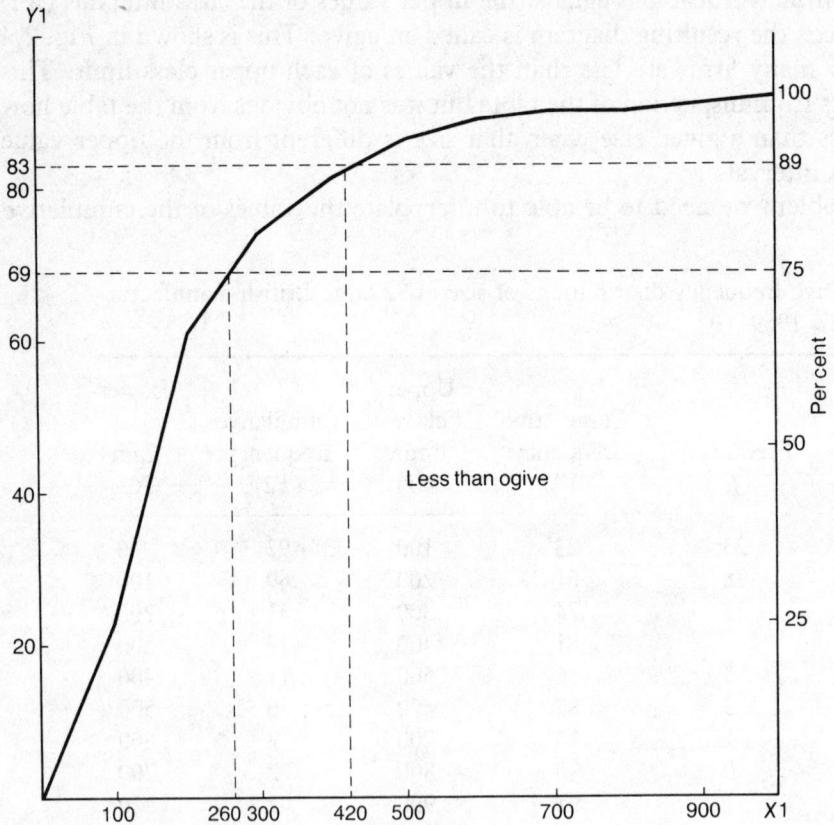

Figure 2.4  Ogives for size of 92 large British manufacturing enterprises (£m), 1969–70

two types of ogives are closely related. Each is in fact a reflection of the other. It is apparent that if, say, 23 out of 92 firms are less than, or equal to £100m in size, the remaining 69 must be bigger. This close relationship can be seen in the diagrams by considering $X1 = X2 = 420$. It can be seen that approximately 83 firms (89% of the total) are smaller than this value while the remaining 9 (11% of the total) are bigger.

## 2.3   Scatter diagrams

At the heart of most empirical research is the investigation of relationships between and amongst variables. The simplest such relationship is that between two variables $X$ and $Y$. For example $X$ might be the incidence of smoking and $Y$ the incidence of lung cancer. Or, $X$ might be the level of economic development and $Y$ the standard of medicine. If data are available for the two variables concerned, we can get an initial indication of the presence of a relationship by presenting them in a *scatter diagram*.

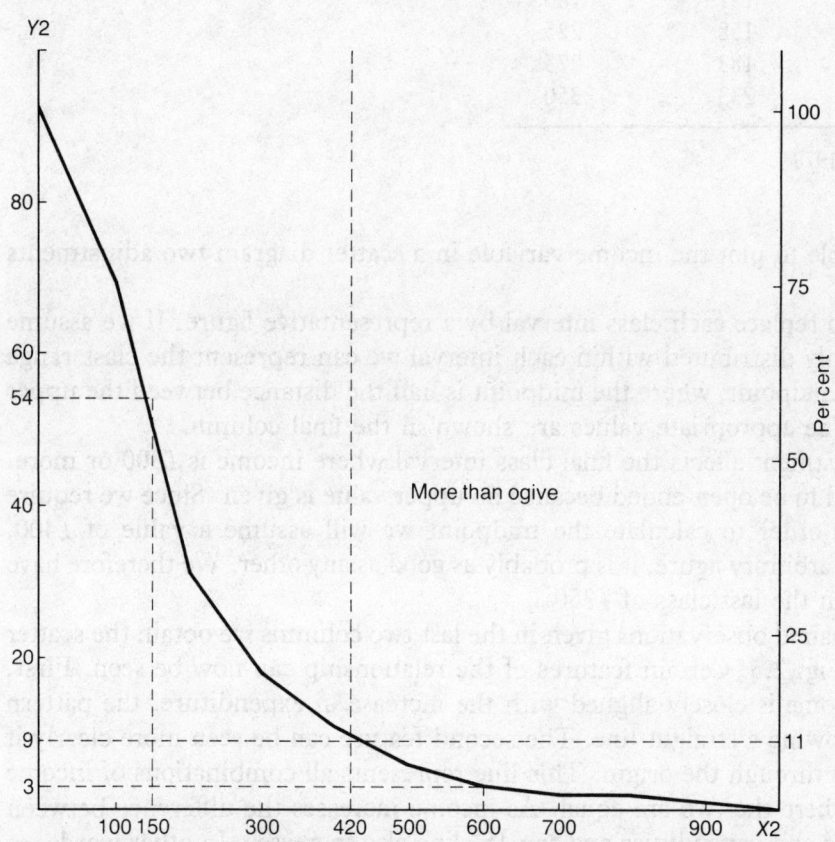

Figure 2.4   *Continued*

In economic theory there is good reason to believe that people's weekly expenditure is closely related to their weekly income. We can begin to investigate this suggestion by taking data from the *Family Expenditure Survey*. The relevant data for households are reproduced in Table 2.6 where the total expenditure figure has been rounded to the nearest whole number.

Table 2.6  Weekly income and expenditure of households

| Gross normal weekly income (£ per week) | Total expenditure (£ per week) | Midpoint of income |
|---|---|---|
| Under 40 | 33 | 20 |
| 40 and under  60 | 53 | 50 |
| 60 and under  80 | 70 | 70 |
| 80 and under 120 | 90 | 100 |
| 120 and under 160 | 110 | 140 |
| 160 and under 200 | 131 | 180 |
| 200 and under 250 | 158 | 225 |
| 250 and under 300 | 183 | 275 |
| Over 300 | 233 | 350 |

Compiled from *FES*, 1978

In order to be able to plot the income variable in a scatter diagram two adjustments are required.

First, we need to replace each class interval by a representative figure. If we assume that income is evenly distributed within each interval we can represent the class range in each case by its midpoint, where the midpoint is half the distance between the upper and lower limit. The appropriate values are shown in the final column.

The second adjustment affects the final class interval where income is £300 or more. This interval is said to be open-ended because no upper value is given. Since we require an upper value in order to calculate the midpoint we will assume a value of £400. Although this is an arbitrary figure, it is probably as good as any other. We therefore have a midpoint value in the last class of £350.

By plotting the paired observations given in the last two columns we obtain the scatter diagram given in Fig. 2.5. Certain features of the relationship can now be seen. First, the increase in income is closely aligned with the increase in expenditure, the pattern approximately following a straight line. The second feature can be seen more clearly if we draw a 45° line through the origin. This line represents all combinations of income and expenditure where the two are equal. As income increases the difference between the trend in income and expenditure and the 45° line also increases. In other words, as

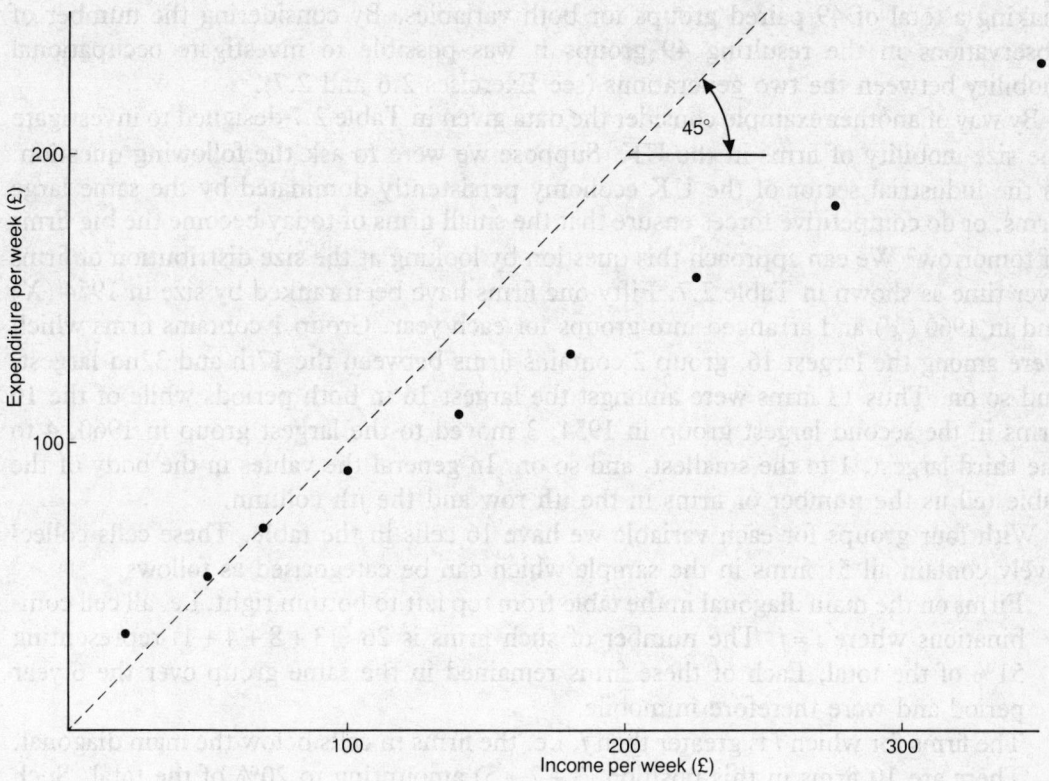

Figure 2.5   Scatter diagram of expenditure and income

income increases the proportion of income devoted to expenditure decreases. Although we are not yet able to quantify these two features their presence has been brought to light by a simple scatter diagram.

## 2.4   Two-way tables of classification

We have seen that a frequency distribution shows the number of observations in each class interval for a given variable $X$. We now go on to consider *two-way tables of classification* which show the number of observations there are jointly in each pair of class intervals for two variables $X$ and $Y$. Such tables are also called *joint frequency distributions*.

An example of a two-way table of classification can be found in Chapter 2 of *Social Mobility* by A. Heath (Fontana, 1981). In the early 1970s each respondent in a sample of 10 000 males was asked to record his own occupation $(X)$ and that of his father $(Y)$. For each variable the occupations given were classified into seven separate groups making a total of 49 paired groups for both variables. By considering the number of observations in the resulting 49 groups it was possible to investigate occupational mobility between the two generations (see Exercises 2.6 and 2.7).

By way of another example consider the data given in Table 2.7 designed to investigate the size mobility of firms in the UK. Suppose we were to ask the following question: Is the industrial sector of the UK economy persistently dominated by the same large firms, or do competitive forces ensure that the small firms of today become the big firms of tomorrow? We can approach this question by looking at the size distribution of firms over time as shown in Table 2.7. Fifty-one firms have been ranked by size in 1954 ($X$) and in 1960 ($Y$) and arranged into groups for each year. Group 1 contains firms which were among the largest 16, group 2 contains firms between the 17th and 32nd largest, and so on. Thus 13 firms were amongst the largest 16 in both periods while of the 16 firms in the second largest group in 1954, 3 moved to the largest group in 1960, 4 to the third largest, 1 to the smallest, and so on. In general the values in the body of the table tell us the number of firms in the $i$th row and the $j$th column.

With four groups for each variable we have 16 cells in the table. These cells collectively contain all 51 firms in the sample which can be categorised as follows.

1  Firms on the main diagonal in the table from top left to bottom right, i.e. all cell combinations where $i = j$. The number of such firms is 26 $(13 + 8 + 4 + 1)$ representing 51% of the total. Each of these firms remained in the same group over the 6-year period and were therefore immobile.

2  The firms for which $i$ is greater than $j$, i.e. the firms in cells below the main diagonal. There are 10 firms in this position $(3 + 2 + 5)$ amounting to 20% of the total. Such firms are mobile upwards, i.e. they become relatively bigger over time.

3  The firms for which $i$ is less than $j$, i.e. firms above the main diagonal. The remaining 15 firms (29% of the total) are in this position. These firms are mobile downwards,

Table 2.7 Two-way table of classification of 51 large companies by size in 1954 and 1960

| Rank in 1954 ($X$) \ Rank in 1960($Y$) | 1–16 | 17–32 | 33–48 | 49–60 | Total |
|---|---|---|---|---|---|
| 1–16 | 13 | 3 | 0 | 0 | 16 |
| 17–32 | 3 | 8 | 4 | 1 | 16 |
| 33–48 | 0 | 2 | 4 | 7 | 13 |
| 49–60 | 0 | 0 | 5 | 1 | 6 |
| Total | 16 | 13 | 13 | 9 | 51 |

Compiled from *Growth, Profitability and Valuation* by A. Singh and G. Whittington (C.U.P., 1968)

becoming relatively smaller over time. Thus, about half of the sample are immobile, while the other half are mobile in either direction.

## 2.5 Relationships involving frequency distributions, scatter diagrams and two-way tables

So far we have introduced different kinds of tables and diagrams in order to present data in summary form. We have introduced each in turn and in isolation from the rest, but in this section we will see that they are very closely related and that by investigating a

Table 2.8   Exam and coursework marks for a sample of 60 students

| Exam mark | Coursework mark | Exam mark | Coursework mark |
| --- | --- | --- | --- |
| 31 | 38 | 30 | 32 |
| 38 | 45 | 60 | 50 |
| 41 | 52 | 50 | 54 |
| 61 | 71 | 72 | 74 |
| 52 | 52 | 61 | 54 |
| 57 | 57 | 78 | 70 |
| 52 | 78 | 52 | 59 |
| 61 | 65 | 78 | 62 |
| 53 | 58 | 36 | 34 |
| 60 | 64 | 57 | 58 |
| 55 | 51 | 79 | 69 |
| 76 | 70 | 52 | 47 |
| 44 | 54 | 62 | 50 |
| 64 | 74 | 69 | 66 |
| 56 | 68 | 42 | 31 |
| 66 | 67 | 64 | 61 |
| 46 | 48 | 62 | 59 |
| 58 | 52 | 54 | 47 |
| 59 | 64 | 78 | 64 |
| 58 | 52 | 48 | 32 |
| 49 | 58 | 63 | 66 |
| 68 | 56 | 78 | 55 |
| 54 | 61 | 56 | 47 |
| 78 | 63 | 67 | 58 |
| 54 | 62 | 47 | 53 |
| 52 | 54 | 65 | 54 |
| 55 | 58 | 57 | 42 |
| 79 | 72 | 65 | 52 |
| 56 | 59 | 58 | 51 |
| 72 | 78 | 66 | 48 |

data set using different tables and diagrams simultaneously we get various insights which no single approach could provide. To illustrate this we will use the data given in Table 2.8 showing the coursework and exam marks for a group of 60 students.

Our first task is to obtain the frequency distributions for exam and coursework marks. Using class intervals of 30–40, 40–50, ..., 70–80 we obtain the distributions given in Table 2.9 and the histograms in Fig. 2.6. From these we can obtain a cumulative frequency distribution and an ogive, and this is left as an exercise for the reader (see Exercise 2.12). Using the same class intervals the data can also be arranged into the two-way table given in Table 2.10. Finally they can be presented in a scatter diagram as shown in Fig. 2.7.

From the frequency distributions we can see that the general distribution of exam marks is very similar to the distribution of coursework marks, with a tendency for more students to get exam marks 60 or above compared with coursework marks. Moreover, from Table 2.10 we see that 47% of the sample (i.e. the 28 observations falling on the main diagonal from top left to bottom right) fall in the same class range for both coursework and exam. Of the remainder, 20% (those in cells above the main diagonal)

Table 2.9 Frequency distributions of exam and course-work marks for sample of 60 students

| Mark ($X_i$) | Frequency (exam) | Frequency (coursework) |
|---|---|---|
| 30 up to but less than 40 | 4 | 5 |
| 40 up to but less than 50 | 7 | 7 |
| 50 up to but less than 60 | 22 | 26 |
| 60 up to but less than 70 | 17 | 14 |
| 70 up to but less than 80 | 10 | 8 |
| | 60 | 60 |

Table 2.10 Two-way classification of exam and coursework marks for sample of 60 students

| Exam \ Coursework | 30–40 | 40–50 | 50–60 | 60–70 | 70–80 | Total |
|---|---|---|---|---|---|---|
| 30–40 | 3 | 1 | 0 | 0 | 0 | 4 |
| 40–50 | 2 | 1 | 4 | 0 | 0 | 7 |
| 50–60 | 0 | 4 | 13 | 4 | 1 | 22 |
| 60–70 | 0 | 1 | 8 | 6 | 2 | 17 |
| 70–80 | 0 | 0 | 1 | 4 | 5 | 10 |
| Total | 5 | 7 | 26 | 14 | 8 | 60 |

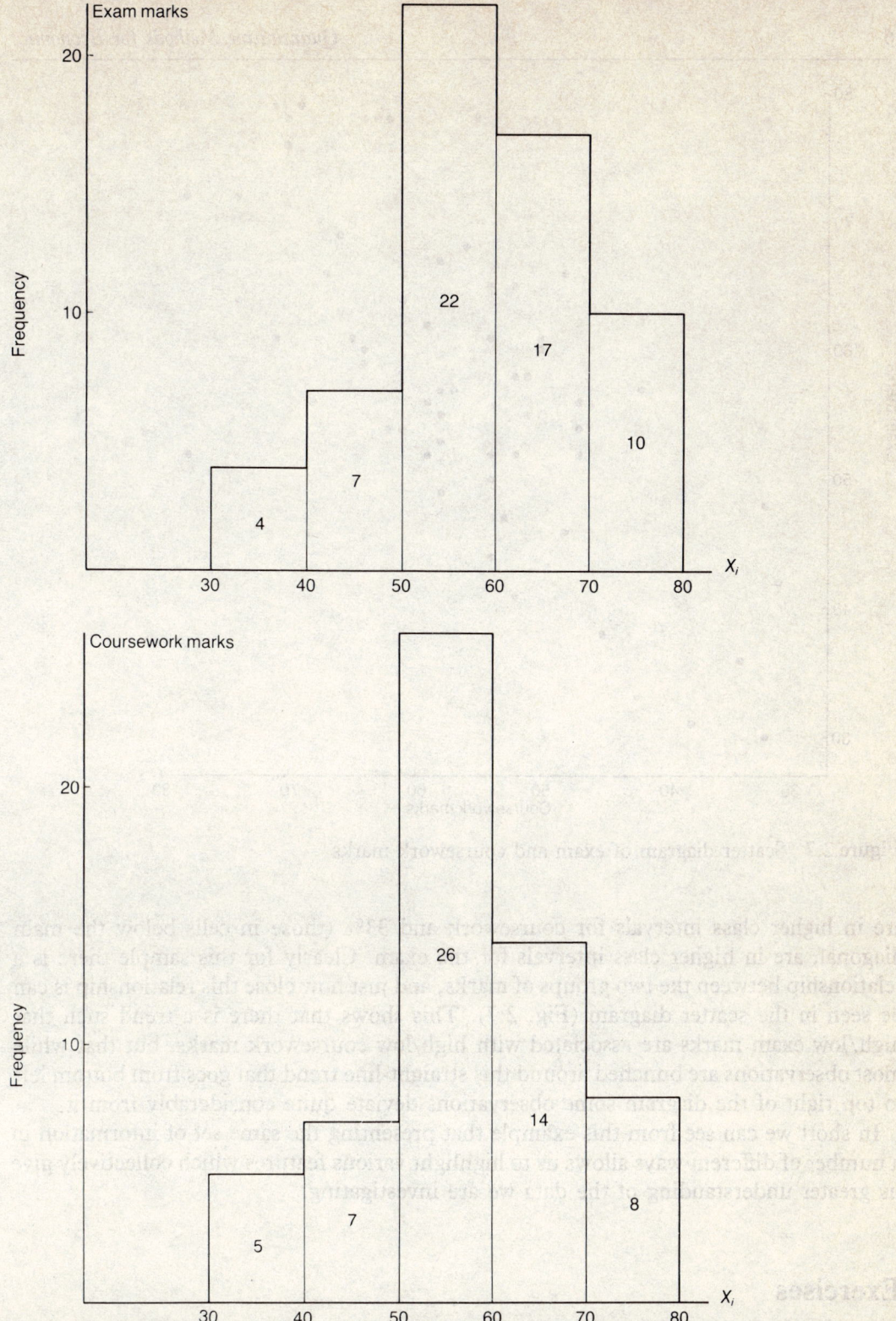

Figure 2.6  Histograms of exam and coursework marks of sample of 60 students

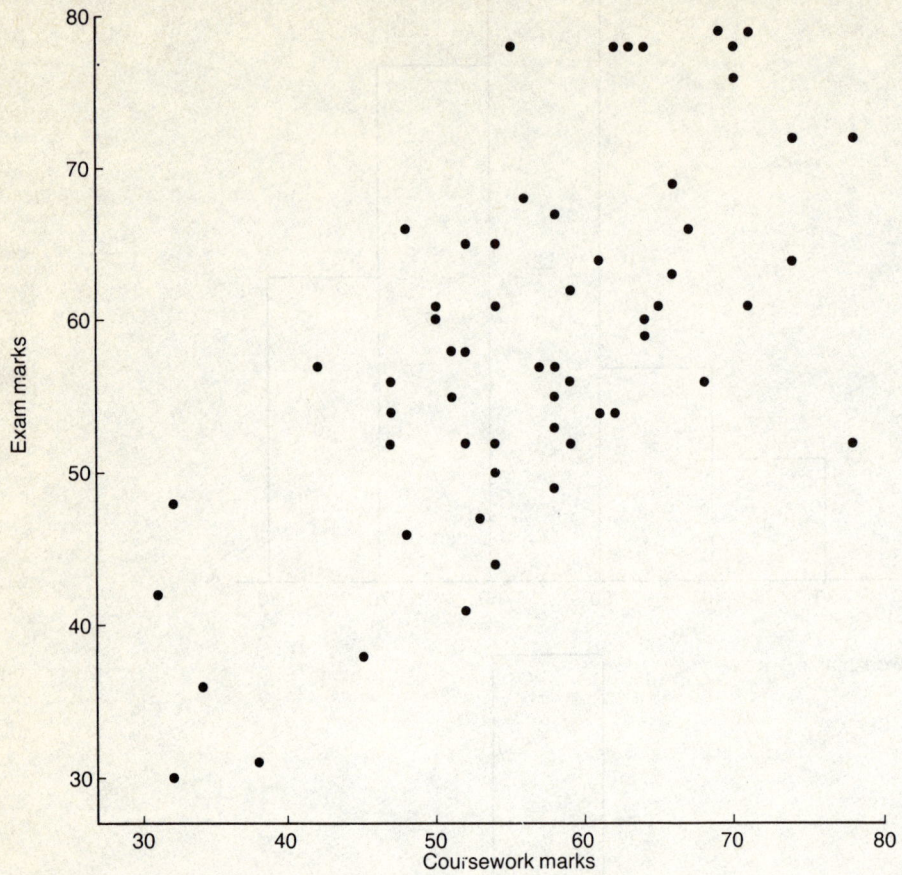

Figure 2.7   Scatter diagram of exam and coursework marks

are in higher class intervals for coursework and 33% (those in cells below the main diagonal, are in higher class intervals for the exam. Clearly for this sample there is a relationship between the two groups of marks, and just how close this relationship is can be seen in the scatter diagram (Fig. 2.7). This shows that there is a trend such that high/low exam marks are associated with high/low coursework marks, but that while most observations are bunched around this straight-line trend that goes from bottom left to top right of the diagram some observations deviate quite considerably from it.

In short we can see from this example that presenting the same set of information in a number of different ways allows us to highlight various features which collectively give us greater understanding of the data we are investigating.

## Exercises

**2.1**   The data below show changes in the level of the FT Index for 90 days from the beginning of March 1984.

| +0.7 | +6.7 | −0.8 | +6.7 | +4.2 | −6.2 |
|------|------|------|------|------|------|
| +8.5 | −4.0 | +12.8 | +7.3 | −5.1 | −11.6 |
| +10.6 | +0.4 | −14.2 | +2.3 | +6.7 | −1.4 |
| −6.3 | −18.3 | −7.7 | +11.8 | +11.0 | +9.2 |
| +9.0 | −0.4 | −18.6 | +4.7 | +18.7 | −1.6 |
| −6.2 | +5.4 | −11.0 | +22.3 | −11.2 | +1.8 |
| +2.3 | +11.0 | −10.9 | −1.1 | +14.5 | +11.4 |
| +3.2 | −17.3 | −0.4 | +0.2 | +3.8 | +7.5 |
| +3.2 | +4.2 | +4.3 | +8.5 | −11.4 | +2.5 |
| +20.9 | −7.4 | −4.5 | −11.9 | +1.5 | +6.6 |
| −0.4 | +1.0 | −0.7 | +19.2 | −1.9 | −20.0 |
| −3.2 | +12.3 | −5.1 | −5.8 | −14.6 | +4.6 |
| +6.4 | −9.1 | +11.5 | +9.1 | +0.2 | +8.8 |
| −13.3 | +10.8 | −20.9 | −8.0 | +6.6 | −8.6 |
| −1.8 | +4.2 | +8.2 | −7.5 | −4.8 | −3.8 |

(a)  Using class intervals 10 units wide as in Table 2.2 obtain the frequency distribution and draw the resulting histogram.

(b)  Do you think that an alternative choice of intervals is preferable for these figures? Give reasons for your answer.

**2.2**  Draw the histogram in Fig. 2.1 and the frequency polygon in Fig. 2.2 as one combined figure. Hence show that the areas under both are equal.

**2.3**  For the data given below construct a frequency distribution with unequal class intervals. Draw the resulting histogram:

(a)  before adjusting for unequal class intervals;

(b)  after adjusting for unequal class intervals.

Compare and discuss your results.

Sales of 92 of the largest British manufacturing enterprises (£m), 1969–70

| 64 | 132 | 115 | 100 | 144 | 67 | 145 | 404 |
|-----|-----|-----|-----|-----|-----|-----|-----|
| 148 | 98 | 126 | 315 | 115 | 382 | 163 | 117 |
| 174 | 133 | 113 | 228 | 83 | 447 | 243 | 563 |
| 184 | 970 | 165 | 488 | 299 | 86 | 204 | 69 |
| 68 | 125 | 346 | 503 | 209 | 262 | 72 | 155 |
| 97 | 76 | 359 | 174 | 301 | 121 | 161 | 495 |
| 82 | 161 | 140 | 75 | 338 | 113 | 71 | 113 |
| 104 | 78 | 512 | 402 | 75 | 294 | 166 | 90 |
| 72 | 172 | 251 | 67 | 176 | 898 | 179 | 152 |
| 84 | 267 | 69 | 268 | 627 | 152 | 76 | 268 |
| 124 | 194 | 314 | 116 | 156 | 95 | 237 | 157 |
| 177 | 92 | 107 | 190 | | | | |

Channon D. F., *Strategy and Structure of British Enterprise*, Macmillan, 1973, pp 52–63

**2.4**  Six companies have been omitted from the sample of firms given in the last question. The values of sales for these firms in 1969–70 were 1467, 1120, 2243, 2352, 1145 and 1355. Construct a frequency distribution with unequal class intervals for all 98 firms. Compare the resulting distribution with the one obtained in the previous exercise. Comment.

**2.5**  The data below show weekly income and percentage of households in each group owning each of a number of durable goods. For each durable good:
(a)  Draw the scatter diagram between the durable good and income;
(b)  Investigate the visual presentation in the scatter diagram to see whether it is an accurate picture of the actual relation;
(c)  If the actual scatter diagram is more non-linear than linear, draw a rough sketch to indicate the nature of non-linearity present.

| Gross normal weekly income (£) | Households (%) with | | |
|---|---|---|---|
| | One car | Refrigerator | Telephone |
| Under 30 | 10.6 | 74.9 | 31.3 |
| 30 and under 40 | 3.6 | 81.2 | 38.6 |
| 40 and under 50 | 14.2 | 90.2 | 50.3 |
| 50 and under 60 | 26.9 | 91.0 | 57.4 |
| 60 and under 70 | 34.3 | 92.0 | 58.3 |
| 70 and under 80 | 40.2 | 94.0 | 61.1 |
| 80 and under 100 | 45.0 | 95.1 | 66.9 |
| 100 and under 120 | 52.4 | 95.6 | 68.0 |
| 120 and under 140 | 59.1 | 97.1 | 75.1 |
| 140 and under 160 | 59.8 | 98.0 | 78.2 |
| 160 and under 180 | 65.1 | 97.9 | 80.1 |
| 180 and under 200 | 62.3 | 99.6 | 85.6 |
| 200 and under 250 | 61.5 | 99.5 | 89.0 |
| 250 and under 300 | 53.4 | 100.0 | 93.5 |
| 300 and under 350 | 44.1 | 100.0 | 94.1 |
| 350 or more | 28.9 | 100.0 | 95.6 |

*FES*, 1980, Table 4

**2.6**  In a sample survey each of 150 respondents was asked to record his own social class and that of his father. Six classes were defined with class I being of high social standing and class VI being of low social standing. The results were as follows:

| Father's class \ Respondent's class | I | II | III | IV | V | VI |
|---|---|---|---|---|---|---|
| I | 10 | 3 | 2 | 0 | 0 | 0 |
| II | 6 | 15 | 4 | 1 | 0 | 0 |
| III | 4 | 10 | 8 | 5 | 1 | 0 |
| IV | 1 | 6 | 6 | 12 | 3 | 1 |
| V | 0 | 0 | 5 | 10 | 10 | 4 |
| VI | 0 | 0 | 0 | 6 | 8 | 9 |

Discuss the nature and the amount of social mobility revealed by the data.

**2.7**  For the data in Exercise 2.6 construct a table in which the 6 classes have been replaced by 3 as follows:

Class A = Classes I and II combined
Class B = Classes III and IV combined
Class C = Classes V and VI combined

If we now define movements between the resulting adjacent classes as short-range movements and other movements as long-range movements, discuss the upward and downward mobility revealed by the table.

**2.8**
(a)  For the data given below obtain the frequency distributions for $X$ and $Y$ using constant class intervals 1–15, 16–30, ..., 61–75, 76–90.
(b)  Using the same class intervals for $X$ and $Y$ construct a two-way table of classification showing the mobility of firms between 1970 and 1980. Briefly discuss your results.
(c)  Draw a scatter diagram for $X$ and $Y$. Use the resulting diagram to briefly discuss the mobility of firms.

| Company name | Rank in 1980/1 ($Y$) | Rank in 1970/1 ($X$) | Company name | Rank in 1980/1 ($Y$) | Rank in 1970/1 ($X$) |
|---|---|---|---|---|---|
| Shell Transport | 2 | 1 | British Leyland | 10 | 8 |
| British Petroleum | 1 | 2 | General Electric | 12 | 9 |
| Br. American Tobacco | 3 | 3 | Courtaulds | 20 | 10 |
| ICI | 4 | 4 | Esso Petroleum | 8 | 11 |
| Unilever | 5 | 5 | GKN | 17 | 12 |
| Imperial Tobacco | 6 | 6 | Dunlop | 26 | 14 |
| Shell Mex & B.P. | 9 | 7 | Ford | 7 | 15 |

*Continued*

| Company name | Rank in 1980/1 ($Y$) | Rank in 1970/1 ($X$) | Company name | Rank in 1980/1 ($Y$) | Rank in 1970/1 ($X$) |
|---|---|---|---|---|---|
| Gallaher | 23 | 16 | Joseph Lucas | 52 | 44 |
| Dalgety | 58 | 17 | C. Czarnikow | 31 | 46 |
| BICC | 50 | 18 | Tesco | 27 | 47 |
| Hawker Siddeley | 48 | 19 | Tate & Lyle | 43 | 49 |
| Distillers | 59 | 21 | Boots | 40 | 50 |
| Great Universal Stores | 34 | 22 | Brooke Bond Liebig | 90 | 51 |
| Marks & Spencer | 22 | 23 | Vauxhall Motors | 70 | 52 |
| Rank Hovis | 30 | 24 | Wimpey & Co. | 67 | 53 |
| Allied Breweries | 13 | 26 | Metal Box | 51 | 54 |
| RTZ | 11 | 27 | Thomas Tilling | 29 | 55 |
| Bass Charrington | 46 | 29 | Sainsbury | 44 | 56 |
| Reed International | 24 | 30 | Consolidated Gold | 56 | 57 |
| Woolworth | 64 | 31 | P. & O. Steam | 32 | 58 |
| Unigate | 47 | 32 | Gill & Duffus | 81 | 60 |
| Rolls Royce | 66 | 33 | EMI | 65 | 63 |
| Tube Investments | 38 | 34 | Spillers | 77 | 64 |
| Union International | 53 | 35 | Whitbread | 76 | 65 |
| Bowring & Co. | 33 | 36 | Guinness | 83 | 69 |
| Sears Holdings | 36 | 37 | British Oxygen | 37 | 70 |
| Coats Patons | 85 | 38 | Beecham | 60 | 71 |
| Bowater | 21 | 39 | Reckitt & Colman | 88 | 72 |
| Amalgamated Metal | 42 | 40 | Lonrho | 35 | 75 |
| Thorn Electrical | 39 | 41 | Philips | 80 | 78 |
| Cadbury's | 54 | 42 | Ready Mixed Concrete | 75 | 88 |
| Burmah Oil | 41 | 43 | IBM | 74 | 90 |

*The Times 1000*, 1970 and 1980

**2.9** Draw the histogram and frequency polygon for Table 2.3.

**2.10** Plot the frequencies given in column 2 of Table 2.4 against the class widths given in column 3 of the same table. Compare the resulting histogram with the one given in Fig. 2.3. Discuss.

**2.11** The data below show the number of hours per week spent watching television by a sample of children.

| Hours per week | Number of children |
|---|---|
| 0 and less than 2 | 1 |
| 2 and less than 4 | 2 |

*Continued*

| Hours per week | Number of children |
|---|---|
| 4 and less than 6 | 1 |
| 6 and less than 8 | 5 |
| 8 and less than 10 | 15 |
| 10 and less than 12 | 35 |
| 12 and less than 14 | 17 |
| 14 and less than 16 | 7 |
| 16 and less than 18 | 3 |
| 18 and less than 20 | 1 |

Draw two histograms, the first having frequency on the vertical axis and the second having frequency density on the vertical axis. Compare and discuss the two histograms.

**2.12**  Obtain the cumulative frequency distributions and the resulting ogives for both the exam and coursework marks given in Table 2.8. What fresh insights do they give which were not discussed in Section 2.5?

**2.13**  The estimated probabilities of takeover for a sample of firms who were the targets of takeovers and a sample who were not the targets of takeovers are given below. Express the frequencies of each distribution in percentage terms. Use the resulting values to draw the histograms of both distributions on the same diagram. Briefly discuss the results.

| Estimated probability of takeover | Target firms (frequency) | Non-target firms (frequency) |
|---|---|---|
| 0.000 up to but less than 0.040 | 6 | 37 |
| 0.040 up to but less than 0.080 | 23 | 74 |
| 0.080 up to but less than 0.120 | 35 | 60 |
| 0.120 up to but less than 0.160 | 36 | 48 |
| 0.160 up to but less than 0.200 | 23 | 19 |
| 0.200 up to but less than 0.240 | 22 | 12 |
| 0.240 up to but less than 0.280 | 8 | 4 |
| 0.280 up to but less than 0.320 | 5 | 0 |
| 0.320 up to but less than 0.360 | 2 | 1 |
| 0.360 up to but less than 0.400 | 2 | 1 |
| | 162 | 256 |

Adapted from *Journal of Accounting and Economics*, 1986

# 3 Describing frequency distributions

3.1 Measures of location
3.2 Measures of dispersion
3.3 Combining the mean and standard deviation
3.4 Comparing different average measures
3.5 Appendix
Exercises

In the previous chapter our aim was to summarise a large amount of data by presenting it in tabular and diagrammatic form. In this way we were able to highlight visually important features which might otherwise be hidden amongst the mass of detail. Our aim in this chapter is similar in that we again wish to summarise large amounts of data, but now we do so by introducing formulae which allow us to describe distributions numerically.

There are a variety of measures which can be used to describe different features of a frequency distribution numerically. They may be divided into two groups: the first consisting of measures to locate strategic points of interest including the mean, median, mode, quartiles, deciles and percentiles; the second group designed to measure the spread of a distribution including the range, the semi-interquartile range and the standard deviation. The relative usefulness of these measures depends in part on the shape of the distribution under consideration.

In the case of a normal distribution the main average measure of interest is the mean and the main measure of spread is the standard deviation. These two are of particular interest because they can be combined to define characteristics of a normal distribution which are of central importance for much of the inferential statistical analysis which follows in later chapters.

## 3.1 Measures of location

There are various ways of calculating an average value for a distribution. The most common amongst them is the arithmetic mean or, as it is more commonly known, the *mean* ($\overline{X}$).

### Mean using ungrouped data

The mean value of a series of figures is simply the sum total of the values divided by the number of observations. So if there are $N$ observations of a variable $X$, the mean

Table 3.1 Average annual rate of inflation (%), June 1979 to May 1984

|      | 1979 | 1980 | 1981 | 1982 | 1983 | 1984 |
|------|------|------|------|------|------|------|
| Jan  |      | 18.4 | 13.0 | 12.0 | 4.9  | 5.1  |
| Feb  |      | 19.1 | 12.5 | 11.0 | 5.3  | 5.1  |
| Mar  |      | 19.8 | 12.6 | 10.4 | 4.6  | 5.2  |
| Apr  |      | 21.8 | 12.0 | 9.4  | 4.0  | 5.2  |
| May  |      | 21.9 | 11.7 | 9.5  | 3.7  | 5.1  |
| Jun  | 11.4 | 21.0 | 11.3 | 9.2  | 3.7  |      |
| Jul  | 15.6 | 16.9 | 10.9 | 8.7  | 4.2  |      |
| Aug  | 15.8 | 16.3 | 11.5 | 8.0  | 4.6  |      |
| Sep  | 16.5 | 15.9 | 11.4 | 7.3  | 5.1  |      |
| Oct  | 17.2 | 15.4 | 11.7 | 6.8  | 5.0  |      |
| Nov  | 17.4 | 15.3 | 12.0 | 6.3  | 4.8  |      |
| Dec  | 17.2 | 15.1 | 12.0 | 5.4  | 5.3  |      |

*Observer*, July 1, 1984

value of $X$ using summation notation (see Section 3.5) is given by:

$$\bar{X} = \sum X_i / N$$

In Table 3.1 we have figures showing the average annual rate of inflation for each month of each of the first five years of Mrs Thatcher's Government. Since there are 60 observations in all we can calculate the mean as follows:

$$\bar{X} = (X_1 + X_2 + \cdots + X_{60})/N$$
$$= (11.4 + 15.6 + \cdots + 5.1)/60$$
$$= 10.93$$

The mean value of the annual rate of inflation for this period is therefore 10.93%. This of course is a representative figure for the whole period and may not be equal to any individual value given in the series.

## Mean using grouped data

Where data are presented in a frequency distribution, the formula above for calculating the mean has to be adjusted. Assume that the data in Table 3.1 have been arranged into class intervals as shown in Table 3.2. When data are presented in this form we may not know the values of the individual observations, in which case we have to choose a figure to represent each group. In general the midpoint ($x_i$) is the obvious choice and this is shown for each class interval in column 3. Our formula for the mean now becomes:

$$\bar{X} = \sum f_i x_i / N$$

Note here that the summation sign relates to the number of classes not the number

Table 3.2  Calculating mean ($\overline{X}$), median and standard deviation ($s$) of the average annual rate of inflation

| Class interval ($X_i$) | Frequency ($f_i$) | Midpoint ($x_i$) | $f_ix_i$ | cum $f_i$ | $f_ix_i^2$ |
|---|---|---|---|---|---|
| 3 up to 7 | 20 | 5 | 100 | 20 | 500 |
| 7 up to 11 | 8 | 9 | 72 | 28 | 648 |
| 11 up to 15 | 14 | 13 | 182 | 42 | 2366 |
| 15 up to 19 | 13 | 17 | 221 | 55 | 3757 |
| 19 up to 23 | 5 | 21 | 105 | 60 | 2205 |
|  | 60 |  | 680 |  | 9476 |

$$\overline{X} = \frac{\Sigma f_ix_i}{N} = \frac{680}{60} = 11.33$$

$$\text{Median} = 11 + \left[\left(\frac{30-28}{14}\right) \times 4\right] = 11.57$$

$$s = \sqrt{\frac{9476}{60} - (11.33)^2} = 5.43$$

of observations. Since there are five class intervals in our example we can expand the formula and use it to calculate the mean value as follows:

$$\overline{X} = (f_1x_1 + f_2x_2 + f_3x_3 + f_4x_4 + f_5x_5)/60$$
$$= (100 + 72 + 182 + 221 + 105)/60$$
$$= 11.33$$

Using the new formula the mean value is now 11.33%. But how can the same data yield two different mean values? The reason is that by presenting the data in the form of a distribution we have lost some of the original information. For example we know that 20 observations have values between 3 and 7, but we no longer know exactly what these values are and we have chosen the midpoint to represent them. If the values are equally distributed within each class interval the two different formulae will give the same answer. The difference between the two answers is a reflection on the accuracy of our use of the midpoint as a representative figure for each class interval. Although the first of the two formulae above is more accurate in general, in many practical situations only the second can be used.

## Median using ungrouped data

Our second average measure is the *median* which is defined as the value of the middle observation when all observations have been arranged in ascending order. If there is an even number of observations the median value is the midpoint between the two middle observations. For the values given in Table 3.1 the appropriate arrangement of values can be shown as follows

$$3.7, \ 3.7, \ ..., \qquad 11.3, \ 11.4, \ ..., \qquad 21.8, \ 21.9$$

Smallest                Values of 30th and                Largest
value                    31st observations                value

The median value for this series is therefore:

$$\text{med } X_i = (11.3 + 11.4)/2 = 11.35$$

since the median value is midway between the 30th and 31st observations.

## Median using grouped data

In order to calculate the median for data arranged into a distribution, we once again have to introduce an approximation because we do not know the exact value of each observation. The formula used in this case is:

$$\text{med } X_i = L + \left(\frac{N/2 - \sum f}{f_{med}}\right) C$$

where    $L$ = lower boundary of the class containing the median observation
$N/2$ = position of median observation (This is an approximation which is sufficiently accurate for our purposes)
$C$ = size of class interval containing the median observation
$\sum f$ = sum of frequencies up to the class containing the median observation
$f_{med}$ = frequency of class containing the median observation

To apply this formula to the data on inflation we need to refer to Table 3.2. In column 5 we have cumulated the values of $f_i$ beginning at the top: this means that we have 20 observations in the first class interval, 28 observations in the first two combined, etc. By inspection we see that the median observation, i.e. the one occupying the 30th position in ascending order, is one of the 14 observations contained in the third class interval. If we now feed the appropriate values into the formula we get

$$\text{med } X_i = 11 + \left[\left(\frac{30 - 28}{14}\right) \times 4\right]$$
$$= 11.57$$

What the formula is saying is that the median observation has a value equivalent to moving into the third class interval by an amount equal to 2/14 of its entire width.

Once again the answers provided by the two formulae differ because of the approximation introduced in the second.

## Mode

The final average measure we shall consider is the *mode* which is defined as the most frequent occurring value in a series. Sometimes a series of observations will have more than one modal value. By inspecting the values given in Table 3.1 we can see that 12.0 and 5.1 each occurs four times. Each value is then said to be a *modal value* and the series as a whole is defined as being bi-modal.

When data have been arranged into class intervals we can readily define the modal class and take the midpoint of this class as the modal value. On this basis we can say that for the data in Table 3.2, the first class interval is the modal class and we can take the midpoint of this class, i.e. 5, as the modal value.

## Other measures of location

We have seen that the median observation divides all observations in the series into two groups of equal size. If we extend this idea we can define observations that divide a series into groups of 4, 5, 10 or 100 and the associated measures are known as *quartiles, quintiles, deciles* and *percentiles*. In each case the formula required is a simple extension of the formula for the median.

To illustrate this we will consider the formulae required for calculating quartiles.

We define the first quartile as that value below which 25% of the observations fall and above which the remaining 75% fall when arranged in ascending order. The second quartile is the value below which 50% fall and above which the remaining 50% fall. Parallel definitions follow for the third and fourth quartiles.

Clearly, the second quartile is synonymous with the median whose formula we already have. Moreover, the fourth quartile must be either the value of the largest observation or the value of the upper interval of the last group of observations. In each case a formula is not required as the value can be obtained by inspection.

We therefore require formulae only for the first (lower) and third (upper) quartiles, which we shall label $Q1$ and $Q3$. For the first quartile we define:

$$Q1 = L + \left( \frac{N/4 - \sum f}{f_{Q1}} \right) C$$

where    $L$ = lower value of class containing the first quartile observation
$\quad\quad\quad N/4$ = position of first quartile observation
$\quad\quad\quad C$ = size of class interval containing the first quartile observation
$\quad\quad\quad \sum f$ = sum of frequencies up to the class containing the first quartile observation
$\quad\quad\quad f_{Q1}$ = frequency of the class containing the first quartile observation

For the data contained in Table 3.2 we find that:

$$Q1 = 3 + \left[ \left( \frac{15 - 0}{20} \right) \times 4 \right]$$

$$= 6.0$$

From what we have said so far about the formula for the median and the first quartile, it is quite easy to obtain the formula for $Q3$ and for any other measures of location referred to above (see Example 3.1 and Exercise 3.3).

# Example 3.1 _____

Given the data in Table 3.2 we could calculate any of the other measures of location discussed in the text. In this example we will calculate the second quintile ($Q^*2$), the third decile ($D3$) and the sixty-fifth percentile ($P65$).

$$Q^*2 = L + \left(\frac{2N/5 - \sum f}{f_{Q^*2}}\right)C$$

$$= 7 + \left(\frac{24 - 20}{8}\right) \times 4$$

$$= 9.0$$

$$D3 = L + \left(\frac{3N/10 - \sum f}{f_{D3}}\right)C$$

$$= 3 + \left(\frac{18 - 0}{20}\right) \times 4$$

$$= 6.6$$

$$P65 = L + \left(\frac{65N/100 - \sum f}{f_{P65}}\right)C$$

$$= 11 + \left(\frac{39 - 28}{14}\right) \times 4$$

$$= 14.1$$

## 3.2  Measures of dispersion

Although the various measures of location introduced so far are useful in describing frequency distributions they are quite limited on their own. To illustrate this, consider the two distributions A and B shown in Fig. 3.1. It is clear that they both have the same kind of bell-type shape and they both have average values in common centring on the vertical axis. And yet they are quite different from each other. In particular the values of the observations in distribution B are far more spread out than those in distribution A, and it is clearly important to be able to measure the spread in each case.

### *Range*

The simplest way of measuring the amount of dispersion is to calculate the *range*. The range for a series of observations is the difference between the lowest and highest values in the sample.

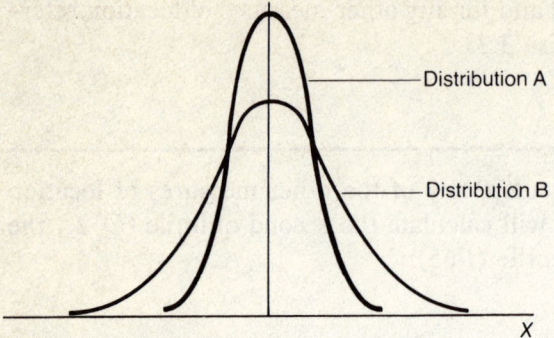

Figure 3.1   Two distributions of a variable $X$

Having previously looked at the inflation figures under the Conservative Government between 1979 and 1984 (shown in Table 3.1), let us now consider the inflation figures during the last five years of the previous Labour Governments. These are shown in Tables 3.3 and 3.4. The lowest figure in Table 3.3 is 7.4% and the highest figure is 26.9%. The range is therefore given by:

Range = 26.9 – 7.4 = 19.5%

Although this is a measure which can be calculated very easily it has a number of disadvantages.

1   While we can say that the larger the value calculated the more dispersed are the data, a single value on its own is of little help when interpreting the data at hand.
2   It is subject to the effect of any freak, atypical values which may be present in the series.

Table 3.3   Average annual rate of inflation (%), June 1974 to May 1979

|      | 1974 | 1975 | 1976 | 1977 | 1978 | 1979 |
|------|------|------|------|------|------|------|
| Jan  |      | 19.9 | 23.4 | 16.4 | 9.9  | 9.3  |
| Feb  |      | 19.9 | 22.9 | 16.2 | 9.5  | 9.6  |
| Mar  |      | 21.2 | 21.2 | 16.7 | 9.1  | 9.8  |
| Apr  |      | 21.7 | 18.9 | 17.5 | 7.9  | 10.1 |
| May  |      | 25.0 | 15.4 | 17.1 | 7.7  | 10.3 |
| Jun  | 16.5 | 26.1 | 13.8 | 17.7 | 7.4  |      |
| Jul  | 17.1 | 26.3 | 12.9 | 17.6 | 7.8  |      |
| Aug  | 16.9 | 26.9 | 13.8 | 16.5 | 8.0  |      |
| Sep  | 17.1 | 26.6 | 14.3 | 15.6 | 7.8  |      |
| Oct  | 17.1 | 25.9 | 14.7 | 14.1 | 7.8  |      |
| Nov  | 18.3 | 25.2 | 15.0 | 13.0 | 8.1  |      |
| Dec  | 19.1 | 24.9 | 15.1 | 12.1 | 8.4  |      |

*Observer*, July 1, 1984

Table 3.4 Distribution of average rate of inflation (%), June 1974 to May 1979

| Class interval | Frequency $(f_i)$ | Midpoint $(x_i)$ | $f_i x_i^2$ |
|---|---|---|---|
| 7 up to 11 | 17 | 9 | 1377 |
| 11 up to 15 | 8 | 13 | 1352 |
| 15 up to 19 | 19 | 17 | 5491 |
| 19 up to 23 | 7 | 21 | 3087 |
| 23 up to 27 | 9 | 25 | 5625 |
| | 60 | | 16932 |

3 Since it uses only two observations from a distribution, it ignores much of the information available which contributes to its overall shape.

## Semi-interquartile range

Our second measure of dispersion makes use of two measures of location discussed in the last section, namely the first and third quartiles ($Q1$ and $Q3$). The semi-interquartile range is defined as being equal to half the difference between $Q3$ and $Q1$, that is:

$$SIR = \tfrac{1}{2}(Q3 - Q1)$$

For the data given in Table 3.4, $Q1 = 10.52\%$ and $Q3 = 19.57\%$ (see Exercise 3.2). It therefore follows that:

$$SIR = \tfrac{1}{2}(19.57 - 10.52)$$
$$= 4.53$$

When we say that a variable is widely dispersed, implicitly we have in mind a fixed point around which dispersal occurs. In the case of the semi-interquartile range, the fixed point is the median. Given that the median value for the data in Table 3.4 is 16.05% (see Exercise 3.2), we can say that the average as measured by the median is 16.05%, and the dispersion measured around the median is 4.53%.

Since the semi-interquartile range uses more of the data available than the range, it is to be preferred as a measure of dispersion. But it still does not use all the information available in the way that our next measure of dispersion does.

## Standard deviation and variance

The most common measure of dispersion is the *standard deviation* (*s*) for which the formula is

$$s = \sqrt{\frac{\Sigma(X_i - \bar{X})^2}{N}}$$

At the heart of the formula is the expression $X_i - \bar{X}$, which is the difference between any value of $X$ and the mean. From this it is apparent that the fixed point around which the spread is measured is the mean. Each difference is squared in order to overcome the problem of large positive and negative differences cancelling each other, giving a small value for data which are highly dispersed. These squared values are then summed and divided by $N$. The result is a measure called the *variance*.

If we take the square root of the variance we obtain the *standard deviation*. Although the variance is as good a measure of dispersion as the standard deviation, it is the latter which receives more emphasis because of its important role in other areas of statistics.

When data have been organised into a frequency distribution the formula to find the standard deviation is:

$$s = \sqrt{\frac{\Sigma (x_i - \bar{X})^2 f_i}{N}}$$

where $x_i$ and $f_i$ are respectively the midpoints and the frequencies of the class intervals.

Although these two formulae make it clear just what the standard deviation is measuring they can be rather unwieldy for practical purposes. For this reason when performing calculations it is preferable to use alternative expressions for the standard deviation. For ungrouped data we use:

$$s = \sqrt{\frac{\Sigma X_i^2}{N} - \bar{X}^2}$$

and for grouped data we use:

$$s = \sqrt{\frac{\Sigma f_i x_i^2}{N} - \bar{X}^2}$$

Given the information in Table 3.4 and the fact that for these data $\bar{X} = 15.87$ (see Exercise 3.5) we have:

$$s = \sqrt{\frac{16\,932}{60} - (15.87)^2}$$
$$= \sqrt{(282.2 - 251.9)} = 5.5$$

At this stage knowing that $s = 5.5$ is in itself not very helpful. But if we also know that the value of $s$ for the data in Table 3.2 is 5.43, we can conclude that the amount of dispersion in the inflation figures for the Conservative and Labour administrations over the ten-year period investigated was approximately the same.

## 3.3  Combining the mean and standard deviation

Among the many possible different shapes of frequency distribution, a few occur frequently. One that is particularly common which is at the heart of statistical analysis in general is the *normal distribution*. For present purposes we can describe the normal distribution as being bell shaped and perfectly symmetrical about the mean. This is illustrated in Fig. 3.1

Another feature of the normal distribution is that it displays various properties based on combining the mean and standard deviation. For example, if we find the values of $X_i$ given by $\bar{X} + s$ and $\bar{X} - s$ (written $\bar{X} \pm s$), and if we project a vertical line through each value until it reaches the curve of the distribution, the area under the curve between these two values is approximately equal to 68% of the total area under the curve. Similarly, if we find values for $X_i$ which are two standard deviations either side of the mean (i.e. $\bar{X} \pm 2s$) and three standard deviations either side of the mean (i.e. $\bar{X} \pm 3s$), the approximate percentages are 95% and 99% respectively.

These three situations are shown in Fig. 3.2. Note in particular that these properties apply to all normal distributions and *only* to normal distributions (see Exercise 3.4).

The areas under the curve defined above are approximations, but it will be seen later that it is possible to define values of $X_i$ for which the areas under the curve are exactly 68%, 95% and 99%. Indeed, it will also be seen that we can take any percentage value

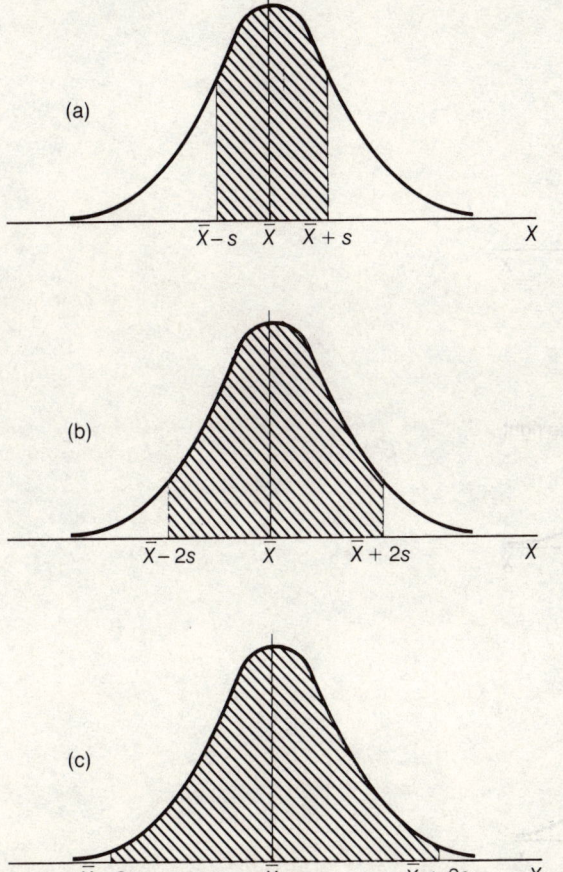

Figure 3.2   Areas under the curve of a normal distribution

for the area under the curve of a normal distribution and obtain the resulting values for $X$ on the horizontal axis.

Since the values $\bar{X}$ and $s$ can vary, there exists an unlimited number of normal distributions, but they all belong to the same family because they are all bell shaped and perfectly symmetrical about the mean value. From amongst this unlimited number there is one of special interest which is called the *standard normal distribution*. For this distribution the mean value ($\bar{X}$) is 0, the standard deviation ($s$) is 1 and the area under the curve is equal to 1 square unit. It is of special interest because of the central role it plays in statistical analysis in general and we shall meet it again in later chapters.

## 3.4   Comparing different average measures

The *mean*, *median* and *mode* are three different measures of the average value for a variable and the relationship between each pair is determined by the overall shape of the distribution.

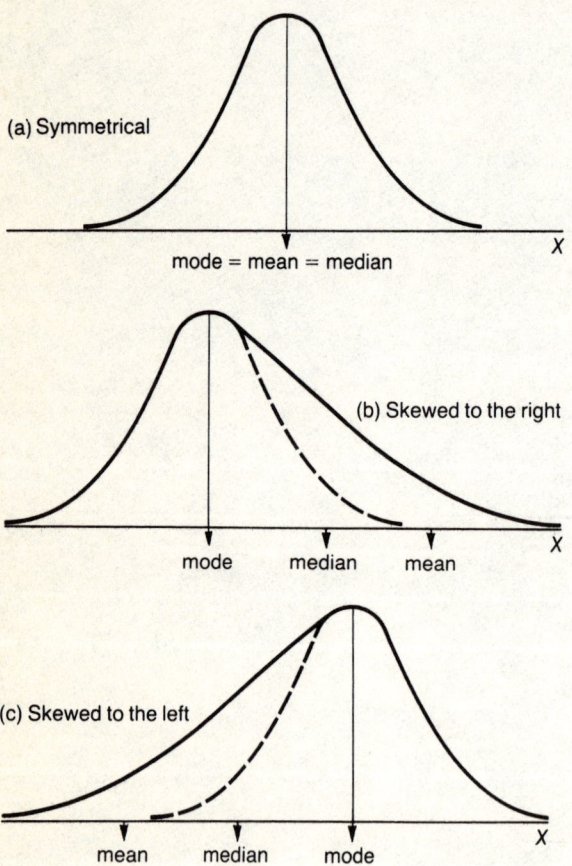

Figure 3.3   Mean, median and mode for differing distributions

Three shapes are shown in Fig. 3.3. In the first case $X$ is normally distributed and the values of all three average measures are the same. Many human characteristics such as height and intelligence display this pattern, as do many economic variables when measured in terms of changes in their levels over time. Although all three measures provide the same answer, the mean is to be preferred over the other two because it uses all the data and therefore makes the best use of the information available.

The second distribution in Fig. 3.3 is said to be skewed to the right because as shown, the right-hand tail is pulled away from normality. The result is that very large values of $X$ are combined with very small values of $f$, causing the mean value to exceed that of the median, and both to exceed the mode. Since the numerical difference between the mean and the median is a positive value, the distribution is also said to be positively skewed. The national distribution of personal income, where relatively few people earn extremely large incomes (see Example 3.2), and the size distribution of firms (see Exercise 2.3 in Chapter 2), where a few firms are relatively very much larger than the rest, are distributions that are positively skewed.

The final distribution in Fig. 3.3 is skewed to the left because the tail is pulled away from normality for low values of $X$. The skew to the left means that very low values of $X$ are combined with low values of $f$ causing the mean value to be less than the median and both to be less than the mode. With the numerical difference between the mean and the median being a negative value, the distribution is said to be negatively skewed. Although one can find distributions that visually appear to be negatively skewed, the numerical difference between the mean and the median in such cases is often positive (see Exercise 3.7). In practice negatively skewed distributions are far less common in economics than are distributions with a positive skew.

When a distribution is heavily skewed either to the right or the left, the mean value is disproportionately affected by very large values of $X$ when the skew is positive and by very small values of $X$ when the skew is negative. In such situations the median is generally a better measure of the average than the mean, and both are generally superior to the mode. In all other situations, given the kind of data we will be encountering, we can take the mean as the best single measure of the average.

# Example 3.2

In the first two columns of the table below we have the frequency distribution of income for all households with no worker in 1982.

| Income (£ per week) | Frequency ($f_i$) | Midpoint ($x_i$) | Cumulative frequency | $f_i x_i$ |
|---|---|---|---|---|
| Under 50 | 697 | 25.0 | 697 | 17 425.0 |
| 50 up to 70 | 636 | 60.0 | 1333 | 38 160.0 |
| 70 up to 100 | 483 | 87.5 | 1816 | 42 262.5 |
| 100 up to 150 | 219 | 125.0 | 2035 | 27 375.0 |

*Continued*

| Income (£ per week) | Frequency ($f_i$) | Midpoint ($x_i$) | Cumulative frequency | $f_i x_i$ |
|---|---|---|---|---|
| 150 up to 200 | 88 | 175.0 | 2123 | 15 400.0 |
| 200 up to 250 | 28 | 225.0 | 2151 | 6 300.0 |
| 250 up to 325 | 21 | 287.5 | 2172 | 6 037.5 |
| 325 and above | 7 | 375.0 | 2179 | 2 625.0 |
|  | 2179 |  |  | 155 585.0 |

*FES*, 1982

By plotting the frequency density against income (see Section 2.1) we can obtain the histogram given below.

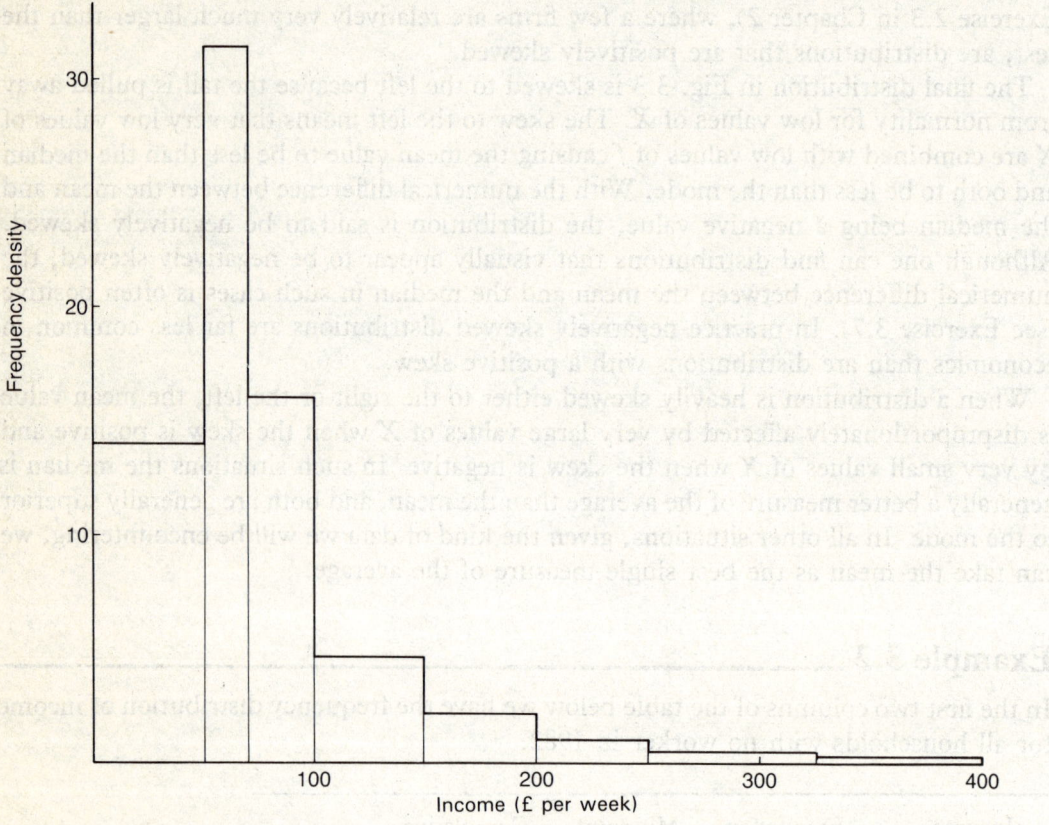

The histogram suggests that the distribution is heavily skewed to the right. This can be confirmed by calculating the mean and the median and comparing their values.

Mean $= \sum f_i x_i / N = 155\ 585 / 2179 = 71.4$

$$\text{Median} = L + \left(\frac{N/2 - \sum f}{f_{med}}\right) C$$

$$= 50 + \left(\frac{1089.5 - 697}{636}\right) \times 20$$

$$= 50 + 0.617 \times 20$$

$$= 62.34$$

Since the difference between the mean (£71.4) and the median (£62.34) is a positive value (+£9.06), we can confirm that the data above are positively skewed.

## 3.5 Appendix

In many of the calculations throughout this book we require the addition of values taken by a variable or the addition of the product of values taken by two variables. A convenient and simple way of expressing this makes use of the summation operator $\Sigma$.

If we have two variables $X_i$ and $Y_i$ with $i = 1, 2, \ldots, N$ we can use the summation operator $\Sigma$ to form the following:

$$\text{sums} \left( \sum_{i=1}^{N} X_i, \sum_{i=1}^{N} Y_i \right)$$

$$\text{sums of squares} \left( \sum_{i=1}^{N} X_i^2, \sum_{i=1}^{N} Y_i^2 \right)$$

$$\text{sum of cross products} \left( \sum_{i=1}^{N} X_i Y_i \right)$$

$$\sum_{i=1}^{N} X_i = X_1 + X_2 + \cdots + X_N$$

$$\sum_{i=1}^{N} Y_i = Y_1 + Y_2 + \cdots + Y_N$$

$$\sum_{i=1}^{N} X_i^2 = X_1^2 + X_2^2 + \cdots + X_N^2$$

$$\sum_{i=1}^{N} Y_i^2 = Y_1^2 + Y_2^2 + \cdots + Y_N^2$$

$$\sum_{i=1}^{N} X_i Y_i = X_1 Y_1 + X_2 Y_2 + \cdots + X_N Y_N$$

Each of the expressions on the left-hand side makes it clear that the values that need to be added begin at the first observation (say $X_1$), ends at the $N$th observation (say $X_N$) and includes all others in between. These expressions can also be simplified to read $\Sigma X_i$, $\Sigma Y_i$, $\Sigma X_i^2$, $\Sigma Y_i^2$ and $\Sigma X_i Y_i$; or even $\Sigma X$, $\Sigma Y$, $\Sigma X^2$, $\Sigma Y^2$ and $\Sigma XY$, where the $i$ subscript is implied, and it is assumed that the addition is from the first to the $N$th observation.

The calculations involved are illustrated below where $N = 5$ and values are given for $X_i$ and $Y_i$ where $X_1 = 4$, $X_2 = 8$, etc.

| $X_i$ | $Y_i$ | $X_i^2$ | $Y_i^2$ | $X_i Y_i$ |
|-------|-------|---------|---------|-----------|
| 4 | 7 | 16 | 49 | 28 |
| 8 | 2 | 64 | 4 | 16 |
| 3 | 4 | 9 | 16 | 12 |
| 2 | 5 | 4 | 25 | 10 |
| 1 | 6 | 1 | 36 | 6 |
| $\Sigma X = 18$ | $\Sigma Y = 24$ | $\Sigma X^2 = 94$ | $\Sigma Y^2 = 130$ | $\Sigma XY = 72$ |

## Exercises

**3.1**   Refer to the *FES* and find at least one example of a variable for which the following have been calculated:
(a)   third decile
(b)   second quintile
(c)   lower (i.e. first) quartile
(d)   median

**3.2**   Calculate the median, first quartile and third quartile for the data given in Table 3.4. Compare the values you obtain for the median and first quartile with the values obtained for the data in Table 3.2 given in the text. Briefly discuss.

**3.3**   Write out in full the formula for each of the following:
(a)   fourth quintile $(Q^*4)$
(b)   third quartile
(c)   sixth decile $(D6)$
(d)   eighty-fourth percentile $(P84)$

**3.4**   The data below show the distribution of marks in a given examination for a sample of 170 students.

| Examination mark (%) | Frequency |
|----------------------|-----------|
| 0 up to but less than 10 | 1 |
| 10 up to but less than 20 | 3 |
| 20 up to but less than 30 | 12 |

*Continued*

| Examination mark (%) | Frequency |
|---|---|
| 30 up to but less than 40 | 33 |
| 40 up to but less than 50 | 38 |
| 50 up to but less than 60 | 50 |
| 60 up to but less than 70 | 26 |
| 70 up to but less than 80 | 4 |
| 80 up to but less than 90 | 2 |
| 90 up to but less than 100 | 1 |

(a) From these data calculate the mean value ($\bar{X}$) and the value of the standard deviation ($s$).

(b) How many of the students are contained between the values $\bar{X} + 2s$ and $\bar{X} - 2s$?

(c) How does this number compare with the number you would expect if the sample was normally distributed? Explain and discuss.

**3.5** Calculate the mean value for the data given in Table 3.4

**3.6** Calculate the mean and standard deviation for each of the two frequency distributions given in Exercise 2.13. Compare and discuss your results.

**3.7** The data below show the frequency distribution of income for all households with three workers:

| Gross Income (£ per week) | Frequency |
|---|---|
| 80 up to 125 | 6 |
| 125 up to 175 | 14 |
| 175 up to 225 | 49 |
| 225 up to 275 | 98 |
| 275 up to 375 | 158 |
| Over 375 | 115 |

*FES*, 1983

(a) Draw the frequency curve for these figures.

(b) How would you define the shape of the distribution?

(c) Calculate the mean and the median. Do your calculations confirm the conclusion reached in (b). If not, why?

**3.8** The data below show the residual error in the UK national income accounts for the period 1964–85.

| | Residual error (£m) | | Residual error (£m) |
|------|------|------|------|
| 1964 | 10 | 1975 | 1061 |
| 1965 | −243 | 1976 | 3167 |
| 1966 | −90 | 1977 | 83 |
| 1967 | 188 | 1978 | 830 |
| 1968 | 287 | 1979 | −154 |
| 1969 | −438 | 1980 | 137 |
| 1970 | −507 | 1981 | 826 |
| 1971 | 453 | 1982 | −1762 |
| 1972 | −439 | 1983 | −957 |
| 1973 | −619 | 1984 | −4734 |
| 1974 | 928 | 1985 | −3276 |

Calculate the mean and standard deviation for the period 1964–74 and for the period 1975–85. Briefly discuss your results. (A definition of residual error can be found in any recent edition of *UK National Accounts* published by HMSO.)

**3.9**  The figures below show the daily changes in the level of the FT Ordinary Share Index for each of 20 trading days between April 5th and May 4th 1984 (Period 1) and 20 trading days between May 5th and June 6th 1984 (Period 2). Calculate the mean and standard deviation for each period. Briefly discuss your results.

Period 1

| April 5 | −1.4 | April 14 | 6.6 | April 27 | 11.5 |
|------|------|------|------|------|------|
| April 6 | 9.2 | April 17 | −20.0 | April 28 | 8.9 |
| April 7 | −1.6 | April 18 | 4.6 | May 1 | 2.1 |
| April 10 | 1.8 | April 19 | 8.8 | May 2 | 5.7 |
| April 11 | 11.4 | April 21 | −8.6 | May 3 | 3.6 |
| April 12 | 7.5 | April 25 | −3.8 | May 4 | 3.4 |
| April 13 | 2.5 | April 26 | 11.4 | | |

Period 2

| May 5 | −7.4 | May 17 | 1.4 | May 26 | 1.5 |
|------|------|------|------|------|------|
| May 9 | −10.6 | May 18 | 5.1 | May 30 | −1.7 |
| May 10 | −8.6 | May 19 | −10.1 | May 31 | −22.8 |
| May 11 | −11.3 | May 22 | 1.8 | June 1 | −6.5 |
| May 12 | −13.9 | May 23 | −19.9 | June 2 | 27.6 |
| May 15 | 3.0 | May 24 | −8.7 | June 6 | −3.2 |
| May 16 | 4.0 | May 25 | −21.2 | | |

**3.10**  If the level of the FT Ordinary Share Index on the morning of April 5th was 859.2

use your answers in the previous exercise to calculate the level after trading on May 4th (assume that missing days during the period were non-trading days).

**3.11** If the level of the FT Ordinary Share Index after trading on June 6th was 840.1 use your calculations in Exercise 3.9 to determine the level of the index on the morning of May 5th (again assume that missing days during the period were non-trading days).

**3.12** Compare and briefly discuss your answers to Exercises 3.10 and 3.11.

**3.13** Use the data given below to obtain the values of the first and third quartiles, the second and fourth deciles and the thirty-fifth and seventy-eighth percentiles.

| No of employees | No of work units (000) |
|---|---|
| 25–49 | 67 |
| 50–99 | 34 |
| 100–199 | 18 |
| 200–499 | 11 |
| 500–999 | 3 |
| 1000–1999 | 1 |
| 2000+ | 1 |

**3.14**
(a) What is meant by the first quartile and the third quartile? How can they be used to provide a measure of dispersion for a given set of data?
(b) Draw an ogive for the frequency distribution given below. Use your diagram to obtain the value of the semi-interquartile range. Briefly discuss your results.

Annual increase in rates in 1986/87 for 43 counties in England and Wales

| $X_i$(%) | $f_i$ |
|---|---|
| less than 10 | 5 |
| 10 up to but less than 15 | 10 |
| 15 up to but less than 20 | 15 |
| 20 up to but less than 25 | 7 |
| 25 up to but less than 30 | 3 |
| 30 up to but less than 35 | 2 |
| more than 35 | 1 |

*Observer*, 1 March 1986

**3.15** Calculate the mean and the median for both distributions given in Exercise 2.13. Compare and discuss your results.

# 4 Probability

In the previous chapters we concentrated on the presentation of data in tabular and graphic form and on developing various measures of location and dispersion which summarise strategically important features of a given set of data. Collectively these areas of analysis are known as descriptive statistics.

In this chapter we are going to introduce the topic of probability and in so doing provide the necessary link between descriptive statistics and inferential statistics.

We begin by developing a simple intuitive approach to the concept of probability after which various formulae and definitions will be introduced. Most of the examples and exercises are based on data taken from the *Family Expenditure Survey* and it would be helpful at this point to refer back to Section 1.5 where the main features of the survey are briefly described.

## 4.1 Relative frequency approach to probability

We can begin our approach to probability by asking the following question: From amongst all households in the UK consisting of at most six people, what is the probability that one household chosen at random will contain exactly two people?

One way of answering this question is to conduct an experiment in which we take a sample of households and count the proportion of the total containing exactly two people. The sample proportion estimated in this way could then be taken as an estimate of the unknown proportion in the population.

However, the accuracy of the resulting estimate will depend on the number of observations (households) in the sample, and it is therefore useful to know how the accuracy varies according to the number of observations used. For this reason it is of interest to conduct a series of sampling experiments in which the number of households in the sample is allowed to vary.

The results that such an experiment might produce are contained in Fig. 4.1 where the proportion of two-person households in each sample is measured vertically and the size of the sample is measured horizontally. From the figure it can be seen that in the

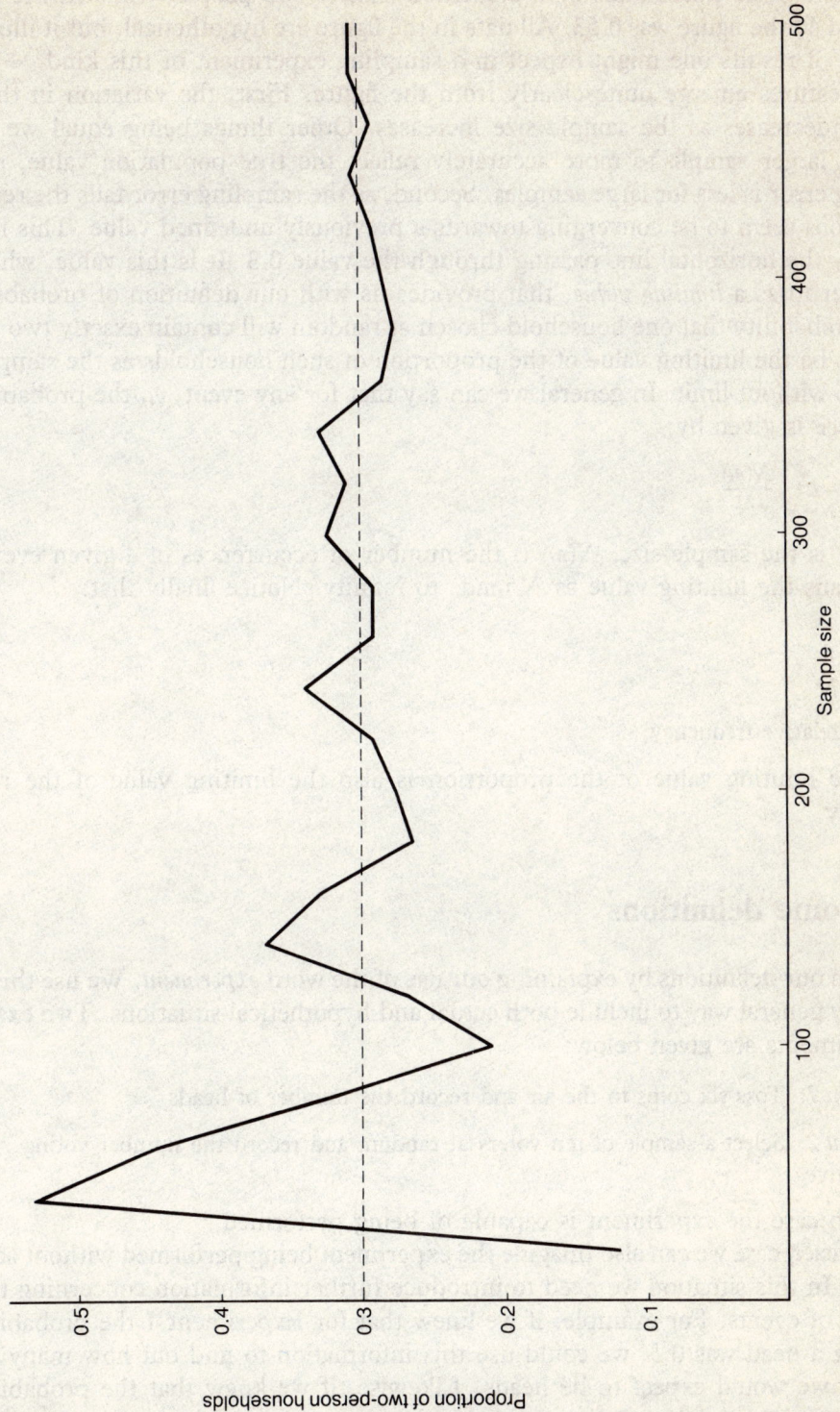

Figure 4.1 Hypothetical proportions in sampling experiment

first sample of 20 households 0.12 contained exactly two people, while in the second sample of 40 the figure was 0.53. All data in the figure are hypothetical, but it illustrates the kind of results one might expect in a sampling experiment of this kind.

Two features emerge quite clearly from the figure. First, the variation in the proportions decreases as the sample size increases. Other things being equal we would expect a larger sample to more accurately reflect the true population value, so that sampling error is less for large samples. Second, as the sampling error falls the resulting proportions seem to be converging towards a previously undefined value. This is illustrated by the horizontal line passing through the value 0.3. It is this value, which we shall refer to as a *limiting value*, that provides us with our definition of probability.

The probability that one household chosen at random will contain exactly two people is said to be the limiting value of the proportion of such households as the sample size increases without limit. In general we can say that for any event, $e_i$, the probability of occurrence is given by:

$$P(e_i) = \underset{N \to \infty}{Lt} \frac{N(e_i)}{N}$$

where $N$ is the sample size, $N(e_i)$ is the number of occurrences of a given event and $\underset{N \to \infty}{Lt}$ means the limiting value as $N$ tends to infinity. Notice finally that:

$$\frac{N(e_i)}{N} = \frac{f_i}{N}$$

$$= \text{relative frequency}$$

Thus the limiting value of the proportion is also the limiting value of the relative frequency.

## 4.2   Some definitions

We begin our definitions by explaining our use of the word *experiment*. We use this word in a fairly general way to include both actual and hypothetical situations. Two examples of experiments are given below:

*Experiment 1*: Toss six coins in the air and record the number of heads

*Experiment 2*: Select a sample of ten voters at random and record the number voting Conservative

In each case the experiment is capable of being performed.

But in each case we can also imagine the experiment being performed without actually doing it. In this situation we need to introduce further information concerning the occurrence of events. For example, if we knew that for Experiment 1 the probability of obtaining a head was 0.5, we could use this information to find out how many of the six coins we would expect to be heads. Likewise, if we knew that the probability of voting Conservative was 0.3, we could calculate how many of the ten voters we would expect to vote Conservative. In each case we have a hypothetical experiment rather than an actual one, and our use of the word experiment is meant to embrace both possibilities.

For each experiment we need to define the *sample space*. The sample space of an experiment lists each possible separate outcome of the experiment. If we select at random one household from amongst all households in the population with at most six people and record the number of people in it, we have six possible outcomes given by:

$e_1$ = household with 1 person
$e_2$ = household with 2 persons
$e_3$ = household with 3 persons
$e_4$ = household with 4 persons
$e_5$ = household with 5 persons
$e_6$ = household with 6 persons

Similarly, if we select at random one worker from a population and record employment status, we might list three possible outcomes as:

$e_1$ = employee
$e_2$ = self-employed
$e_3$ = economically inactive

Each element in a sample space is called a *simple event* (or an outcome or a non-decomposable event). Any collection of simple events is called a *compound event* (or a decomposable event). We use lower case $e$ to refer to the former and capital $E$ to refer to the latter. Given the simple events $e_1$, $e_2$, ..., $e_6$ above for the number of people in a household, we can define $E_1$ as the event of selecting a household with at most three people and $E_2$ as the event of selecting a household with at least four people. We therefore have:

$E_1 = (e_1; e_2; e_3)$
and   $E_2 = (e_4; e_5; e_6)$

A further important distinction centres around the nature of events. Two events are said to be *mutually exclusive* if the occurrence of one precludes the occurrence of the other. The events $E_1$ and $E_2$ as defined in the previous paragraph are mutually exclusive since any randomly selected household conforming to one event cannot at the same time conform to our definition of the other.

However, if we define $E_1$ as the selection of a household with at most four people and $E_2$ as the selection of a household with at least four people, $E_1$ and $E_2$ are *not mutually exclusive*. The occurrence of $E_1$ does not preclude the simultaneous occurrence of $E_2$ since the selection of a household with four people conforms with both events.

These definitions are illustrated in Fig. 4.2. Each part is called a *Venn diagram* and describes the main features of an experiment. Figure 4.2(a) shows the simple events $e_1$, $e_2$, ..., $e_6$ and the mutually exclusive compound events $E_1$ and $E_2$. In Fig. 4.2(b) we have the same six simple events but with $E_1$ and $E_2$ not mutually exclusive. The fact that $E_1$ and $E_2$ are not mutually exclusive is shown in the diagram by the mutual presence of $e_4$.

Finally we notice that in each diagram $E_1$ and $E_2$ embrace all simple events in the sample space and are therefore said to be *exhaustive*. If in Fig. 4.2(a) we were to keep $E_1$

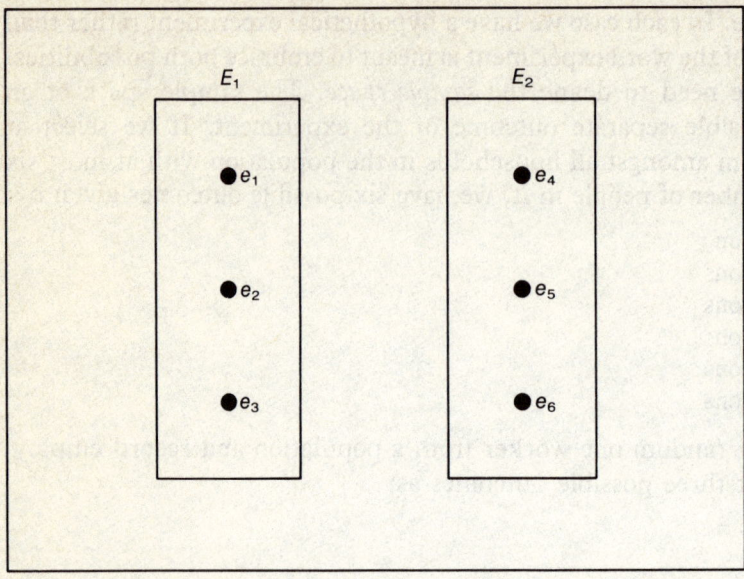

(a) Mutually exclusive

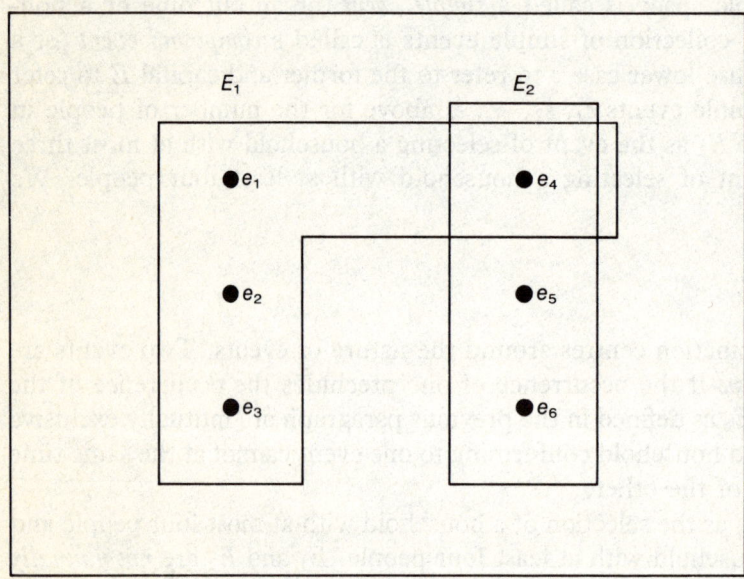

(b) Not mutually exclusive

Figure 4.2   Venn diagrams for events $E_1$ and $E_2$

as previously defined but define $E_2 = (e_4; e_5)$, $E_1$ and $E_2$ would not be exhaustive events because neither contains the simple event $e_6$ which is still an element in the total sample space.

We have previously defined the probability of a simple event and we now need to define the probability of a compound event.

Within the context of a sampling experiment the probability of occurrence for the event $e_1$ is given by:

$$P(e_1) = \underset{N \to \infty}{Lt} \frac{N(e_1)}{N}$$

If the composite event $E_1 = (e_1; e_2)$ then $E_1$ occurs if either $e_1$ or $e_2$ occurs, and we can therefore define the probability of $E_1$ as:

$$P(E_1) = \underset{N \to \infty}{Lt} \left( \frac{N(e_1) + N(e_2)}{N} \right)$$

$$= \underset{N \to \infty}{Lt} \frac{N(e_1)}{N} + \underset{N \to \infty}{Lt} \frac{N(e_2)}{N}$$

$$= P(e_1) + P(e_2)$$

The probability of $E_1$ is therefore equal to the sum of the probabilities of the simple events $e_1$ and $e_2$.

In general we can say that the probability of occurrence of a compound event is equal to the sum of the probabilities of the simple events of which it is composed.

From our definitions various probability axioms follow.

*First*:

$$0 \leqslant P(E_i) \leqslant 1$$

The probability of any event has a maximum value of 1 and a minimum value of 0. If we define $E_7$ as the event of selecting a household with more than six people, it is impossible for $E_7$ to occur, i.e. $P(E_7) = 0$. And if we define $E_A$ as the event of selecting a household with at least one person $P(E_A) = 1$ because it is certain to occur if the experiment is performed.

*Second*, for events that are mutually exclusive and exhaustive the sum of the probabilities is 1. If we have $K$ events for each of which $P(E_i) = N(E_i)/N$ where $N(E_i)$ is the number of simple events in the composite events $E_i$ and $N$ is the total number of simple events in the sample space it follows that

$$\sum_{i=1}^{K} P(E_i) = \frac{N(E_1)}{N} + \frac{N(E_2)}{N} + \cdots + \frac{N(E_k)}{N}$$

$$= \frac{N(E_1) + N(E_2) + \cdots + N(E_k)}{N} = \frac{N}{N} = 1$$

*Third*, in some situations it is easier to calculate $P(E_i)$ by first calculating the probability of $E_i$ not occurring, i.e. $P(\bar{E}_i)$. Since it is certain that an event $E_i$ will either occur or not occur it follows that:

$$P(E_i) + P(\bar{E}_i) = 1$$

and

$$P(E_i) = 1 - P(\bar{E}_i)$$

See Exercises 4.1, 4.2 and 4.3.

## 4.3  Addition rule of probability

In many practical situations it is not possible to conveniently list the sample space or work out probabilities from Venn diagrams and it becomes necessary to develop various formulae.

We begin by considering two events $E_1$ and $E_2$ and ask: what is the probability that either or both events will occur? In symbols we have:

$$P(E_1 \text{ or } E_2)$$

The solution depends on the nature of the event being considered.

Figure 4.3 contains a Venn diagram showing two events $E_1$ and $E_2$ which are not mutually exclusive. The shaded area in the diagram represents the simple events common to both compound events $E_1$ and $E_2$. The required probability $P(E_1 \text{ or } E_2)$ is given by all simple events in $E_1$ and $E_2$ as a fraction of the total sample space.

But if we add all simple events in $E_1$ to all those in $E_2$ we will double count all those in the shaded area. To overcome this problem we can define $N(E_1 \text{ and } E_2)$ as the number

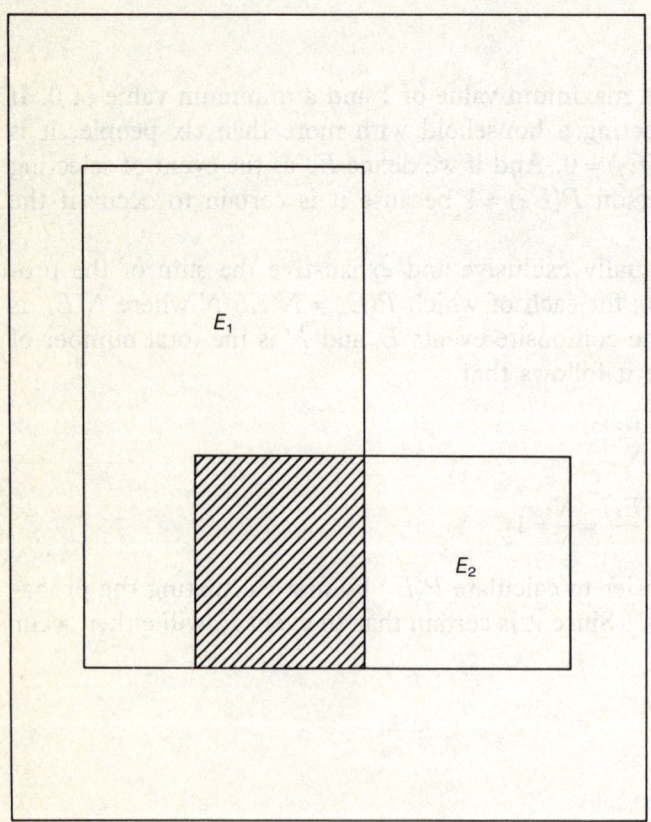

Figure 4.3  Venn diagram for events $E_1$ and $E_2$

of simple events in $E_1$ also occurring in $E_2$ and the required probability becomes:

$$P(E_1 \text{ or } E_2) = \frac{N(E_1)}{N} + \frac{N(E_2)}{N} - \frac{N(E_1 \text{ and } E_2)}{N}$$

$$= P(E_1) + P(E_2) - P(E_1 \text{ and } E_2)$$

This then is the *addition rule* of probability for two events which are not mutually exclusive.

This rule can be extended to incorporate more than two events which are not mutually exclusive, though the formula that results depends upon the particular areas of overlap in any given situation.

The simplest possibility is shown in Fig. 4.4 where the overlap is fully contained in

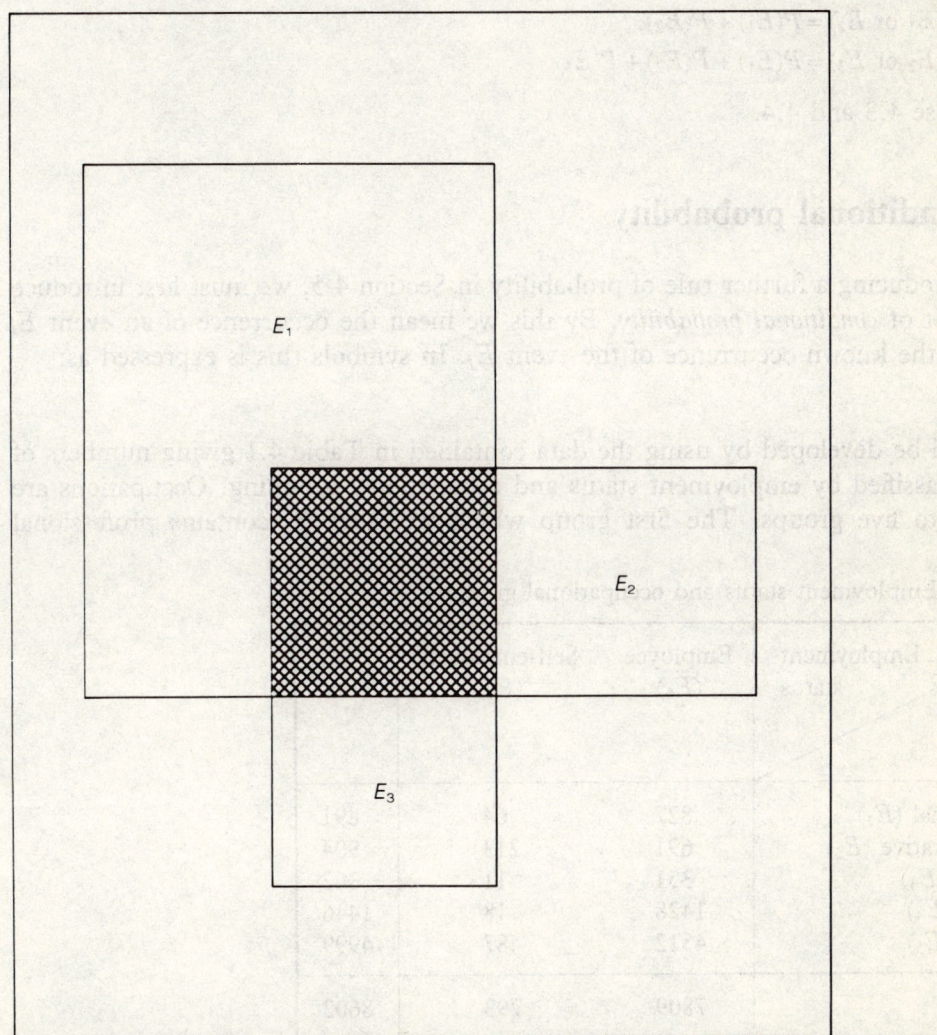

Figure 4.4 Venn diagram for events $E_1$, $E_2$ and $E_3$

the shaded area common to all three events. If we add all simple events in all three compound events, some of the former will be counted three times and the appropriate adjustment results in the following:

$$P(E_1 \text{ or } E_2 \text{ or } E_3) = P(E_1) + P(E_2) + P(E_3) - 2P(E_1 \text{ and } E_2 \text{ and } E_3)$$ □

In general, for three events which are not mutually exclusive we have:

$$P(E_1 \text{ or } E_2 \text{ or } E_3) = P(E_1) + P(E_2) + P(E_3) - P(E_1 \text{ and } E_2) - P(E_1 \text{ and } E_3)$$
$$- P(E_2 \text{ and } E_3) - 2P(E_1 \text{ and } E_2 \text{ and } E_3)$$

If the compound events under consideration are mutually exclusive areas of overlap do not exist and each probability of the form $P(E_i \text{ and } E_j)$ is 0. The addition rules for two or three events therefore become:

$$P(E_1 \text{ or } E_2) = P(E_1) + P(E_2)$$
$$P(E_1 \text{ or } E_2 \text{ or } E_3) = P(E_1) + P(E_2) + P(E_3)$$

See Exercise 4.3 and 4.4.


## 4.4  Conditional probability

Before introducing a further rule of probability in Section 4.5, we must first introduce the concept of *conditional probability*. By this we mean the occurrence of an event $E_i$ subject to the known occurrence of the event $E_j$. In symbols this is expressed as:

$P(E_i/E_j)$

This will be developed by using the data contained in Table 4.1 giving numbers of workers classified by employment status and occupational grouping. Occupations are divided into five groups. The first group which we label $E_1$ contains professional

Table 4.1  Employment status and occupational grouping

| Occup. grouping \ Employment status | Employee ($E_6$) | Self-employed ($E_7$) | Total |
|---|---|---|---|
| Professional ($E_1$) | 827 | 64 | 891 |
| Administrative ($E_2$) | 691 | 213 | 904 |
| Teacher ($E_3$) | 351 | 11 | 362 |
| Clerical ($E_4$) | 1428 | 18 | 1446 |
| Manual ($E_5$) | 4512 | 487 | 4999 |
| Total | 7809 | 793 | 8602 |

*FES*, 1979

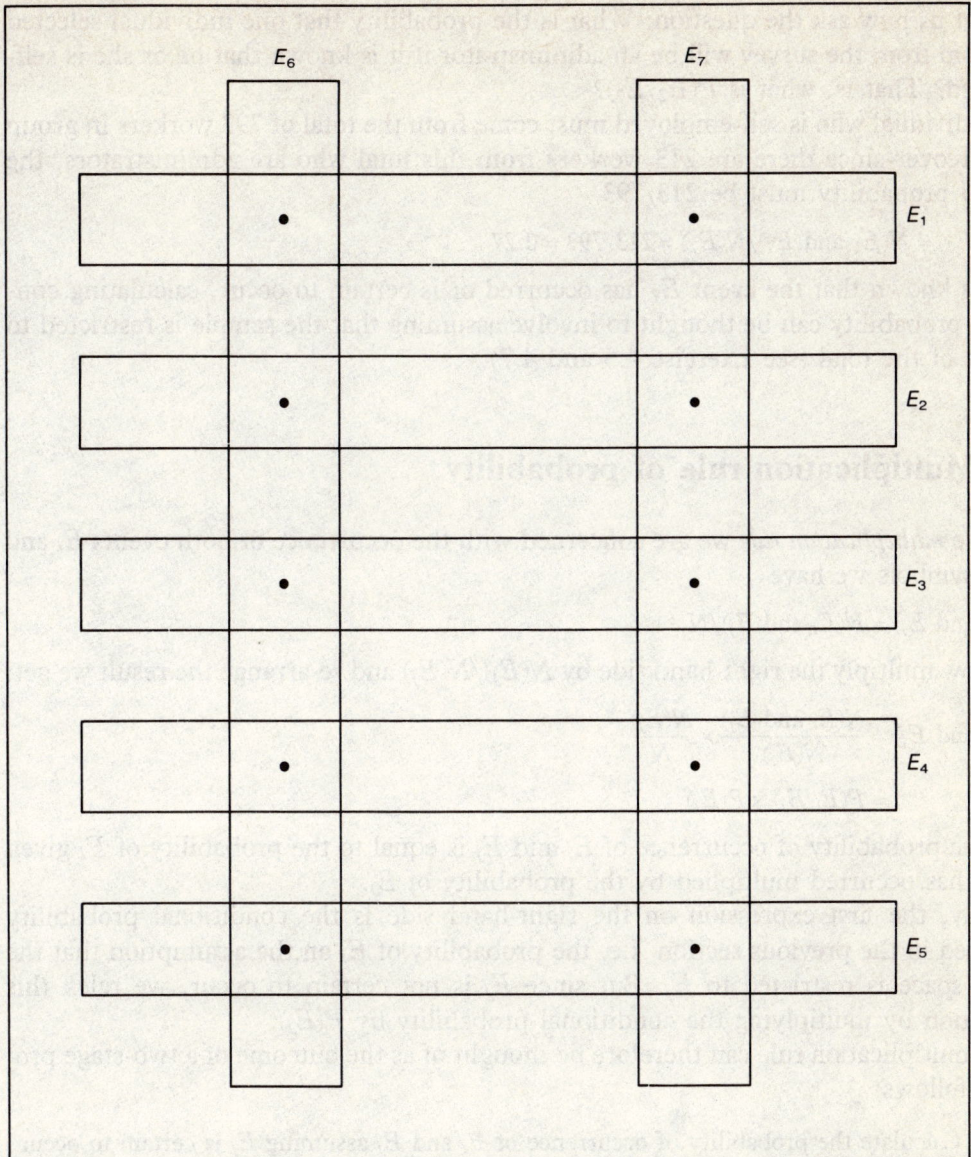

Figure 4.5   Venn diagram for employment status and occupational grouping

workers, the second group $E_2$ contains administrative workers, etc. Employment status is broken down into two groups containing employees labelled $E_6$ and self-employed labelled $E_7$. The associated Venn diagram is shown in Fig. 4.5.

With these figures we can calculate the probability of occurrence of each event. For example:

$$P(E_1) = N(E_1)/N = 891/8602 = 0.103$$

But let us now ask the question: What is the probability that one individual selected at random from the survey will be an administrator if it is known that he or she is self-employed? That is, what is $P(E_2/E_7)$?

An individual who is self-employed must come from the total of 793 workers in group $E_7$. Moreover since there are 213 workers from this total who are administrators, the required probability must be 213/793.

$$P(E_2/E_7) = N(E_2 \text{ and } E_7)/N(E_7) = 213/793 = 0.27$$

If it is known that the event $E_7$ has occurred or is certain to occur, calculating conditional probability can be thought to involve assuming that the sample is restricted to a subset of the total (see Exercise 4.5 and 4.7).

## 4.5  Multiplication rule of probability

With the *multiplication rule* we are concerned with the occurrence of both events $E_i$ and $E_j$. In symbols we have

$$P(E_i \text{ and } E_j) = N(E_i \text{ and } E_j)/N$$

If we now multiply the right-hand side by $N(E_j)/N(E_j)$ and re-arrange the result we get:

$$P(E_i \text{ and } E_j) = \frac{N(E_i \text{ and } E_j)}{N(E_j)} \times \frac{N(E_j)}{N}$$

$$= P(E_i/E_j) \times P(E_j)$$

Thus the probability of occurrence of $E_i$ and $E_j$ is equal to the probability of $E_i$ given that $E_j$ has occurred multiplied by the probability of $E_j$.

Clearly, the first expression on the right-hand side is the conditional probability developed in the previous section, i.e. the probability of $E_i$ on the assumption that the sample space is restricted to $E_j$. But since $E_j$ is not certain to occur, we relax this assumption by multiplying the conditional probability by $P(E_j)$.

The multiplication rule can therefore be thought of as the outcome of a two-stage process as follows:

*Stage 1*: Calculate the probability of occurrence of $E_i$ and $E_j$ assuming $E_j$ is certain to occur

*Stage 2*: Relax the assumption of certainty of occurrence of $E_j$ and allow for its possible non occurrence

See Exercise 4.6.

## Example 4.1 _____

From Table 4.1 we see that $E_2$ = probability of being an administrator and $E_7$ = probability of being self-employed.

It follows then that:

$$P(E_2 \text{ and } E_7) = P(E_2/E_7) \times P(E_7)$$
$$= 0.27 \times (793/8602)$$
$$= 0.27 \times 0.09$$
$$= 0.025$$

Note: by inspection $P(E_2 \text{ and } E_7) = 213/8602$
$$= 0.025$$

## 4.6 Statistical independence

There are some occasions when the multiplication rule as presented above can be simplified. This is so when events are *statistically independent*, i.e. the occurrence of one event is unaffected by the occurrence of another. In more formal terms we can say that two events are statistically independent if, and only if, in each case the conditional probability of occurrence equals the unconditional probability of occurrence:

$$P(E_i/E_j) = P(E_i)$$

*and*

$$P(E_j/E_i) = P(E_j)$$

We can illustrate this by using the hypothetical data in Table 4.2 which shows occupational status and gender for a number of individuals. Four events are defined as follows:

$E_1$ = male
$E_2$ = female
$E_3$ = employee
$E_4$ = self-employed

We can calculate the conditional probabilities:

$$P(E_1/E_3) = 300/450 = 2/3$$

and

$$P(E_3/E_1) = 300/400 = 3/4$$

Table 4.2 Employment status and gender (hypothetical data)

| Gender \ Status | Employee ($E_3$) | Self-employed ($E_4$) | Total |
|---|---|---|---|
| Male ($E_1$) | 300 | 100 | 400 |
| Female ($E_2$) | 150 | 50 | 200 |
| Total | 450 | 150 | 600 |

and the unconditional probabilities:

$P(E_1) = 400/600 = 2/3$

and

$P(E_3) = 450/600 = 3/4$

Clearly:

$P(E_1/E_3) = P(E_1) = 2/3$

and

$P(E_3/E_1) = P(E_3) = 3/4$

Knowing that an individual is an employee does not help in predicting whether or not the worker is male, and knowing that the worker is male does not help in predicting whether or not he is an employee.

In the light of our understanding of statistical independence we can look further at our rule of multiplication.

If:

$P(E_i/E_j) = P(E_i)$

the multiplication rule of probability previously given by:

$P(E_i \text{ and } E_j) = P(E_i/E_j) \times P(E_j)$

can now be replaced by:

$P(E_i \text{ and } E_j) = P(E_i) \times P(E_j)$

Moreover if we have three events $E_i$, $E_j$ and $E_k$ with each pair being statistically independent, the multiplication rule for all three events can be written

$P(E_i \text{ and } E_j \text{ and } E_k) = P(E_i) \times P(E_j) \times P(E_k)$

See Exercise 4.7.

## Example 4.2

Calculate the conditional and unconditional probability for the events $E_1$ and $E_6$ in Table 4.1. Are these two events statistically independent? How are your conclusions affected if the answers are given to one decimal place?

$P(E_1/E_6) = 827/7809 = 0.106$
$P(E_6/E_1) = 827/891 = 0.928$
$P(E_1) = 891/8602 = 0.104$
$P(E_6) = 7809/8602 = 0.908$

Since $P(E_1/E_6) \neq P(E_1)$ and $P(E_6/E_1) \neq P(E_6)$ the events are not statistically independent.

If answers are given to one decimal place

$$P(E_1/E_6) = P(E_1) = 0.1$$
$$P(E_6/E_1) = P(E_6) = 0.9$$

In this case $E_1$ and $E_6$ are statistically independent.

In such a situation we can conclude that strictly speaking events $E_1$ and $E_6$ are not statistically independent, but for practical purposes they may be considered as such. In practice, knowing that an individual is an employee does not help in predicting professional status or otherwise.

## Exercises

**4.1**  The *FES* classifies those households with married women according to: (1) the working status of the married woman (working; not working) and (2) the number of children the married woman has (0; 1; 2; 3; 4).

Define the sample space for an experiment in which one household is chosen at random from:
(a)  all households with married women,
(b)  all households with married women not working,
(c)  all households with married women with at least 3 children,
(d)  all households with married women with more than 1 but less than 4 children.

**4.2**  The *FES* provides data on the personal characteristics of individuals taking part in the survey. Individuals are classified, among other categories, according to gender (male; female) and employment status (employee at work; employee temporarily away from work; employee out of a job; self-employed; seeking occupation but not yet working).

Given this information define experiments of your own consisting of events $E_1$ and $E_2$ where these events are:
(a)  exhaustive and mutually exclusive,
(b)  mutually exclusive and not exhaustive,
(c)  not mutually exclusive and not exhaustive.

**4.3**  The data below are taken from *FES*, 1979, Table 1.
(a)  Construct the sample space for an experiment consisting of selecting one household at random and recording the size of household.
(b)  Calculate the probability that one household chosen at random from the *FES* survey will contain:
  (i)    1 or 3 persons
  (ii)   an even number of people
  (iii)  less than 4 people

| Size of household (persons) | % of households | No of households |
|---|---|---|
| 1 | 22.0 | 1494 |
| 2 | 32.1 | 2176 |
| 3 | 16.3 | 1101 |
| 4 | 18.5 | 1254 |
| 5 | 7.4 | 502 |
| 6 | 2.5 | 167 |
| 7 | 0.8 | 57 |
| 8 | 0.2 | 11 |
| 9 or more | 0.2 | 15 |
| Total | 100.0 | 6777 |

(iv)  an even number of people or a number less than 3 or greater than 6
(v)   an odd number of people or greater than 5
(vi)  a number of people between 2 and 6 or between 4 and 8
In each case draw the associated Venn diagram.

**4.4**  Write out the addition rule of probability for the three events given in each of the diagrams below:

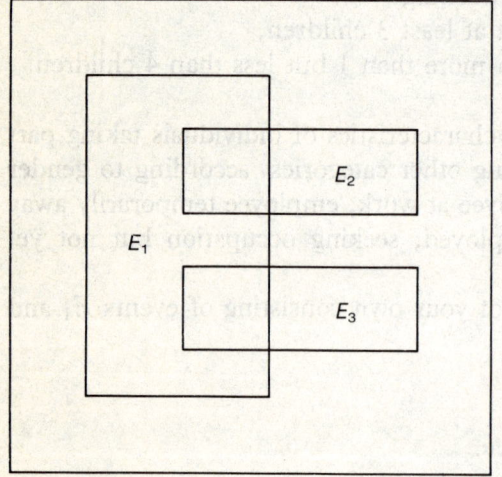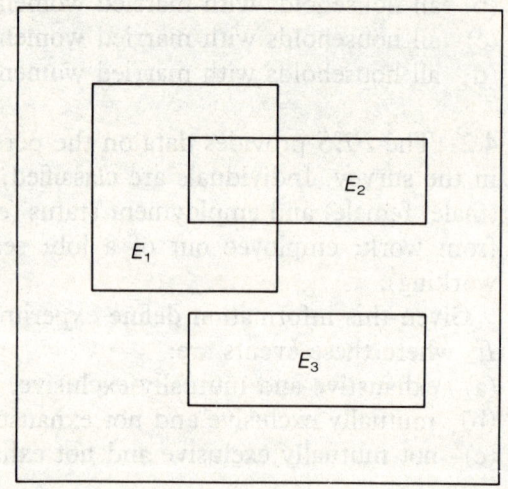

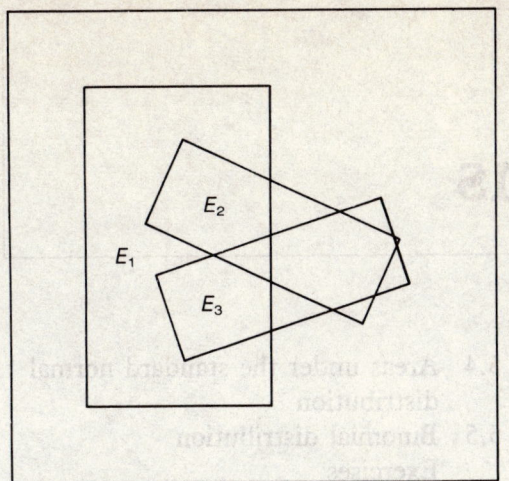

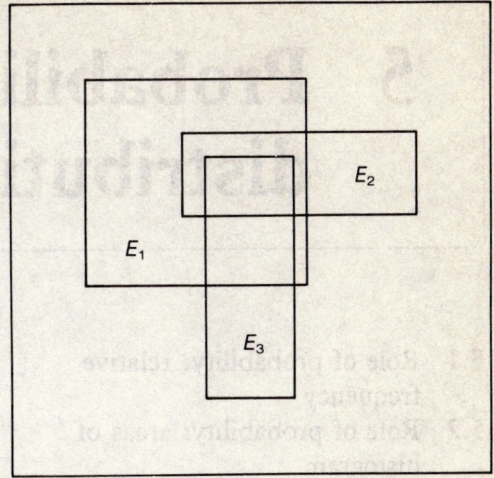

**4.5** Given the data contained in Table 4.1 calculate:
(a) $P(E_1/E_6)$
(b) $P(E_6/E_4)$
(c) $P(E_5/E_7)$
(d) $P(E_7/E_2)$

**4.6** For the data in Table 4.1 use the multiplication rule to calculate:
(a) $P(E_1 \text{ and } E_7)$
(b) $P(E_6 \text{ and } E_5)$
(c) $P(E_3 \text{ and } E_6)$
(d) $P(E_4 \text{ and } E_7)$

**4.7** Use the data in Table 4.1 to calculate the conditional probabilities $P(E_i/E_j)$, $P(E_j/E_i)$ and the unconditional probabilities $P(E_i)$, $P(E_j)$ for each of the following:
(a) $E_5$ and $E_7$
(b) $E_2$ and $E_7$
(c) $E_3$ and $E_6$
(d) $E_4$ and $E_6$
Say whether or not each pair is statistically independent.

# 5 Probability distributions

From our previous discussion we know that statistical analysis involves the use of information contained in a sample, and that the sample represents the population from which it is taken. So a frequency distribution of a variable $X$ based on sample data is an estimate of the distribution of $X$ in the population. We also know that the presence of sampling error means that the sample is not a completely accurate reflection of the population.

Nevertheless, experience has shown that certain shapes of frequency distribution continually recur, and two of these form the focal point of the material in this chapter. But our concern here is not with distributions whose shape is generated by sample data, but with distributions whose shape is determined by a formula.

Before introducing these distributions let us see in the next two sections how our discussion of probability in Chapter 4 relates to our understanding of frequency distributions.

## 5.1 Role of probability: relative frequency

Developing our discussion in Sections 3.1 and 3.2, let us define:

$\bar{X}$ = sample mean
$s$ = sample standard deviation
$\mu$ = population mean
$\sigma$ = population standard deviation

$$\bar{X} = \frac{\sum_{i=1}^{K} f_i X_i}{N}$$

$$= \sum_{i=1}^{K} x_i \times \frac{f_i}{N}$$

But we also know that $f_i/N$ is the relative frequency of the $i$th class interval which is an estimate of the true population probability. Therefore we can say that the population mean, $\mu$, is given by:

$$\mu = \sum_{i=1}^{K} x_i \times P(x_i)$$

Likewise we know that the standard deviation for the sample is given by:

$$s = \sqrt{\frac{\sum_{i=1}^{K}(x_i - \bar{X})^2 \times f_i}{N}} = \sqrt{\sum_{i=1}^{K}(x_i - \bar{X})^2 \times \frac{f_i}{N}}$$

and that $f_i/N$ is an estimate of the unknown population probability. Therefore we can say that the population standard deviation, $\sigma$, is given by:

$$\sigma = \sqrt{\sum_{i=1}^{K}(x_i - \bar{X})^2 \times P(x_i)}$$

## 5.2 Role of probability: areas of histogram

We can also show how the concept of relative frequency relates to the histogram. Consider the histogram shown in Fig. 2.1 and the corresponding frequency distribution shown in Table 2.2. Suppose we wish to calculate the total area of the histogram. This is given by the sum of the areas of the separate rectangles:

area $= (3 \times 10) + (12 \times 10) + (9 \times 10) + (6 \times 10)$
$= 300$ square units

Now suppose we wish to normalise the histogram by reducing its area to one square unit. We do this by dividing throughout by 300:

$$\text{normalised area} = \frac{(3 \times 10)}{300} + \frac{(12 \times 10)}{300} + \frac{(9 + 10)}{300} + \frac{(6 \times 10)}{300}$$

$$= \frac{f_1}{N} + \frac{f_2}{N} + \frac{f_3}{N} + \frac{f_4}{N}$$

$$= 1 \text{ square unit}$$

So the area of each rectangle is now expressed in terms of its appropriate relative frequency and we can ask, e.g. What proportion of the changes in the FT Index fall between $-10$ and $+10$? The required proportion is given by:

$$\frac{\text{shaded area}}{\text{total area}} = \frac{(12 \times 10) + (9 \times 10)}{300} = \frac{12/30 + 9/30}{1} = 0.7$$

We can therefore think of relative frequencies as being equivalent to areas under certain parts of the curve for a normalised histogram.

## 5.3  Normal distribution

The normal distribution is probably the single most important distribution in statistical analysis. This is so for two reasons. First, experience has shown that many variables such as height, weight and intelligence are approximately normally distributed. Second, because it is at the heart of much of the inferential statistics to be introduced later.

We have already come across the normal distribution in Section 3.3 where it was defined as being bell shaped and perfectly symmetrical about its vertical axis. More formally we can say that the normal distribution for a variable $X_i$ is given by the expression:

$$f(X_i) = \frac{1}{\sqrt{2\pi\sigma^2}} \times e^{-1/2[(X_i-\mu)/\sigma]^2}$$

where  $f(X_i) =$ frequency of $X_i$
$\quad\quad\quad \mu =$ mean of $X_i$
$\quad\quad\quad \sigma =$ standard deviation of $X_i$
$\quad\quad\quad \pi = 3.14$
$\quad\quad\quad e = 2.72$

Since $\pi$ and e are constants it is clear from the formula that the normal distribution depends entirely upon the values of $X$, the mean and the standard deviation. Moreover, since $\mu$ and $\sigma$ will vary for different sets of data there is, in practice, an infinite number of different normal distributions.

Consider the two distributions shown in Fig. 5.1. Both are normally distributed but the one on the left has a smaller mean value and a smaller standard deviation than the one on the right. We can therefore say that the formula for the normal distribution given above expresses a family of distributions in which each is different from the rest but all are closely related to each other.

A problem arises, however, when we wish to compare two normal distributions with differing means and differing standard deviations. For example, we may wish to compare

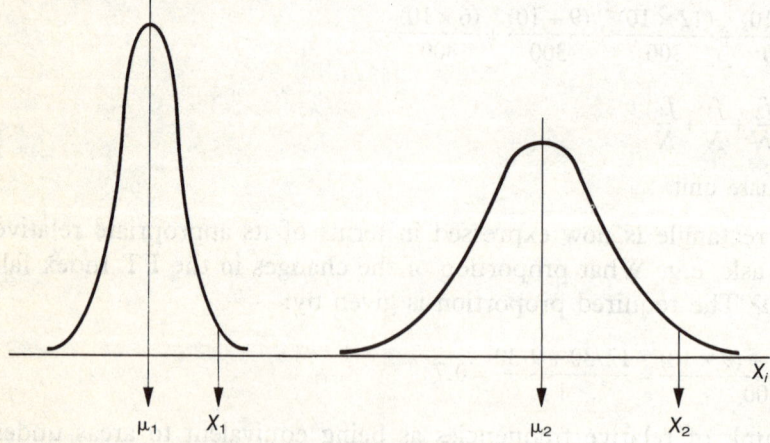

Figure 5.1  Two different normal distributions

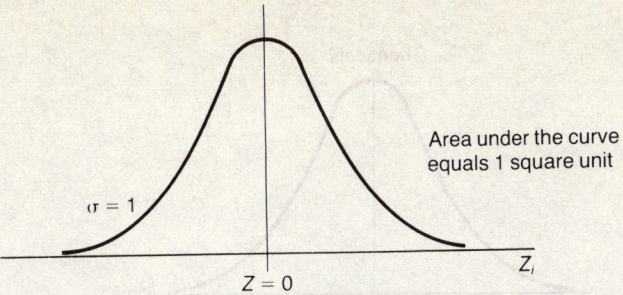

Figure 5.2   Standard normal distribution

the value $X_1$ in the left-hand distribution with the value $X_2$ in the right-hand distribution. In absolute terms it is obvious that $X_2$ is greater than $X_1$ but it is not obvious, for example, whether $X_1$ is further from $\mu_1$ in relative terms than $X_2$ is from $\mu_2$.

To make such a comparison we need to introduce a particular kind of normal distribution called the *standard normal distribution* (SND). A standard normal distribution is a normal distribution whose mean value is 0, standard deviation is 1 and whose area under the curve is equal to 1 square unit. Such a curve is illustrated in Fig. 5.2 where the horizontal axis is now labelled $Z_i$.

This distribution is the reference point which makes possible comparison between all other non-standard normal curves. Any non-SND can be reduced to an SND by use of the transformation given by:

$$Z_i = (X_i - \mu)/\sigma$$

where $Z_i$ = the point on the SND corresponding to $X_i$ on the non-SND

$\mu$ = mean value of the non-SND

$\sigma$ = standard deviation of the non-SND

The calculations involved are illustrated in Example 5.1 (see also Exercises 5.1 and 5.2).

# Example 5.1

The growth rates of sales (%) over the period 1980–5 for firms in the food and chemicals industries are normally distributed with means and standard deviations as follows:

|          | Food | Chemicals |
|----------|------|-----------|
| $\mu$    | 5.2  | 10.3      |
| $\sigma$ | 0.8  | 1.4       |

Two firms are selected at random. Firm 1 from the food industry has a growth rate of sales of 6.4% and Firm 2 from the chemicals industry has a growth rate of sales of 12.4%. The performance of both firms in relation to the industries from which they

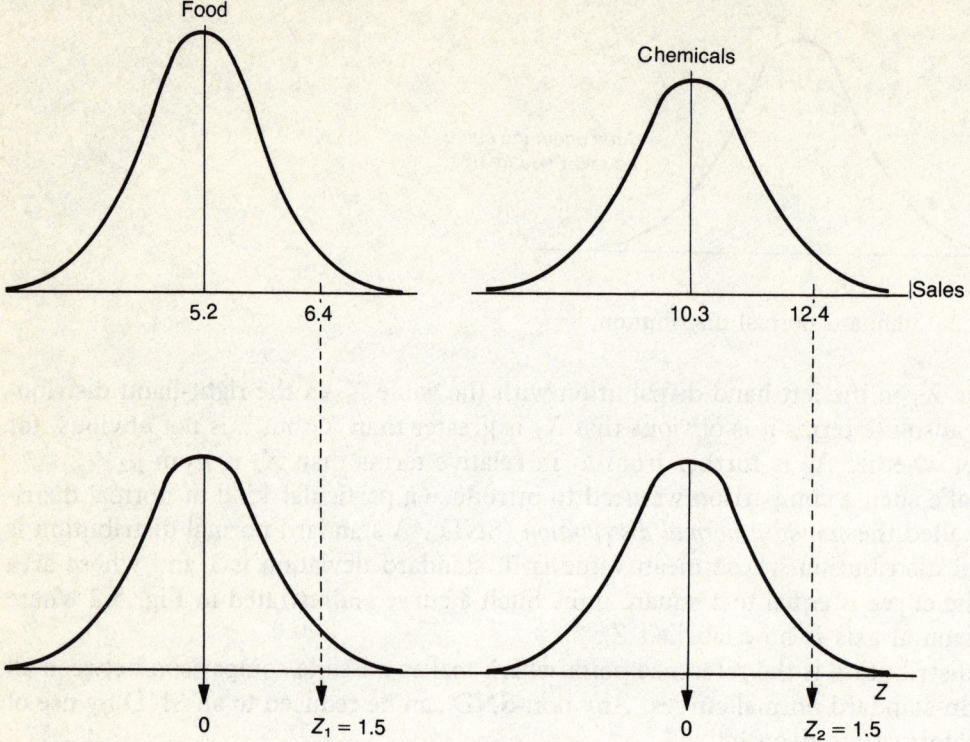

Figure 5.3   SND and non-SND curves for the food and chemicals industries

come is illustrated in Fig. 5.3. For Firm 1 a value of 6.4% provides a value on the SND given by:

$$Z_1 = (6.4 - 5.2)/0.8 = 1.5$$

Similarly for Firm 2 a value of 12.4% provides a value on the SND given by:

$$Z_2 = (12.4 - 10.3)/1.4 = 1.5$$

From this we can see that the performance of both firms, relative to the industry from which each comes, is the same.

## 5.4   Areas under the standard normal distribution

In Chapter 3 we saw that one of the properties of the normal distribution is that approximately 95% of the area under the curve is contained between values of $X$ given by $\mu \pm 2\sigma$.

With the help of the SND we can in fact go further and say exactly how much of the area is contained between these values. Indeed it is possible to define any two values of

$X$ and say how much of the area under the curve is contained between them. To do this we need to extend our understanding of the SND.

The table in Appendix A shows areas under the curve of an SND for given values of $Z$. Numbers contained in the first column and the first row when combined express values of $Z$ to two decimal places, while values given in the rest of the table are corresponding areas under the curve.

For example, beginning at the row labelled 1.9 and reading along to the column headed 0.06 we obtain the value 0.4750. The numbers 1.9 and 0.06 combined gives the $Z$ ordinate of 1.96, so that 0.4750 square units are contained between the values $Z = 0$ (the mean of the SND) and $Z = 1.96$. Since by definition the entire area equals 1 square unit, the values of $Z$ defined contain 47.5% of the entire area. In addition it follows that since the curve is perfectly symmetrical about the mean, 95% of the area under the curve is contained between the values of $Z = \pm 1.96$.

In general the table can be used to calculate areas under the curve for any two values of $Z$. This is illustrated in Fig. 5.4. If we wish to find the area between $Z_3$ and $Z_4$, we can find the areas between 0 and $Z_3$ and between 0 and $Z_4$ and calculate the sum of the two. Or if we wish to find the area between $Z_1$ and $Z_2$, we can find the areas between 0 and $Z_1$ and between 0 and $Z_2$ and subtract the latter from the former. Finally, to find the non-shaded area to the right of $Z_4$ we can find the area between 0 and $Z_4$ and subtract the value from 0.5 since half the total area lies to the right of the mean value of $Z = 0$.

As well as finding areas under the curve for given values of $Z$, we can find values of $Z$ for given areas under the curve. If, for example, we are told that a given area lies between $Z = 0$ and a value of $Z$ which is to the right of the mean, we can find the area in the body of the table and read the resulting value of $Z$. Example 5.2 illustrates the calculations involved in finding both ordinates and areas of the SND (see also Exercises 5.3 to 5.8).

We have seen earlier in this chapter that areas under the curve of a normalised histogram can be thought of as being equivalent to relative frequencies and that relative frequencies are estimates of probabilities. From this we can see that areas under the curve of the SND, which is a normalised distribution, are equivalent to probability values. So when finding the area under the curve for two values of $Z$, say $Z_1$ and $Z_2$,

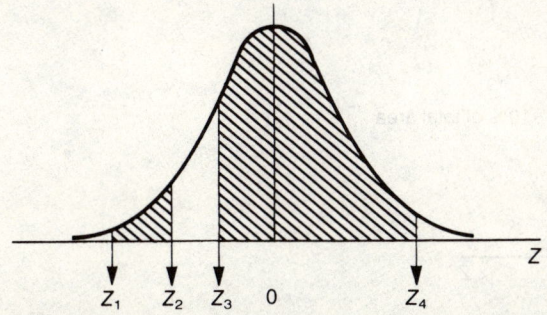

Figure 5.4   Calculating areas of the SND for given values of $Z$

we are also finding the probability that the variable $Z$ will lie between $Z_1$ and $Z_2$ (see Exercise 5.6).

# Example 5.2

In Fig. 5.5 the values of $Z_i$ are $Z_1 = -2.04$, $Z_2 = -1.62$, $Z_3 = -0.81$ and $Z_4 = 1.52$.
First we can calculate the area between $Z_3$ and $Z_4$.

area between 0 and    $1.52 = 0.4357$
area between 0 and $-0.81 = 0.2881$
$$\overline{\phantom{xxxxxxxx}}$$
required area $= 0.7238$

Next we can calculate the area between $Z_1$ and $Z_2$.

area between 0 and $-2.04 = 0.4793$
area between 0 and $-1.62 = 0.4474$
$$\overline{\phantom{xxxxxxxx}}$$
required area $= 0.0319$

To find $Z$ values from given areas refer to Fig. 5.6. From Appendix A we see that an

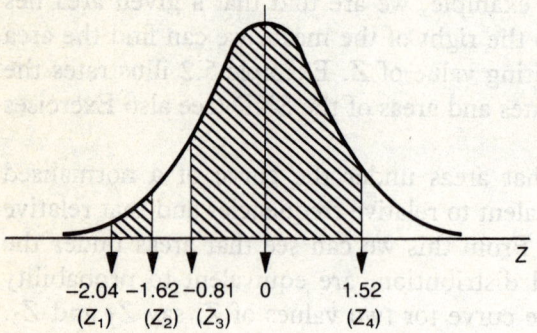

Figure 5.5   Calculating areas of the SND given $Z$

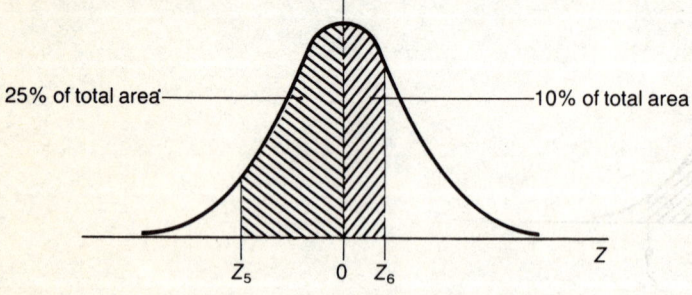

Figure 5.6   Calculating values of $Z$ given the areas of the SND

area of 0.25 gives a $Z$ value of 0.67. Since we are dealing with 25% of the area to the left of the mean the $Z$ value must be negative. Therefore $Z_5 = -0.67$. Similarly 10% of the area means finding a $Z$ value for 0.1 in the body of the table. The value is 0.25 and since the area concerned is to the right of the mean the value for $Z_6$ is $+0.25$. Therefore we can say there is 35% probability that for the SND the value of $Z$ varies between $-0.67$ and $+0.25$.

## 5.5 Binomial distribution

The second distribution of interest is the binomial distribution. A variable $X$ is said to be binomially distributed if there are only two possible outcomes to an experiment.

If the variable $X$ measures voting in a particular constituency and if the only outcomes are defined as voting Conservative or not voting Conservative, $X$ is binomially distributed. Other variables which are binomially distributed when defined as given include gender (male or female), number of persons in household (less than two, two or more), income (less than £150 per week, at least £150 per week) and company size (sales less than £100m per year, sales at least £100m per year).

In each case one outcome is labelled a success and one is labelled failure. The sole basis on which these labels are introduced is convenience and no moral or value judgement is involved; an event labelled success in one situation may well be labelled failure in another.

It is also necessary to assign probabilities to each of the two events. We will let the probability of success be $p$ and the probability of failure be $q$. By definition $p + q = 1$. For example, if $X$ measures voting behaviour as defined above and if the probability of voting Conservative ($p$) is 0.3, then the probability of not voting Conservative ($q$) is 0.7.

In order to develop further the binomial distribution we will consider more fully the example given above in which $X$ measures company size. Let us assume that companies in a given industry with sales less than £100m per year are considered small and those with sales at least £100m per year are considered large. We will further assume that amongst the many companies in the industry, exactly half are small and half are large so that $p = q = 0.5$. Given this information we now ask: What is the sample space for an experiment in which 4 companies are selected at random from the industry?

The solution is shown in Fig. 5.7 and is developed as follows. The first company will be either large (L) or small (S).

If it is large it will be followed by the second company which will be either large or small. So at this stage we have two outcomes: either 2 large companies (LL) or 1 large followed by 1 small (LS).

But the first company may be small and this will be followed by a second which may be large or small. So we have two further possibilities: 1 small company followed by 1 large company (SL) or 2 small companies (SS). Thus after considering only the first 2 companies we have four possible outcomes: LL, LS, SL, SS.

If we pursue the same logic for all 4 companies we will finish with sixteen simple

| First company | Second company | Third company | Fourth company |
|---|---|---|---|

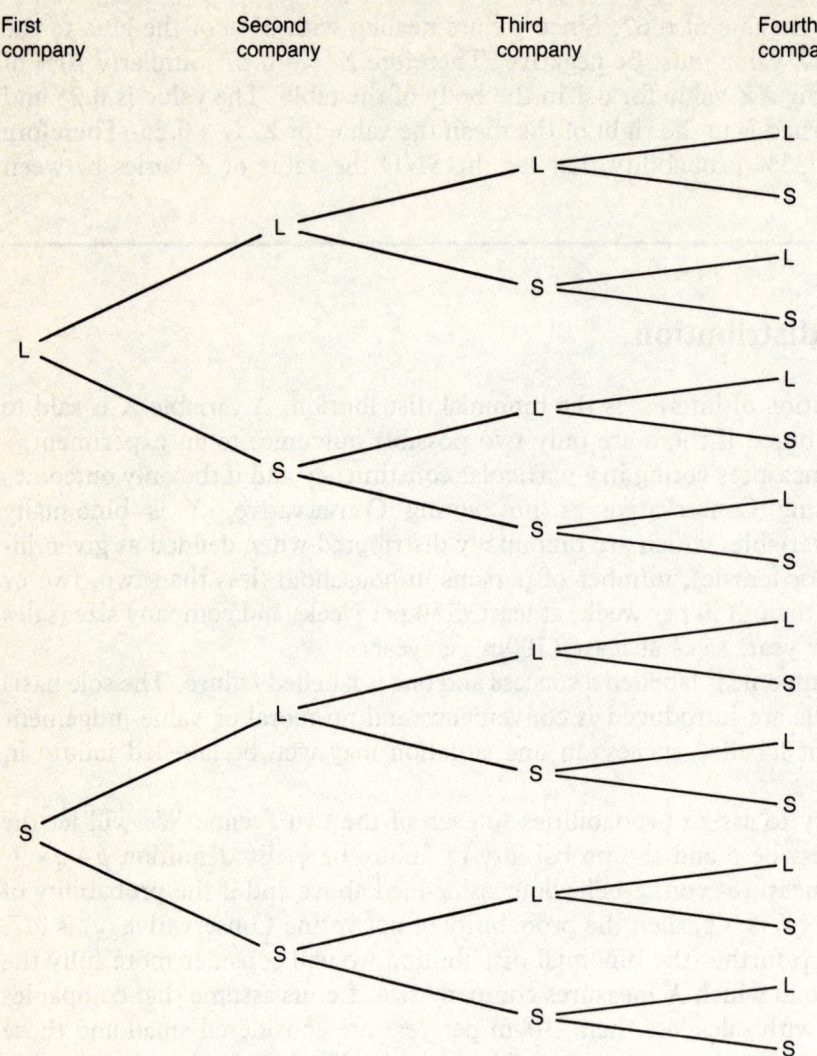

Figure 5.7  Sample space for binomial distribution

events as shown in the last column of the diagram. The first consists of 4 large companies, the second consists of 3 large and 1 small, etc.

If we ignore the order of companies within each event given in the final column, we can arrange them into a frequency distribution as follows:

|  | 4 large + 0 small | 3 large + 1 small | 2 large + 2 small | 1 large + 3 small | 0 large + 4 small |
|---|---|---|---|---|---|
| Frequency | 1 | 4 | 6 | 4 | 1 |

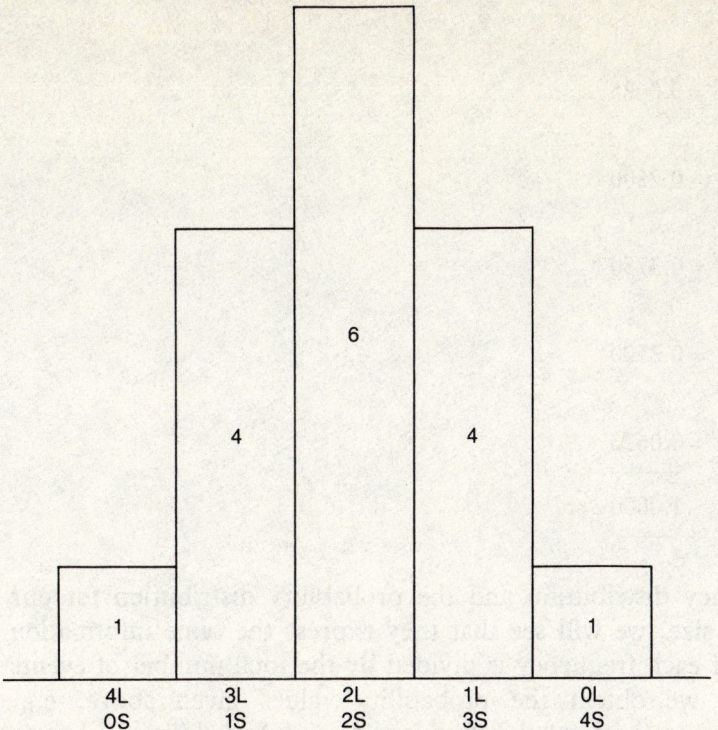

Figure 5.8  Histogram for binomial distribution

The frequency distribution is also shown in Fig. 5.8.

Although the approach outlined in Fig. 5.7 is simple to follow, it becomes very tedious to list the sample space when we have a large number of observations in the sample. Also, though we have listed and counted all possible outcomes we have so far said nothing about the probability of occurrence of events. Both of these limitations can be overcome by introducing the formula for the *binomial probability distribution*:

$$P(X) = \frac{N!}{X! \times (N-X)!} \times p^X q^{N-X}$$

where $P(X)$ = probability of obtaining $X$ successes in $N$ trials
$N! = N \times (N-1) \times (N-2) \times \cdots \times 1$
$p$ = probability of success of a given simple event
$q$ = probability of failure of a given simple event

In order to apply this formula two details should be noted. First, the expression $N!$ is read as '$N$ factorial' and is the sequential product of the first $N$ natural numbers, e.g. $4! = 4 \times 3 \times 2 \times 1 = 24$. Second, we state without proof that $0! = 1$ and that any number raised to the power zero equals 1, so that $\frac{1}{2}^0 = 1$.

We are now in a position to apply the formula to our example of company size. If we define large as a success and given that $N = 4$, $p = 0.5$, $q = 0.5$ and $X = 0, 1, 2, 3, 4$ we obtain the following:

$$P(X=0) = \frac{4!}{0! \times 4!} \times 0.5^0 \times 0.5^4 = 0.0625$$

$$P(X=1) = \frac{4!}{1! \times 3!} \times 0.5 \times 0.5^3 = 0.2500$$

$$P(X=2) = \frac{4!}{2! \times 2!} \times 0.5^2 \times 0.5^2 = 0.3750$$

$$P(X=3) = \frac{4!}{3! \times 1!} \times 0.5^3 \times 0.5 = 0.2500$$

$$P(X=4) = \frac{4!}{4! \times 0!} \times 0.5^4 \times 0.5^0 = 0.0625$$

$$1.0000$$

By comparing the frequency distribution and the probability distribution for our example involving company size, we will see that they express the same information although in different ways. If each frequency is divided by the total number of events in the sample space (16), we obtain the probability values given above, e.g. $1/16 = 0.0625$. Once again we see how relative frequencies and probabilities relate to each other. We should also note that individual probability values can be added to find the probabilities of combined events as illustrated in Example 5.3.

Having now considered the normal distribution and the binomial distribution separately we will conclude by briefly discussing the way in which they are related to each other. From Fig. 5.8 it can be seen that the binomial distribution shown resembles the normal distribution in that it is perfectly symmetrical about the vertical axis. This is no accident. If we increased the number of firms from 4 to 100, 500 or 1000, we would find that the resulting binomial distribution would look more and more like a normal distribution. For this reason we can say that the normal distribution is the limiting case of the binomial distribution as the number of observations tends towards infinity. The normal distribution can therefore be seen to be a special case of the binomial distribution (see Exercises 5.9 to 5.15).

# Example 5.3

If all firms in an industry are classified large or small, and if the probability of being large or small are equal at 0.5, find the probability that in a randomly selected group of 4 firms more than 1 but less than 4 will be large.

The condition more than 1 but less than 4 will be met if either 2 or 3 of the 4 are large. If we define large as a success and $X$ as the number of successes, we therefore need to calculate $P(X=2)$ and $P(X=3)$ and add the two together.

$$P(X=2) = \frac{4!}{2! \times 2!} \times 0.5^2 \times 0.5^2 = 0.3750$$

$$P(X=3) = \frac{4!}{3! \times 1!} \times 0.5^3 \times 0.5 = 0.2500$$

The required probability therefore equals $0.3750 + 0.2500 = 0.6250$.

---

## Exercises

In the exercises below it is always useful to draw diagrams where possible.

**5.1** The arrival time of passengers for a given train is normally distributed about a mean value of 08.00 hours with a standard deviation of 3 minutes. Find the values of $Z$ on the SND corresponding to arrival times of:
(a) 2 minutes before 08.00 hours
(b) 1 minute before 08.00 hours
(c) 90 seconds after 08.00 hours
(d) 5 minutes past 08.00 hours

**5.2** If $X$ is the distribution of arrival time in the previous question, find the values of $X$ corresponding to $Z$ values:
(a) 1.92
(b) 0.61
(c) −1.12
(d) −2.01

**5.3** Find the area under the standard normal curve between:
(a) $Z = 0.91$ and $Z = 1.45$
(b) $Z = -0.62$ and $Z = 1.01$
(c) $Z = -2.39$ and $Z = -1.23$
(d) $Z = 1.10$ and $Z = +\infty$
(e) $Z = -0.32$ and $Z = 2.51$

**5.4** Find the ordinates of the standard normal curve that contain:
(a) 40% of the area under the curve immediately to the right of the mean;
(b) 90% of the area under the curve with 42% to the right of the mean and 48% to the left.

**5.5** The variable $X$ is normally distributed with mean 20 and standard deviation 5. Find the area under the curve for values of $X$ between:
(a) 20 and 30
(b) 15 and 24
(c) 24 and 28
(d) 12 and 19

**5.6**   A variable $Y$ is normally distributed with mean 40 and standard deviation 10. What is the probability that the value of $Y$:
(a)   is greater than 50
(b)   is less than 32
(c)   is between 25 and 46

**5.7**   A variable $Y$ is distributed normally about a mean value of 25 with a standard deviation of 10. Find the areas under the curve for values of $Y$ between:
(a)   $-5$ and 15
(b)   23 and 50
(c)   28 and 30
(d)   22 and 26

**5.8**   A variable $X$ is normally distributed with mean 4 and standard deviation 8. What is the probability that the value of $X$:
(a)   lies between $-16$ and $-10$
(b)   is greater than $-10$
(c)   is less than 14

**5.9**   In a given university it is known that the probability of a student, chosen at random, being politically active is 0.3, while the probability of not being politically active is 0.7. Find the probability that in a sample of 5 students:
(a)   exactly 2 will be politically active;
(b)   at least 4 will be politically inactive;
(c)   the number of politically active students will be larger than the number of politically inactive ones.

**5.10**   Six coins are tossed in the air. Find the probability distribution $P(X)$ where $X$ is the number of heads obtained and $X = 0$, 1, 2, 3, 4, 5, 6. Graph the resulting distribution.

**5.11**   On the basis of past experience it is known that the probability of a first year student correctly spelling the word 'Quantitative' is 0.6. Find the probability that in a sample of 8 students:
(a)   at least 7 will spell the word correctly;
(b)   more than 3 but less than 6 will spell it incorrectly;
(c)   none will spell it correctly.

**5.12**   Find the binomial probability distribution $P(X)$ for $X = 0$, 1, 2, 3, 4 with:
(a)   $p = 0.2$ and $q = 0.8$
(b)   $p = 0.8$ and $q = 0.2$
(c)   $p = 0.5$ and $q = 0.5$
Draw the graph for each distribution and compare the resulting shapes.

**5.13**

(a)  During the course of a given year the stock market index fell on 30 of the total
     number of 250 trading days. Use the binomial distribution to determine the
     probability that the stock market index will fall on at most 3 of the 20 trading days
     during the month of July in the following year.

(b)  Do you think that it is valid to apply the binomial distribution to the problem
     outlined in (a)? Give reasons for your answer.

**5.14**  In a soccer match between two local teams the probability of an individual chosen
at random from the crowd being a supporter of the home team is 0.6, while the
probability of him being a supporter of the away team is 0.4.

(a)  Obtain the frequency distribution for a sample of 5 supporters chosen at random.
     Draw the relevant histogram.

(b)  Find the probability that in a sample of 5 chosen at random more will support the
     away team than support the home team.

(c)  What would you expect to happen to the shape of the distribution if the probability
     of an individual being a home team supporter increased to 0.8?

**5.15**  In the population of quoted companies in the UK 30% of companies earn above
average profits. Find the probability that in a sample of 6 companies:

(a)  exactly 1 will earn above average profits;

(b)  only 3 will earn above average profits;

(c)  none will earn above average profits.

# 6 Sampling and sampling distributions

6.1 Constructing a sampling distribution of a mean

6.2 Characteristics of the sampling distribution of a mean

6.3 Sampling distribution of a mean and the $Z$ distribution

6.4 Other sampling distributions

Exercises

With the advent of national opinion polls, most people are familiar with the idea of taking a sample in order to say something about the population from which it comes. Few, however, are aware of the logistics of sampling. Although there are many ways in which a sample can be taken, two in particular are worth mentioning.

The first is *random sampling* in which every member of the population has an equal probability of being selected in the sample. For example, selecting any name from all those contained in a telephone book would be random sampling providing each name appeared only once.

A second way of taking a sample is to take a *stratified sample* in which certain known characteristics are constrained to appear in the sample. For example, if we were investigating a racial issue in a constituency where whites outnumbered blacks by 3 to 1, we might want to choose the sample in such a way that its members accurately reflect this racial mix.

In this chapter we will develop further our understanding of sampling by introducing a distribution known as a sampling distribution. We will assume that our samples are selected randomly, though our analysis would not be materially affected if alternative methods of sampling were used.

Although it is possible to develop a sampling distribution theoretically from first principles we shall adopt a practical approach in which we will construct sampling distributions experimentally. For each sampling distribution we need to choose a particular statistic of interest. Since the mean is the simplest statistic we begin by considering the sampling distribution of a mean.

## 6.1 Constructing a sampling distribution of a mean

In order to construct a sampling distribution of a mean we take repeated samples from a given population. For each sample we calculate the mean value and arrange the resulting values into a frequency distribution.

Consider an experiment in which a sample of 30 individuals is chosen at random from an overall population in which income is normally distributed with mean $\mu$ and standard deviation $\sigma$. If we record the income of each member of the sample we can calculate the mean value, call it $\bar{X}_1$, which is an estimate of unknown $\mu$. The resulting sample mean may be a good estimate of $\mu$ or it may not. This will depend upon the amount of sampling error present.

Assume now that we repeat the process selecting at random a different set of 30 individuals and calculate the resulting mean value for income which we will call $\bar{X}_2$. Once again sampling error will be present and in general we would not expect $\bar{X}_1$ and $\bar{X}_2$ to be equal.

If we continued taking further samples, keeping the number of observations equal for all samples, we would finish with a very large number of separate mean values $\bar{X}_1$, $\bar{X}_2$, $\bar{X}_3$, ..., where the subscript indicates the number of the sample. These values for $\bar{X}$ can be arranged in the form of a frequency distribution in the same way that observations for a variable $X$ were arranged into a frequency distribution in Chapter 3. The resulting distribution is known as a *sampling distribution of a mean*.

The final situation is illustrated in Fig. 6.1 which shows the original population from which the samples were taken and the sampling distribution of a mean that results. Notice particularly the label of each horizontal axis. In the population it is the variable $X$ which is being distributed, but in the sampling distribution it is the variable $\bar{X}$. Notice

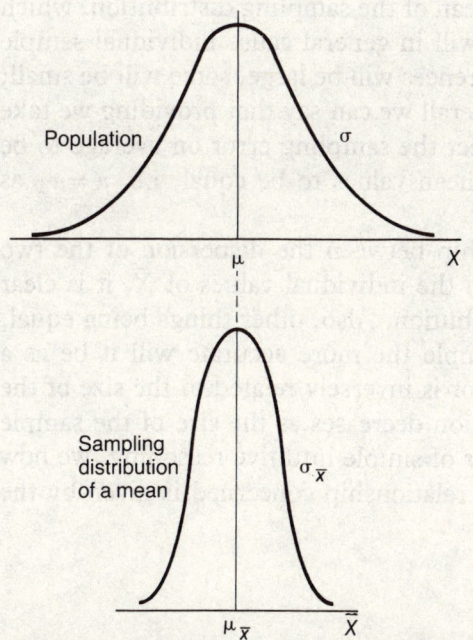

Figure 6.1   The distribution of $X$ and the sampling distribution of $\bar{X}$

also that each distribution has its own mean value (labelled $\mu$ and $\mu_{\bar{X}}$) and each has its own measure of spread (labelled $\sigma$ and $\sigma_{\bar{X}}$).

## 6.2  Characteristics of the sampling distribution of a mean

With the resulting sampling distribution, as with any distribution, there are three main characteristics of interest:

1  the shape
2  the average value (in this case the mean)
3  the spread (in this case the standard deviation)

What then can we say about the sampling distribution of $\bar{X}$ given that the population variable $X$ is normally distributed with a mean value $\mu$ and a standard deviation $\sigma$?

The first thing we can say concerns the shape of the resulting distribution. If the population is normally distributed the sampling distribution will also be normally distributed. Since the former generated the latter this is intuitively reasonable. But it can also be shown that even if the original population is not normally distributed the resulting sampling distribution will become more and more normal as the size of the sample increases. Although this is not intuitively obvious it can be demonstrated by use of a theorem known as the *central limit theorem*. So for practical purposes we can say that the sampling distribution of a mean is normally distributed and therefore possesses all the properties of a normal curve discussed in Chapter 5.

The second characteristic concerns the mean. What relationship should we expect between the mean of the population $\mu$ and the mean of the sampling distribution, which we will call $\mu_{\bar{X}}$? We know that sampling error will in general cause individual sample mean values to differ from $\mu$. Some of these differences will be large, some will be small; some will be positive, some will be negative. Overall we can say that providing we take a large enough number of samples, we can expect the sampling error on average to be zero. This being so we would expect the two mean values to be equal, i.e. $\mu = \mu_{\bar{X}}$ as shown in Fig. 6.1.

Finally, what can we say about the relationship between the dispersion of the two distributions? Since sampling error is present in the individual values of $\bar{X}$, it is clear that this affects the spread of the sampling distribution. Also, other things being equal, we can say that the larger the size of each sample the more accurate will it be as a measure of the population, so that sampling error is inversely related to the size of the sample. So the spread of the sampling distribution decreases as the size of the sample increases. Having reached this point on the basis of simple intuitive reasoning, we now state without proof that the exact nature of the relationship concerned is given by the expression:

$$\sigma_{\bar{X}} = \frac{\sigma}{\sqrt{N}}$$

where $\sigma_{\bar{X}}$ = the standard error of $\bar{X}$

$\sigma$ = the standard deviation of $X$

$N$ = the number of observations in each sample.

Notice in particular our terminology with regard to $\sigma_{\bar{X}}$. Instead of referring to the standard *deviation* of $\bar{X}$, we refer to the standard *error* of $\bar{X}$. We shall see in later sections of this chapter that for each of the other sampling distributions that we will be dealing with, we refer to the standard error rather than the standard deviation. In general we can say that the standard deviation is a measure of spread for frequency and probability distributions, and that the standard error is a measure of spread for sampling distributions.

The relationships between the population and the sampling distribution and the symbols used are shown in Fig. 6.1.

## 6.3 Sampling distribution of a mean and the *Z* distribution

We can summarise Section 6.2 by saying that our variable $\bar{X}$ is normally distributed with a mean value $\mu_{\bar{X}}$ and a standard error $\sigma_{\bar{X}}$. The fact that it is normally distributed is important because it follows from this that the variable $\bar{X}$ possesses all the properties of the normal distribution.

For example, we know that if $X$ is normally distributed with mean $\mu$ and standard deviation $\sigma$, 95% of the area under the curve is contained within the values $\mu \pm 1.96\sigma$. It therefore follows that for the sampling distribution of a mean with mean value $\mu_{\bar{X}}$ and standard error $\sigma_{\bar{X}}$ 95% of the area under the curve is contained between the values

$$\mu_{\bar{X}} \pm 1.96\sigma_{\bar{X}}$$

It is also possible to relate the $Z$ distribution to the sampling distribution by making use of an appropriate $Z$ transformation. We know that for the variable $X_i$

$$Z_i = (X_i - \mu)/\sigma$$

Similarly we can define a point $Z_i$ corresponding to the point $\bar{X}_i$ as follows:

$$Z_i = (\bar{X}_i - \mu_{\bar{X}})/\sigma_{\bar{X}}$$

where $\bar{X}_i$ = the point on the sampling distribution of a mean corresponding to $Z_i$ on the standard normal curve;

$\mu_{\bar{X}}$ = the mean of the sampling distribution of a mean;

$\sigma_{\bar{X}}$ = the standard error of the sampling distribution of a mean.

All of this is illustrated in Fig. 6.2. Notice in particular the different variables on the three axes $X$, $\bar{X}$ and $Z$. It is also important to understand how these three distributions are related.

We begin with the population distribution of $X$. From this we construct the sampling distribution of $\bar{X}$ from which we can obtain the relevant values of $Z$ and the consequent areas under the curve. See Example 6.1 and Exercises 6.1 to 6.6.

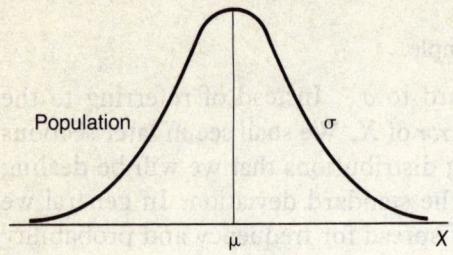

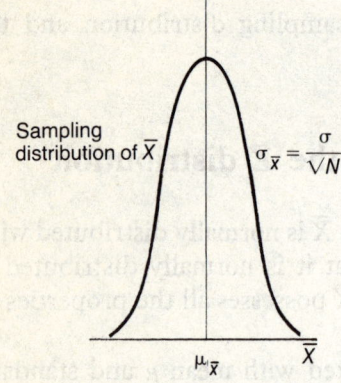

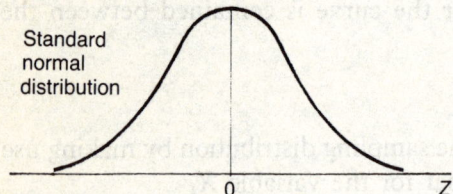

Figure 6.2    Population, sampling distribution of a mean and the standard normal distribution

# Example 6.1

Given that $X$ is normally distributed with mean 22 and standard deviation 4, find the probability that a sample mean $\bar{X}$ with $N = 64$ will exceed 23.

Since $\mu = 22$, $\sigma = 4$ and $N = 64$ it follows that $\mu_{\bar{X}} = 22$ and $\sigma_{\bar{X}} = 4/8 = 0.5$.

To find the required probability we need to obtain the $Z$ value (say $Z_1$) corresponding to $\bar{X} = 23$ as shown in Fig. 6.3:

$$Z_1 = (23 - 22)/0.5 = 2.0$$

From the $Z$ tables (Appendix A) the area from $Z = 0$ to $Z = 2.0$ equals 0.4772. The area to the right of $Z = 2.0$ is therefore 0.0228.

Therefore the probability that $\bar{X}$ will exceed 23 is 0.0228.

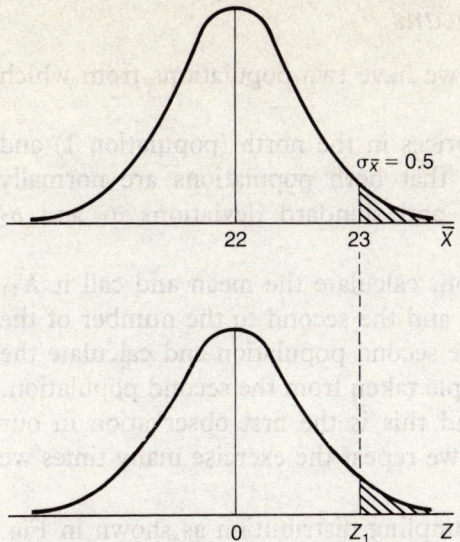

Figure 6.3  Obtaining $Z$ for given $X$

## 6.4  Other sampling distributions

So far we have concentrated on the sampling distribution of a mean, but there are three other statistics of interest each of which gives rise to a separate sampling distribution: proportion, difference in means and difference in proportions. We shall discuss each of these in turn emphasising the way in which the distribution is generated, the characteristics of the resulting sampling distribution and the formula for the $Z$ transformation.

### *Sampling distribution of a proportion*

The statistic of interest here is the proportion of a sample with a given characteristic, for example, the proportion who are unemployed. Repeated samples are taken with the number of observations in each being fixed. For each sample the proportion unemployed is recorded giving a series of proportions $\hat{p}_1$, $\hat{p}_2$, $\hat{p}_3$, ... These values are then arranged into a frequency distribution giving a sampling distribution of a proportion. The characteristics of this distribution and the relevant $Z$ transformation formula are:

$$\text{shape} = \text{normally distributed}$$
$$\text{mean } \mu_{\hat{p}} = p$$
$$\text{standard error } \sigma_{\hat{p}} = \sqrt{pq/N}$$
$$Z_i = (\hat{p}_i - p)/\sigma_{\hat{p}}$$
$$\text{where } p = \text{population proportion with given characteristic}$$
$$q = (1 - p)$$

## Sampling distribution of differences in means

The essential feature of this distribution is that we have two populations from which samples are drawn.

Let us assume that we are measuring house prices in the north (population 1) and house prices in the south (population 2), and that both populations are normally distributed with means $\mu_1$ and $\mu_2$ respectively and standard deviations $\sigma_1$ and $\sigma_2$ respectively.

We can take a sample from the first population, calculate the mean and call it $\bar{X}_{11}$ where the first subscript refers to the population and the second to the number of the sample. Similarly, we can take a sample from the second population and calculate the mean calling it $\bar{X}_{21}$, i.e. the mean of the first sample taken from the second population. The difference between the two is $\bar{X}_{11} - \bar{X}_{21}$ and this is the first observation in our sampling distribution of differences in means. If we repeat the exercise many times we obtain $\bar{X}_{11} - \bar{X}_{21}$, $\bar{X}_{12} - \bar{X}_{22}$, ...

These observations are then arranged into a sampling distribution as shown in Fig. 6.4. The number of observations in all samples from the first population is $N_1$, and the number of observations in all samples from the second population is $N_2$. $N_1$ and $N_2$ are not necessarily equal.

The main characteristics of the resulting sampling distribution of differences in means and the relevant $Z$ transformation formula are:

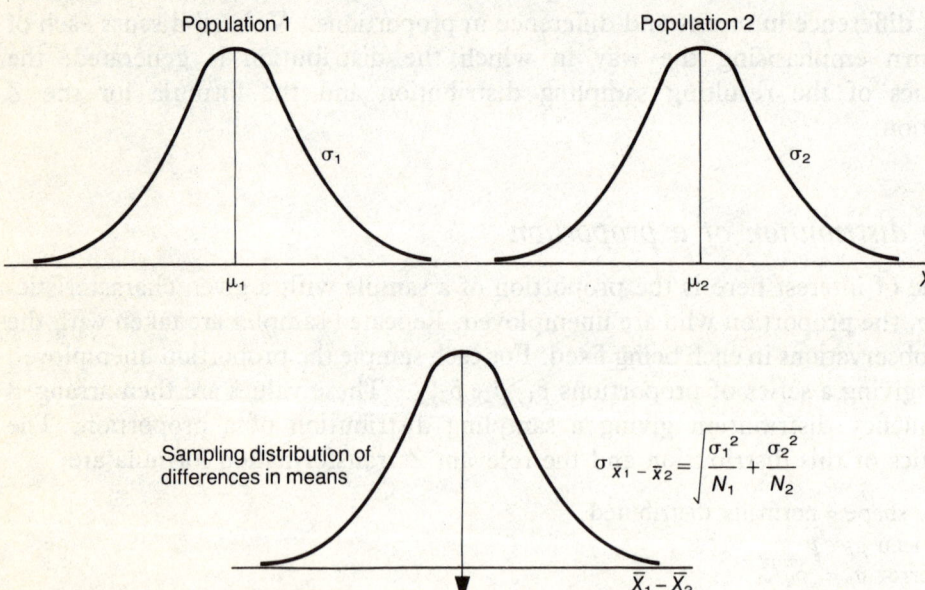

shape = normally distributed

mean $\mu_{\bar{X}_1 - \bar{X}_2} = \mu_1 - \mu_2$

Population 1

$\sigma_1$

$\mu_1$

Population 2

$\sigma_2$

$\mu_2$

$X$

Sampling distribution of differences in means

$$\sigma_{\bar{X}_1 - \bar{X}_2} = \sqrt{\frac{\sigma_1^2}{N_1} + \frac{\sigma_2^2}{N_2}}$$

$\bar{X}_1 - \bar{X}_2$

$\mu_{\bar{X}_1 - \bar{X}_2}$

Figure 6.4  Sampling distribution of differences in mean values

standard error $\sigma_{\bar{X}_1 - \bar{X}_2} = \sqrt{\dfrac{\sigma_1^2}{N_1} + \dfrac{\sigma_2^2}{N_2}}$

$$Z_i = \frac{(\bar{X}_{1i} - \bar{X}_{2i}) - (\mu_1 - \mu_2)}{\sigma_{\bar{X}_1 - \bar{X}_2}}$$

Example 6.2 illustrates the calculations involved.

## *Sampling distribution of differences in proportions*

Once again the central feature of this sampling distribution is the fact that samples are selected from two populations. Consider, for example, two populations where the first consists of all men in employment and the second consists of all women in employment. We further assume that we are interested in the proportion of workers in each population who are trade union members.

We can take a sample from the male population, calculate the proportion who are union members and call it $\hat{p}_{11}$. Similarly, we can take a sample from the female population and call the resulting proportion who are union members $\hat{p}_{21}$. The difference between the two is $\hat{p}_{11} - \hat{p}_{21}$. By repeating the process many times we obtain a series of differences in proportions, i.e. $\hat{p}_{1i} - \hat{p}_{2i} = \hat{p}_{11} - \hat{p}_{21}, \hat{p}_{12} - \hat{p}_{22}, \ldots$

If these observations are arranged into convenient class intervals we obtain a sampling distribution of differences in proportions. As before $N_1$ is the number of observations in samples chosen from the first population, $N_2$ is the number of observations in each sample chosen from the second population and $N_1$ and $N_2$ are not necessarily equal.

The characteristics of the resulting sampling distribution and the appropriate $Z$ transformation are as follows:

shape = normally distributed

mean $\mu_{\hat{p}_1 - \hat{p}_2} = p_1 - p_2$

standard error $\sigma_{\hat{p}_1 - \hat{p}_2} = \sqrt{\dfrac{p_1 q_1}{N_1} + \dfrac{p_2 q_2}{N_2}}$

$$Z_i = \frac{(\hat{p}_1 - \hat{p}_2) - (p_1 - p_2)}{\sigma_{\hat{p}_1 - \hat{p}_2}}$$

where $p_1$ is the proportion with the given characteristic in the first population and $q_1 = 1 - p_1$. Similar definitions follow for $p_2$ and $q_2$.

The illustration introduced above involving union membership is developed further in Example 6.3

## Example 6.2 ⎯⎯⎯⎯⎯⎯⎯⎯⎯⎯⎯⎯⎯⎯⎯⎯⎯⎯⎯⎯⎯⎯⎯⎯⎯

The prices of 3-bedroomed houses in the south and the north are normally distributed with means and standard deviations as shown in the table.

What is the probability that in a sample of 100 houses from the south and 100 houses from the north, the difference between average house prices will be greater than £11 000 but less than £12 000?

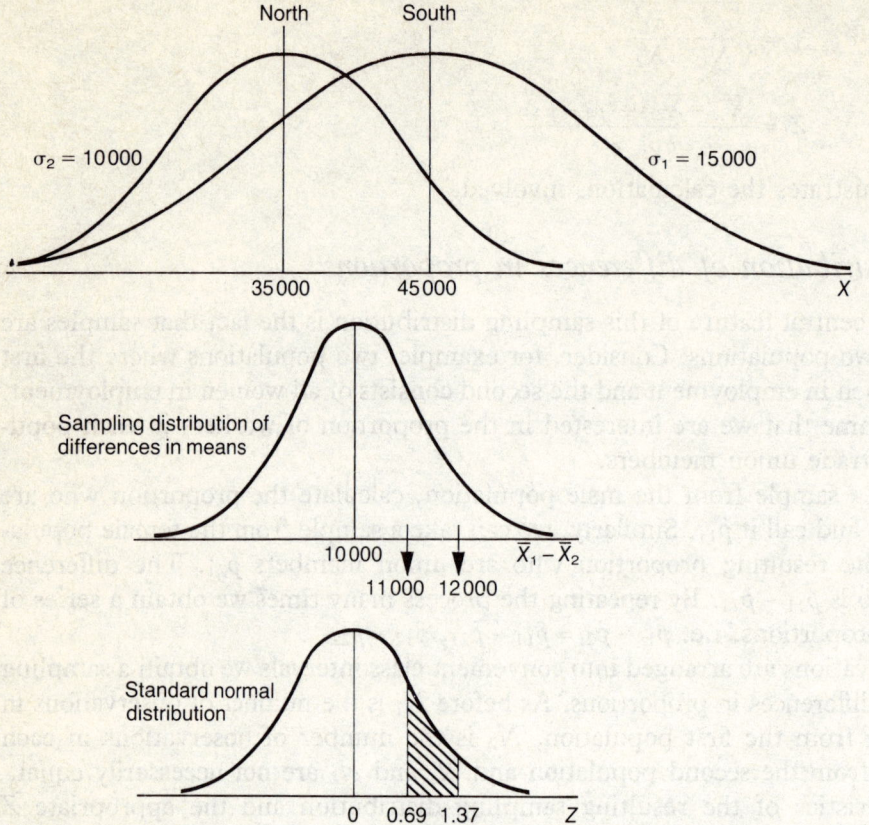

Figure 6.5   Three-tiered diagram for sampling distribution of differences in means

|                    | South (£)   | North (£)   |
|--------------------|-------------|-------------|
| Mean               | 45 000      | 35 000      |
| Standard deviation | 15 000      | 10 000      |

The information given is shown in Fig. 6.5.

$$\mu_{\bar{X}-\bar{X}_2} = 45\,000 - 35\,000 = £10\,000$$

and   $$\sigma_{\bar{X}_1-\bar{X}_2} = \sqrt{\frac{(15\,000)^2}{200} + \frac{(10\,000)^2}{100}} = £1458$$

The required $Z$ value for £11 000, say $Z_1$, is

$$Z_1 = \frac{11\,000 - (45\,000 - 35\,000)}{1458} = 0.69$$

The required $Z$ value for £12 000, say $Z_2$, is

$$Z_2 = \frac{12\,000 - (45\,000 - 35\,000)}{1458} = 1.37$$

The area under the curve from $Z = 0$ to $Z_2 = 1.37$ to 0.4147. The area under the curve from $Z = 0$ to $Z_1 = 0.69$ is 0.2549. Therefore the shaded area in Fig. 6.5 equals $0.4147 - 0.2549$ giving the required probability of 0.1598.

## Example 6.3

The proportions of workers who are trade union members in the male and female labour forces are 0.5 and 0.2 respectively. If samples of 50 men and 100 women are selected at random what is the probability that the difference in resulting proportions is greater than 0.45?

We are given $p_1 = 0.5$, $p_2 = 0.2$, $N_1 = 50$ and $N_2 = 100$. From this it follows that:

$$\mu_{\hat{p}_1 - \hat{p}_2} = 0.3$$

and

$$\sigma_{\hat{p}_1 - \hat{p}_2} = \sqrt{\frac{0.5 \times 0.5}{50} + \frac{0.2 \times 0.8}{100}} = 0.081$$

We can therefore draw the sampling distribution of $\hat{p}_1 - \hat{p}_2$ and the $Z$ distribution as shown in Fig. 6.6. We need to find the value of $Z$ corresponding to $\hat{p}_1 - \hat{p}_2 = 0.45$. This is given by:

$$Z = (0.45 - 0.3)/0.081 = 1.85$$

The area under the curve to the right of this value is $0.5 - 0.4678 = 0.0322$, and this is therefore the required probability.

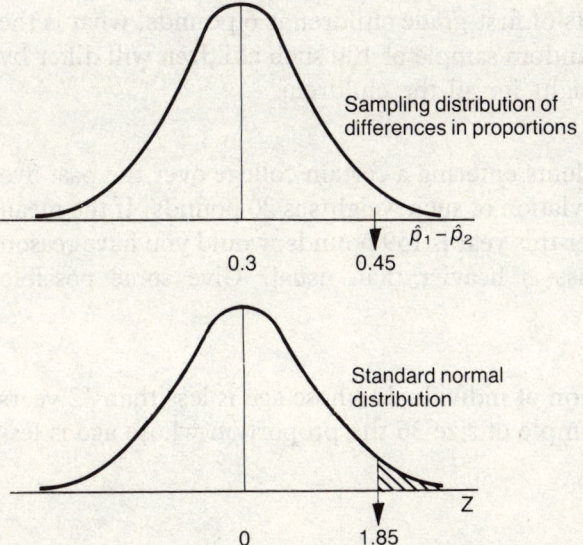

Sampling distribution of differences in proportions

$\hat{p}_1 - \hat{p}_2$

0.3          0.45

Standard normal distribution

$Z$

0          1.85

Figure 6.6   Sampling distribution of differences in proportions and standard normal curve

## Exercises

**6.1**  Given that $X$ is normally distributed with mean 22 and standard deviation 4, calculate the probability that the sample mean $\bar{X}$, based on a sample of size 64, will:
(a)  exceed 23
(b)  exceed 21.5
(c)  lie between 21 and 23
(d)  exceed 24.

**6.2**  Given that $X$ is normally distributed with mean 25 and standard deviation 8, calculate the probability that the sample mean $\bar{X}$, based on a sample size 16, will:
(a)  be less than 27
(b)  exceed 32
(c)  exceed 23
(d)  be less than 20
(e)  lie between 28 and 29.

**6.3**  Sketch on the same diagram the graph of a normal curve with mean 10 and standard deviation 2 and the graph of the corresponding sampling distribution of a mean curve for a sample of size 9.

**6.4**  What would the graph of the $\bar{X}$ curve in Exercise 6.3 have looked like if the sample size had been 36?

**6.5**  If the standard deviation of weights of first-grade children is 6 pounds, what is the probability that the mean weight of a random sample of 100 such children will differ by more than 1 pound from the mean weight for all the children?

**6.6**  The mean weight of first year students entering a certain college over the past five years is 153 pounds and the standard deviation of such weights is 20 pounds. If the mean weight of the first 100 students to register this year is 159 pounds, would you have reason to believe that the new first year class is heavier than usual? Give some possible explanations.

**6.7**  In a given population the proportion of individuals whose age is less than 12 years is 0.6. Find the probability that in a sample of size 36 the proportion whose age is less than 12 is:
(a)  less than 0.5
(b)  between 0.62 and 0.72
(c)  more than 0.66
(d)  less than 0.52 or more than 0.73.

**6.8**  Two separate normally distributed populations have mean values and standard deviations:

$$\mu_1 = 25 \qquad \sigma_1 = 8$$
$$\mu_2 = 20 \qquad \sigma_2 = 10$$

A sample of size 25 is taken from the first population and a sample of size 36 is taken from the second. Find the probability that the difference between the mean values of the samples is:
(a)   negative
(b)   greater than 3
(c)   less than 6 or more than 8
(d)   more than 2 and less than 6 or more than 7.5 and less than 9.

**6.9**  In two separate populations the proportions whose IQ is less than 100 are:

$$\hat{p}_1 = 0.55 \quad \text{and} \quad \hat{p}_2 = 0.48$$

If a sample of size 40 is taken from each population find the values of $\hat{p}_1 - \hat{p}_2$ for each diagram given below:

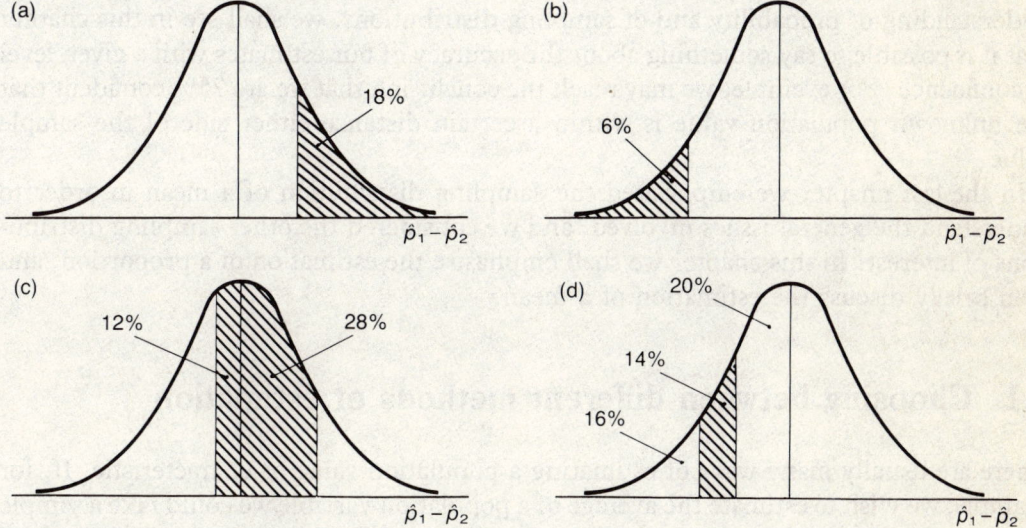

**6.10**  Given the information in Exercise 6.7 calculate the 80% and 92% values for the sample proportion.

**6.11**  For the data given in Exercise 6.8 calculate the 75% and 88% values for the difference in sample means.

# 7 Estimation

| | |
|---|---|
| 7.1 Choosing between different methods of estimation | 7.4 Interval estimates of a mean Exercises |
| 7.2 Point and interval estimates | |
| 7.3 Interval estimates of a proportion | |

We have pointed out that the main purpose of taking a sample is to provide an estimate of the unknown population value. For example, $\bar{X}$ is an estimate of unknown $\mu$ and $\hat{p}$ is an estimate of unknown $p$. The question that now must be asked is: How accurate is our estimate?

Because the population coefficient is unknown and because of the presence of sampling error, we are unable to say anything for certain about our estimates. But, given our understanding of probability and of sampling distributions, we shall see in this chapter that it is possible to say something about the accuracy of our estimates with a given level of confidence. For example, we may reach the conclusion that we are 75% confident that the unknown population value is within a certain distance either side of the sample value.

In the last chapter we emphasised the sampling distribution of a mean in order to understand the general issues involved, and we considered the other sampling distributions of interest. In this chapter we shall emphasise the estimation of a proportion, and then briefly discuss the estimation of a mean.

## 7.1 Choosing between different methods of estimation

There are usually many ways of estimating a population value or characteristic. If, for example, we wish to estimate the average of a population variable we could take a sample and calculate the mean, median or mode. Since these different methods will in general produce different answers, it is of interest to know which method is likely to produce the most accurate answer. The same situation arises if we wish to measure the spread of a population variable. We could take a sample and calculate the variance, standard deviation, range or semi-interquartile range and ask which is likely to be most accurate.

In order to compare different methods of estimating a population value we need to consider various criteria, some of which are of a practical nature, some of which are more statistical in nature. From a practical point of view it is necessary to consider the cost involved in terms of time and money. Data collection is often very expensive and, other things being equal, the cheapest method is to be preferred. In addition to financial considerations it may also be possible to introduce miscellaneous information to help in our choice of method. For example, if it is known that the population is heavily skewed, we may conclude that the semi-interquartile range is preferable to the standard deviation as a measure of spread, because the latter will be heavily affected by values at the extreme of the distribution.

In addition to these practical considerations which affect the choice of method of estimation there are also various statistical factors which need to be taken into account. Amongst these factors two are particularly important.

First, it is desirable that a method of estimation be *unbiased*. Because of sampling error any single estimate may be an over-estimate (biased upwards) or an under-estimate (biased downwards). But it is possible that the application of a given method to repeated samples will result in the amount of sampling error on average being zero. When this happens the method of estimation is said to be unbiased. Generally the value of the estimates obtained from repeated samples equals the true, unknown population value. Other things being equal any method which is unbiased is to be preferred to an alternative which is biased.

A second desirable feature of a method of estimation is that it should be *efficient*. If a method of estimation is applied to repeated samples, the spread of the sampling distribution which results is a measure of the amount of sampling error present. Since different methods of estimation will produce different sampling distributions, we can compare methods by comparing the resulting standard errors. Thus, if methods A and B are unbiased, we can say that method A is preferred to method B if the standard error of its sampling distribution is less than that of method B, in which case the former method is said to be more efficient than the latter. For example, for normal distributions both the mean and the median are unbiased estimates of the average, but it can be shown that the former method is more efficient than the latter.

## 7.2 Point and interval estimates

There are two kinds of estimates of importance when investigating unknown population parameters. The first involves using a single figure as an estimate of the population value.

Consider, for example, the data in Table 7.1 showing the unemployment rate (expressed as the percentage of new UK domiciled graduates whose whereabouts were known at the end of December 1981 and 1982 and who at that time had at best temporary employment) for five separate universities and the total for all 44 UK universities. From the table we can see that the proportion of graduates unemployed at City in 1982 was 0.102 while the figure for Ulster was 0.357. Each of these figures is called a *point estimate* and can be taken as an estimate of the total for all UK universities.

In order to investigate the accuracy of these figures we need to introduce the idea of an *interval estimate*, where a single figure is replaced by a range of figures associated with a given level of probability. The result of this is that we are able to say for a given level of confidence that the unknown population value will be somewhere within the stated

Table 7.1  Proportion unemployed in selected UK universities 1981, 1982

| University | No of new UK domiciled graduates in 1982 whose whereabouts were known at end 1982 | With at best a temporary job at end 1982 (%) | With at best a temporary job at end 1981 (%) |
|---|---|---|---|
| City | 402 | 10.2 | 12.2 |
| Bradford | 936 | 17.0 | 18.6 |
| York | 768 | 15.6 | 18.9 |
| Leeds | 2214 | 22.6 | 16.7 |
| Ulster | 277 | 35.7 | 36.2 |
| Total (44 UK universities) | 59380 | 16.3 | 14.4 |

Adapted from *Financial Times*, 26 January 1984

range. For example, it can be shown that given the value for City of $\hat{p} = 0.102$, we can be 95% confident that the true population proportion will be between 0.066 and 0.138. Also, given the value for York of 0.156, we can be 98% confident that the true population proportion will be between 0.138 and 0.2. Exactly how these figures can be obtained is explained in Section 7.3 (see also Exercises 7.1 and 7.2).

## 7.3  Interval estimates of a proportion

From Table 7.1 we can see that the number of students in the sample for City University is 402. Let us therefore consider the experiment of taking repeated samples with $N = 402$ from a population whose unemployment rate is 0.163 (see table). If we measure the amount of unemployment in each sample and draw the resulting sampling distribution, we would obtain the distribution shown in the upper part of Fig. 7.1. From our previous analysis of sampling distributions we know that the central value of the sampling distribution would be 0.163 and the standard error would be given by:

$$\sigma_{\hat{p}} = \sqrt{\frac{pq}{N}} = \sqrt{\frac{0.163 \times 0.837}{402}} = 0.018$$

With this information we can obtain the values of $\hat{p}$ which contain 95% of the area under the curve. These values are given by:

$$0.163 \pm 1.96\sigma_{\hat{p}} = 0.163 \pm 0.036$$

that is 95% of the area under the curve lies between the values 0.127 and 0.199. From this we can conclude that if the experiment of taking repeated samples with $N = 402$

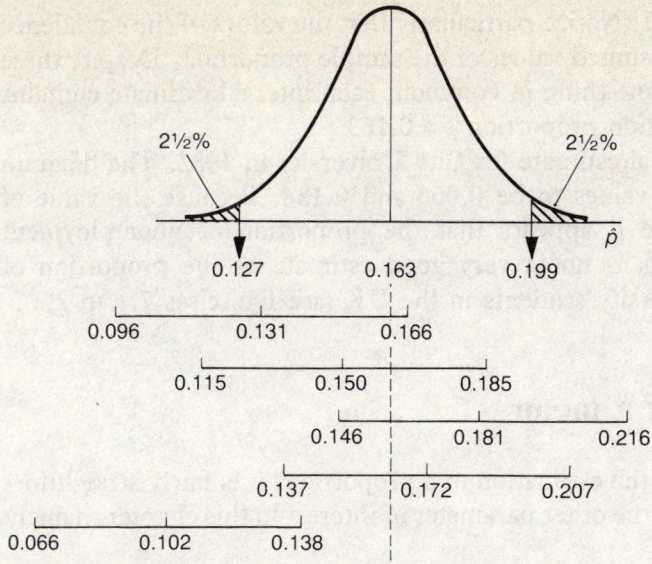

Figure 7.1  Hypothetical sampling distribution of a proportion

were performed let us say 100 times, we would expect 95 of the resulting sample values of $\hat{p}$ to fall between 0.127 and 0.199. Put another way we can say that we are 95% confident that any one of the resulting sample values of $\hat{p}$ will fall between the values of 0.127 and 0.199.

Our argument so far has allowed us to reach a conclusion concerning $\hat{p}$ given the value of $p$. This, however, is the reverse of what we are after. We are not interested here in saying something about the sample given information about the population, but in saying something about the population given information about the sample. In order to do this we need to reverse the conclusion reached in the previous paragraph, that is to say, if we are 95% confident that $\hat{p}$ falls within the range $p \pm 1.96\sigma_{\hat{p}}$ it follows that we must also be 95% confident that $p$ falls in the range $\hat{p} \pm 1.96\sigma_{\hat{p}}$. Put in another way we can say that if:

$$p - 1.96\sigma_{\hat{p}} < \hat{p} < p + 1.96\sigma_{\hat{p}}$$

it necessarily follows that:

$$\hat{p} - 1.96\sigma_{\hat{p}} < p < \hat{p} + 1.96\sigma_{\hat{p}}$$

In the light of this let us now assume that four separate samples are taken with $N = 402$ and that the resulting values for $\hat{p}$ are as follows, with 95% confidence limits (i.e. $\hat{p} \pm 1.96\sigma_{\hat{p}}$) given in brackets:

$\hat{p}_1 = 0.131$ (95% confidence limits = 0.096 and 0.166)
$\hat{p}_2 = 0.150$ (95% confidence limits = 0.115 and 0.185)
$\hat{p}_3 = 0.181$ (95% confidence limits = 0.146 and 0.216)
$\hat{p}_4 = 0.172$ (95% confidence limits = 0.137 and 0.207)

These values are shown in Fig. 7.1. Notice particularly that the values of the confidence limits change depending on the assumed values of the sample proportion. Despite these changes, however, they all have one thing in common: each interval estimate contains within it the value of the population proportion $p = 0.163$.

But this is not so for the interval estimate for City University in 1982. The diagram shows the 95% confidence limit values to be 0.066 and 0.138. Because the value of $p = 0.163$ falls outside this range it appears that the proportion of unemployment amongst City University students is not a very good estimate of the proportion of unemployment amongst all university students in the UK (see Exercises 7.1 to 7.3).

## 7.4   Interval estimates of a mean

Having considered in some detail the estimation of a proportion, it is fairly straightforward to consider the estimation of the other parameter of interest in this chapter, namely the mean.

To obtain interval estimates of a mean we need to make use of the following general formula which follows from our discussion in the previous section.

sample mean $\pm Z$ value $\times$ standard error

Taking our formula for the standard error from the last chapter we can obtain interval estimates of the mean by calculating:

$$\bar{X} \pm Z\sigma_{\bar{x}}$$

It is important to see the role that $N$ plays in our analysis. As $N$ increases the standard error falls (since $\sigma_{\bar{x}} = \sigma/\sqrt{N}$) and the values defining the range of our interval estimate become narrower. Consequently our accuracy of estimation increases in the sense that for a given level of confidence we expect the true population coefficient to vary between narrower limits than with smaller values of $N$. This is illustrated in Exercise 7.5. The calculations involved in estimating a mean are illustrated in Example 7.1 (see also Exercises 7.4 and 7.6).

## Example 7.1 _____

The average IQ of a sample of 50 adults is calculated to be 107 with a standard deviation of 20. Calculate the 95% interval estimate for the sample mean and compare your result with an assumed value for $\mu$ of 100.

The 95% interval estimate for $\bar{X} = 107$ is given by:

$\bar{X} \pm 1.96\sigma_{\bar{x}}$

(where   $\sigma_{\bar{x}} = S/\sqrt{N} = 20/\sqrt{50} = 2.83$)

i.e.   $107 \pm 1.96 \times 2.83$

giving a range from 101.5 to 112.5

The value of $\mu = 100$ is usually taken as a measure of average intelligence. Since the value of $\mu = 100$ is not contained within the range calculated, it appears that our sample value of $\bar{X} = 107$ is not a very accurate estimate of the intelligence of the population as a whole. It is more likely to be a good estimate of a sub group of the overall population in which intelligence is higher than the norm.

## Exercises

**7.1** Using the analysis in Section 7.3 and the data contained in Table 7.1, show that the 95% confidence limits for City in 1982 are 0.066 and 0.138 and that the 98% limits for York in the same year are 0.138 and 0.2.

**7.2** Given the data in Table 7.1 showing proportions unemployed in 1982, determine which of the following is larger:
(a) The 90% upper limit for York or the 95% upper limit for Bradford.
(b) The 98% lower limit for Bradford or the 92% lower limit for Leeds.
(c) The 99% lower limit for Ulster or the 98% upper limit for Leeds.

**7.3** Calculate the 90% confidence limits for the proportion of students unemployed at Bradford University given the data in Table 7.1. Do you think that the sample proportion for Bradford is a good estimate if it is known that the proportion of graduates unemployed in universities in the north of England is 0.21?

**7.4** Draw the sampling distribution of a mean given that $\mu = 15$, $\sigma = 21$ and $N = 49$. On the same diagram show the 95% interval estimates for each of the following sample means which are based on samples of size 49.

$$\bar{X}_1 = 18$$
$$\bar{X}_2 = 13$$
$$\bar{X}_3 = 22$$

Briefly discuss your results.

**7.5** Refer to Example 7.1. Re-calculate the interval estimates assuming that the sample values given are based on a sample of $N = 100$. Comment on the results obtained in relation to those given in the example.

**7.6** In a sample of 30 schoolchildren the mean amount of time spent watching television was 2.1 hours per day with a standard deviation of 0.8 hours. Calculate the 98% interval estimate of a mean for these figures. What happens to the estimate if the level of confidence is reduced to 92%? Briefly discuss.

# 8 Tests of hypotheses—parametric tests

In economics students are often faced with the problem of choosing between competing theories. This choice is usually made by seeing how closely observed data relate to predictions made by the different theories. In this and the next chapter we will introduce a range of tests which will help us to make such a choice. Chapter 8 is concerned with parametric tests in which the variable of interest is assumed to be normally distributed. Wherever it is not possible to say how the variable of interest is distributed it is necessary to use a non-parametric test, examples of which are given in Chapter 9.

The essential features at the heart of hypothesis testing are the same for both parametric and non-parametric tests and will be summarised at this point by giving an example. Results published by Gallup for the UK show that in samples taken in 1964 and 1984 the percentage of those polled who were smokers fell from 49% to 39%. The question then arises: Can we conclude that there has been a fall in the proportion of smokers in the populations from which the samples were taken? There are two possible answers.

1 The observed difference in sample proportions is the result of sampling error and there is therefore *no statistically significant difference* in the proportion of smokers in the UK between 1964 and 1984.

2 The observed difference in sample proportions reflects a change in smoking behaviour at the national level in which case there is *a statistically significant difference* in the proportion of smokers in the UK between 1964 and 1984.

On the basis of available evidence we have to choose between these two competing conclusions. It is possible to say straight away that, other things being equal, the larger the difference in the sample proportions the more likely it is that the second conclusion is correct. But how large must the difference be, in order to accept the second conclusion and, therefore, reject the first?

The rest of this chapter attempts to explain how we can answer this kind of question which arises in the context of a number of different kinds of parametric tests of hypotheses.

## 8.1  What is being tested?

In any test of hypothesis the first question to ask is: What is being tested? This involves identifying the central variable of interest and consequently identifying the required sampling distribution. We have outlined in previous chapters four sampling distributions of interest: the sampling distributions of a mean, difference in means, a proportion and difference in proportion.

To illustrate how to identify the relevant distribution, we will consider the four examples given below which will be investigated in full in subsequent sections of this chapter.

## Case 8.1

At an annual economics conference 72 of the 125 people attending believed that variations in the supply of money were the root cause of inflation, while the remainder attributed the cause to trade union activity. Does this suggest that economists in general prefer the former explanation? Use 95% confidence limits.

## Case 8.2

Two samples of firms are selected at random and for each firm the percentage increase in size over a 5 year period is measured. The data collected gave the following values for the mean, number of observations and the standard deviation:

sample 1: $\bar{X}_1 = 16.3$; $N_1 = 50$; $s_1 = 3.2$
sample 2: $\bar{X}_2 = 14.7$; $N_2 = 60$; $s_2 = 4.5$

Use this information to test at the 0.02 level of the significance whether the samples have been selected from the same population.

## Case 8.3

A travel agent claims that the daily amount of sunshine in a given holiday resort during peak season is 7 hours. A holiday maker who booked a holiday with the agent found that the 30 day holiday gave an average amount of 5.9 hours of sunshine per day with a standard deviation of 1.8 hours. If the daily amount of sunshine is normally distributed, do you think that the holiday maker has reason to believe that the agent has been misleading? Use 0.02 level of significance.

## Case 8.4

In a given university in 1978, 34 graduates out of a total of 515 were unable to find fulltime employment within one year of graduating. In 1986 the figure was 56 out of a total of 485. Has the proportion of graduates unable to find fulltime employment changed significantly been 1978 and 1986?

Given the information in these cases we can now decide in each exactly what is being tested. In Case 8.1 the statistic of interest is the proportion of economists favouring a monetarist explanation of inflation. Since there is only one sample we are testing a proportion, and the sampling distribution of interest is therefore the sampling distribution of a proportion. In Case 8.2 we have two samples which may have been taken from the same population or two different populations. The issue at stake is to be decided by comparing the two sample means so that the statistic of interest is the difference in mean values, and we therefore use the sampling distribution of difference in mean values. In Case 8.3 the statistic of interest is the mean, but since there is only one sample mean value the sampling distribution of interest is the sampling distribution of a mean. Finally, in Case 8.4, we are given the proportion of graduates failing to find fulltime employment within one year of graduation. Although only one university is referred to, samples have been taken from it at two different points of time. We therefore have two populations and the statistic being tested is the difference in two proportions. For this we require the sampling distribution of differences in proportions.

## 8.2  Establish hypotheses

We have previously seen that the purpose of carrying out a significance test is to allow us to choose between competing theories, each of which is designed to explain given empirical data. Our next task therefore is to state clearly the content of these theories.

We do this by specifying two mutually exclusive hypotheses labelled $H_0$ and $H_1$. $H_0$ is the *null hypothesis* whose content usually expresses the idea of no significant relationship or no significant difference between variables. $H_1$ is the *alternative hypothesis* expressing the opposite idea, namely that there *is* a significant relationship or difference between variables. If we refer back to the example of the proportion of smokers in the UK at the beginning of this chapter, we could express $H_0$ and $H_1$ as follows:

$H_0$:  There is *no* significant difference in the proportion of smokers in the UK between 1964 and 1984.

$H_1$:  There *is* a significant difference in the proportion of smokers in the UK between 1964 and 1984.

It is usually possible to express both $H_0$ and $H_1$ more succinctly than we have done above by introducing appropriate symbols. To illustrate this we will consider further Cases 8.1–8.4 discussed in the previous section.

In Case 8.1 we are concerned with the proportion of economists in the population who believe that changes in the supply of money cause inflation. If we call this proportion $p$, its value must be greater than 0.5 if economists in general prefer the monetarist explanation of inflation. If this is not so we can assume that $p$ equals 0.5. Therefore in this example we can express $H_0$ and $H_1$ as follows:

$H_0$: $p = 0.5$

$H_1$: $p > 0.5$

In Case 8.2, the central issue is to use the sample mean values to decide whether or not the two samples have come from the same population. If the samples have come from different populations, then the mean values $\mu_1$ and $\mu_2$ will be different; if not they will be the same. The hypotheses $H_0$ and $H_1$ in this example can be expressed as:

$H_0$: $\mu_1 = \mu_2$  i.e.  $\mu_1 - \mu_2 = 0$

$H_1$: $\mu_1 \neq \mu_2$  i.e.  $\mu_1 - \mu_2 \neq 0$

We know already that the statistic of interest in Case 8.3 is the mean, and it is clear that the hypothesis that needs to be tested is the agent's claim that $\mu$ equals 7 hours. Moreover, if the holiday maker has been misled it is important to know whether it is detrimental, that is, whether $\mu$ is less than 7 hours. Our null and alternative hypotheses therefore become:

$H_0$: $\mu = 7$

$H_1$: $\mu < 7$

Finally, in Case 8.4, we have two proportions of graduates who are unable to find fulltime employment within one year of graduation. We therefore have two populations whose proportions are $p_1$ and $p_2$. We need to decide whether or not these two values have remained constant over the period 1978–86. We can therefore express $H_0$ and $H_1$ as:

$H_0$: $p_1 = p_2$  i.e.  $p_1 - p_2 = 0$

$H_1$: $p_1 \neq p_2$  i.e.  $p_1 - p_2 \neq 0$

Notice that in each of these examples the assumptions listed attempt to summarise the content of the competing theories. In each case the null and alternative hypotheses are expressed in such a way that they are mutually exclusive. This enables us at the end of the testing procedure to accept one hypothesis and therefore, necessarily, to reject the other.

It is also to be noticed that the numerical values contained in $H_0$ and $H_1$ are always population values. Sometimes these values are known and sometimes they are given by assumption. Since $H_0$ and $H_1$ are hypotheses about population values it is inappropriate for them to contain sample values.

## 8.3  Confidence limits

In inferential statistics it is not possible to prove conclusively that one theory is correct and another false. The best we can do is to accept or reject a hypothesis with a given degree of confidence. In order to do this it is necessary to establish the *confidence limits* for any given sampling distribution.

We begin for the sake of argument by accepting the null hypothesis $H_0$ and subsequently developing the sampling distribution that would result if $H_0$ were true. This is illustrated in Fig. 8.1. In order to keep the argument general the horizontal axis of Fig. 8.1 has no label, but if it were a sampling distribution of a mean the label would be $\bar{X}$, or if it were a sampling distribution of differences in proportions the label would be $\hat{p}_1 - \hat{p}_2$.

Because the diagram is drawn assuming $H_0$ is true, the mean value of the sampling distribution (i.e. the value of Mean in the diagram) is equal to the value contained in $H_0$. So if the diagram related to Case 8.3 Mean would be 7 hours or if it related to Case 8.1 Mean would be 0.5. The diagram also shows the values along the horizontal axis which contain 95% of the area under the curve, these values being given by:

Mean $\pm 1.96 \times$ standard error

The resulting values are called the 95% *confidence limits*, and it is ultimately these values that allow us to choose between $H_0$ and $H_1$.

What exactly do these confidence limits tell us? They say that if $H_0$ is true we can expect 95 out of every 100 separate sample values to fall between these limits. Or, to express it another way, if $H_0$ is true we can be 95% confident that any one sample value will fall between them.

With this in mind we can now introduce the following decision rule: if a given sample value falls inside the confidence limits we will accept the hypothesis contained in $H_0$ (and therefore reject $H_1$), or if it falls outside the confidence limits we will reject $H_0$ (and therefore accept $H_1$). In Fig. 8.1 the values on the horizontal axis which fall inside the confidence limits define the *acceptance region* (i.e. the region in which $H_0$ is accepted), while the remaining values on the horizontal axis define the *rejection region* (i.e. the region in which $H_0$ is rejected).

Notice that it is possible to obtain a sample value outside the confidence limits even if $H_0$ is true, in which case to reject $H_0$ would be an incorrect decision. In our example the chances of doing this are quite small, amounting to only 5 chances in 100. Never-

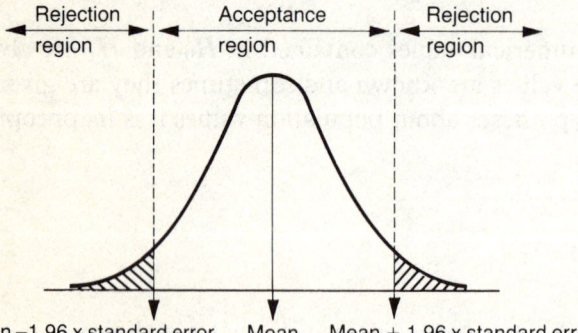

Figure 8.1   Confidence limits and the sampling distribution

theless the fact that we must necessarily take the chance of making an incorrect decision, highlights our statement at the beginning of this section that it is not possible to prove categorically that one theory is correct and another false.

## 8.4   One-tail/two-tail tests

In the previous section we introduced 95% confidence limits with the 5% rejection region distributed equally between the two tails of the distribution. In this section we need to extend our understanding in two ways.

The first concerns our choice of 95% confidence limits. Although our choice of 95% is a generally accepted standard, there are situations in which taking a 5% chance of incorrectly rejecting $H_0$ is either too high or too low a risk to take. Thus we might choose 98% confidence limits in one situation and 90% limits in another.

Second, in our previous discussion the rejection region was distributed between both tails of the distribution. In some situations however, the rejection region is restricted wholly to one or other tail of the distribution. When the rejection region is distributed between both tails we have a *two-tail test* and when it is restricted to just one tail we have a *one-tail test*.

We will pursue both of these issues further by extending our discussion of Cases 8.1–8.4. Figure 8.2 shows the relevant sampling distribution, the area of rejection and the level of significance for each of the four cases. The level of significance refers to the area of rejection; a level of significance of 0.02 means a rejection area equal to 2% which in turn implies confidence limits of 98%.

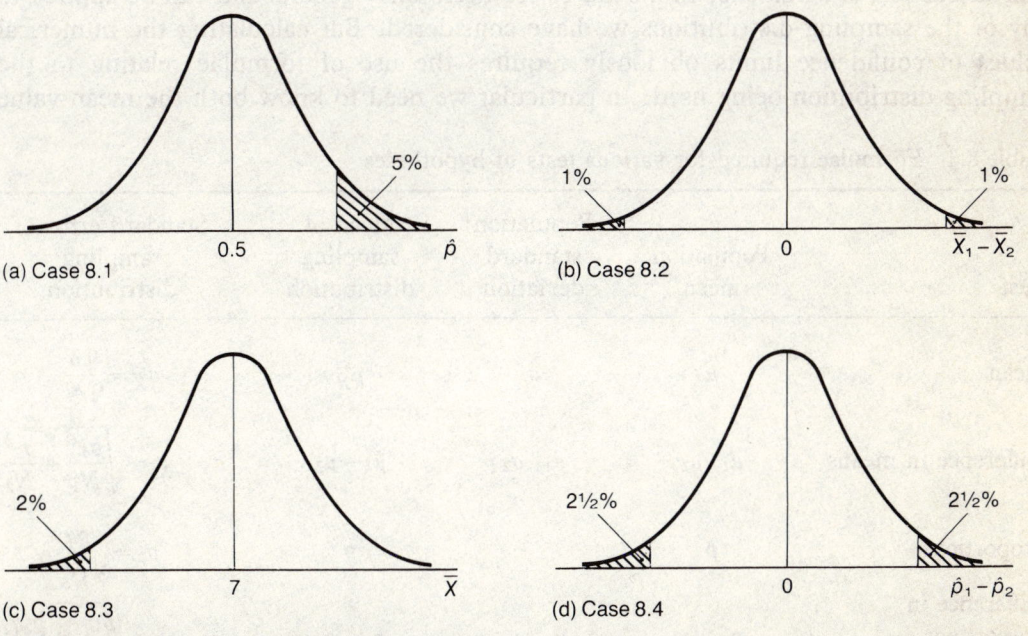

(a) Case 8.1

(b) Case 8.2

(c) Case 8.3

(d) Case 8.4

Figure 8.2   One-tail/two-tail tests

In Case 8.1 we are told to use 95% confidence limits, and we have already seen that the alternative hypothesis $H_1$ ($H_1$: $p > 0.5$) is concerned only with values for $p$ greater than 0.5. From this it is apparent that the 5% rejection area is confined to the right-hand tail of the distribution, i.e. we have a one-tail test as shown in Fig. 8.2(a).

Part (b) of the diagram relates to Case 8.2. From the specification of $H_0$ ($H_0$: $\mu_1 - \mu_2 = 0$), we see that the mean of the sampling distribution of $\bar{X}_1 - \bar{X}_2$ is assumed to be 0. Also, from the specification of $H_1$ ($H_1$: $\mu_1 - \mu_2 \neq 0$), it is clear that the alternative hypothesis may be accepted for positive or negative values of $\bar{X}_1 - \bar{X}_2$, so that we have a two-tail test with a rejection area in each tail. Since we are asked to perform the test at a 0.02 level of significance, it follows that there is a 1% rejection area in each tail with the remaining 98% of the area under the curve in between.

In Case 8.3, shown in Fig. 8.2(c), we have a sampling distribution of $\bar{X}$ whose central value is 7 hours. Once again the alternative hypothesis ($H_1$: $\mu < 7$) makes it clear that we have a one-tail test, but this time the rejection area of 2% (level of significance of 0.02) is contained in the left-hand tail of the distribution.

Figure 8.2(d) shows the sampling distribution of $\hat{p}_1 - \hat{p}_2$ for Case 8.4. Since the proportion of graduates unable to find employment in principle may have risen or fallen over the period 1978 to 1986, the rejection area is distributed over two tails as shown. In this example the level of significance is not stated and we are left to make the final decision at our own discretion. The level chosen is 0.05.

## 8.5  Formulae

Our discussion of confidence limits has so far been fairly general and can be applied to any of the sampling distributions we have considered. But calculating the numerical values of confidence limits obviously requires the use of formulae relating to the sampling distribution being used. In particular we need to know both the mean value

Table 8.1   Formulae required for various tests of hypotheses

| Test | Population mean | Population standard deviation | Mean of sampling distribution | Standard error of sampling distribution |
|---|---|---|---|---|
| Mean | $\mu$ | $\sigma$ | $\mu_{\bar{X}}$ | $\sigma_{\bar{X}} = \sqrt{\dfrac{\sigma}{N}}$ |
| Difference in means | $\mu_1, \mu_2$ | $\sigma_1, \sigma_2$ | $\mu_1 - \mu_2$ | $\sigma_{\bar{X}_1 - \bar{X}_2} = \sqrt{\dfrac{\sigma_1^{2}}{N_1} + \dfrac{\sigma_2^{2}}{N_2}}$ |
| Proportions | $p$ | | $p$ | $\sigma_{\hat{p}} = \sqrt{\dfrac{pq}{N}}$ |
| Difference in proportions | $p_1, p_2$ | | $p_1 - p_2$ | $\sigma_{\hat{p}_1 - \hat{p}_2} = \sqrt{\dfrac{p_1 q_1}{N_1} + \dfrac{p_2 q_2}{N_2}}$ |

and the standard error, and these are tabulated for the four sampling distributions in Table 8.1. The last two columns contain the data necessary to construct each of the required sampling distributions and to calculate the confidence limits on the assumption that $H_0$, as previously discussed, is true.

It is especially important to note that in the final column $\sigma$, $p$ and $q$ are all population coefficients. It often occurs, however, that population coefficients are not available, in which case we are forced to use sample values. This is based on the assumption that the given sample values can be taken as unbiased estimates of population coefficients, an approach which is quite acceptable if the number of observations in each sample is sufficiently large. In practice the sample is usually considered large enough if $N \geqslant 30$ (see Section 7.1 regarding unbiased estimates).

In the case of the sampling distribution of a proportion, however, a complication arises when using sample values in place of population values. In Table 8.1 we see that we require $p_1$ and $p_2$ (and therefore $q_1$ and $q_2$). We also know that under the null hypothesis $p_1 = p_2$. But, because of sampling error it is highly unlikely that $\hat{p}_1 = \hat{p}_2$ and we need to decide how to use our sample information in a way that is consistent with $H_0$. The way we do this is by combining both sets of sample data. In Cast 8.4 $\hat{p}_1 = 34/515 = 0.066$, and $\hat{p}_2 = 56/485 = 0.115$. If we combine both sets of data and call the result $\hat{\hat{p}}$ we find that $\hat{\hat{p}} = (34 + 56)/(515 + 485) = 0.09$. From this we obtain $\hat{\hat{q}} = 1 - \hat{\hat{p}} = 0.91$. We can now use $\hat{\hat{p}}$ as an estimate of $p_1$ and $p_2$ (and $\hat{\hat{q}}$ as an estimate of $q_1$ and $q_2$) and these values are in accord with the null hypothesis of $p_1 = p_2$. This is illustrated in Section 8.7.

## 8.6   Worked example—Case 8.3

We are now in a position to fully work through each of the cases previously discussed. In this section we will work through Case 8.3 and in the next section we will work through Case 8.4 using a slightly different approach. Cases 8.1 and 8.2 are left for the reader to complete (see Exercises 8.1 and 8.2).

## *Case 8.3*

A travel agent claims that the daily amount of sunshine in a given holiday resort during peak season is 7 hours. A holiday maker who booked a holiday with the agent found that the 30 day holiday gave an average amount of 5.9 hours of sunshine a day with a standard deviation of 1.8 hours. If the daily amount of sunshine is normally distributed, do you think that the holiday maker has reason to believe that the agent has been misleading? Use 0.02 level of significance.

From the question and from previous discussion we know:

$H_0$: $\mu = 7$

$H_1$: $\mu < 7$

$\bar{X} = 5.9$

$s = 1.8$

$N = 30$

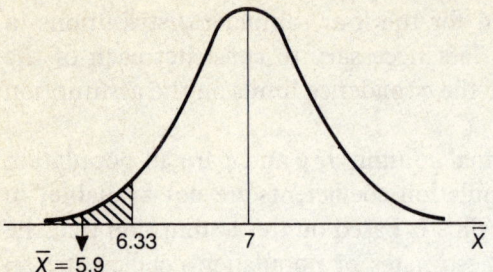

$\bar{X} = 5.9$

**Figure 8.3**  Sampling distribution and confidence limits for Case 8.3

The sampling distribution which results is shown in Fig. 8.3. The standard error (see Table 8.1) is given by:

$$\sigma_{\bar{X}} = \sigma/\sqrt{N} = 1.8/\sqrt{30} = 0.328$$

Appendix A shows that 48% of the area under the standard normal curve lies between the values $Z = 0$ and $Z = \pm 2.05$. Thus the 98% confidence limit is given by

$\mu_{\bar{X}}$ − relevant $Z$ value × standard error
$= 7 - 2.05 \times 0.328$
$= 6.33$

We can therefore say that we are 98% confident that if $H_0$ is true a sample mean value based on $N = 30$ will be at least 6.33 hours. Alternatively we could say that if $H_0$ is true there are only 2 chances in 100 that a sample of 30 observations will give a mean value less than 6.33 hours.

Now it finally remains to see how the actual sample mean given in the question compares with the situation that would arise if $H_0$ were true. From Fig. 8.3 it is clear that the sample mean falls in the rejection region. It is highly unlikely that the given sample mean has been generated by a population whose mean value is 7 hours. We therefore reject $H_0$ and accept $H_1$. It is far more likely that the sample has been selected from a population whose mean value is less than 7 hours and the holiday maker has good reason to believe that the agent has been misleading.

## 8.7  Worked example—Case 8.4

As a further illustration of the calculations involved in hypothesis testing we will work through Case 8.4 in full, though using an approach which is slightly different from that used in Section 8.6.

### *Case 8.4*

In a given university in 1978, 34 graduates out of a total of 515 were unable to find fulltime employment within one year of graduating. In 1986 the figure was 56 out of a total of 485. Has the proportion of graduates unable to find fulltime employment changed significantly between 1978 and 1986?

From our previous discussion we know that:

$H_0: p_1 - p_2 = 0$

$H_1: p_1 - p_2 \neq 0$

$\hat{p} = (34 + 56)/(515 + 485) = 0.09$

giving $\hat{q}$ equal to 0.91. If now we were to calculate the 95% confidence limits we would obtain values of $0 \pm 1.96\sigma_{\hat{p}_1 - \hat{p}_2}$. Since:

$$\sigma_{\hat{p}_1 - \hat{p}_2} = \sqrt{\frac{p_1 q_1}{N_1} + \frac{p_2 q_2}{N_2}}$$

$$= \sqrt{\frac{0.09 \times 0.91}{515} + \frac{0.09 \times 0.91}{485}} = 0.018$$

the resulting values are $\pm 0.035$ as shown in Fig. 8.4, but rather than use the sampling distribution to solve the problem we could use the $Z$ distribution instead. The lower part of Fig. 8.4 shows the 95% limits for the $Z$ distribution which we know to be $\pm 1.96$. We also know that the difference between the two sample proportions is $\hat{p}_1 - \hat{p}_2 = 0.066 - 0.115 = -0.049$. Now we can ask: What is the value of $Z$ that corresponds to the value of $\hat{p}_1 - \hat{p}_2 = -0.049$ and how does it compare with the values of $Z = \pm 1.96$? The required value of $Z$ (making use of the appropriate $Z$ transformation given in Section 6.4) is:

$$Z = \frac{(\hat{p}_1 - \hat{p}_2) - (p_1 - p_2)}{\sigma_{\hat{p}_1 - \hat{p}_2}} = \frac{-0.049}{0.018} = -2.72$$

From Fig. 8.4 it can be seen that the value of $N = -2.72$ falls in the shaded area which

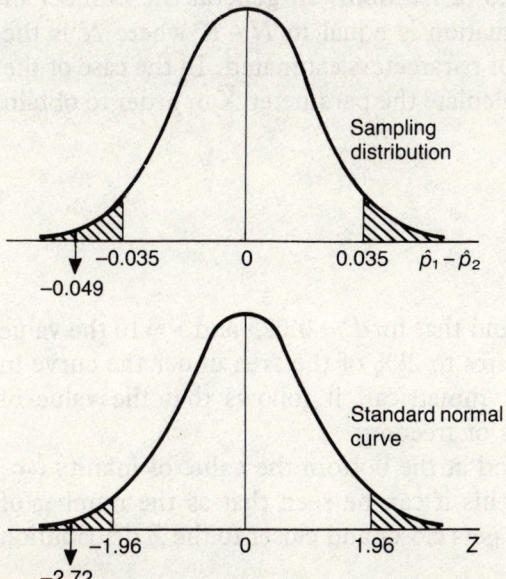

Figure 8.4   Sampling distribution and $Z$ distribution for Case 8.4

is the rejection area for the $Z$ distribution. Given the data in the question there are fewer than 5 chances in 100 of obtaining so large a $Z$ value if $H_0$ is true. We therefore reject $H_0$ and conclude that the proportion of graduates unable to find fulltime employment within one year of graduating has changed significantly between 1978 and 1986.

Although we have reached this conclusion using an alternative approach it should be clear that whichever method we use the conclusion will still be the same. From Fig. 8.4 it can be seen that we finish by rejecting $H_0$ and accepting $H_1$ when using the sampling distribution and also when using the $Z$ distribution; in each case the calculated value of $\hat{p}_1 - \hat{p}_2$ and the corresponding $Z$ value falls in the rejection region. For any given question it is necessary to use only one of the two methods but a full understanding of hypothesis testing will result in an ability to use both.

## 8.8   The $t$ distribution and small sample tests of a mean and difference in means

In our discussion of the sampling distributions of a mean and difference in means we have seen that for samples of size $N \geqslant 30$ we can use sample standard deviations as estimates of population standard deviations, thereby allowing us to use the $Z$ distribution. This, however, is not so in small samples where $N < 30$, and it is therefore necessary to introduce an alternative distribution known as the $t$ distribution, which is an approximation to the $Z$ distribution. From the $t$ distribution we obtain values of the $t$ statistic as illustrated in Table 8.2 (see also Appendix B).

The first row, labelled $p$, contains levels of probabilities corresponding to the shaded area under the curve in the $t$ distribution given in the top right-hand corner. The first column, labelled $v$, contains values of degrees of freedom. In general the number of degrees of freedom available in any given situation is equal to $N - K$ where $N$ is the number of observations and $K$ is the number of parameters estimated. In the case of the standard deviation, for example, we need to calculate the parameter $\bar{X}$ in order to obtain $s$ since

$$s = \sqrt{\frac{\sum (X_i - \bar{X})^2}{N}}$$

in which case $v = N - 1$.

If we now look in the body of the table we find that for $P = 0.025$ and $v = 10$ the value of $t$ is 2.228. Since the value of $P = 0.025$ relates to $2\frac{1}{2}\%$ of the area under the curve in the right-hand tail and since the curve is symmetrical, it follows that the value of $t = \pm 2.228$ are the 95% limits for 10 degrees of freedom.

As we proceed down the first column we find at the bottom the value of infinity $(\infty)$ for which the 95% limits are $\pm 1.96$. From this it can be seen that as the number of degrees of freedom increases the $t$ distribution gets closer and closer to the $Z$ distribution until finally they become synonymous.

When carrying out a small sample test of a mean, the procedure followed is exactly

Table 8.2  Stylised presentation of the *t* table

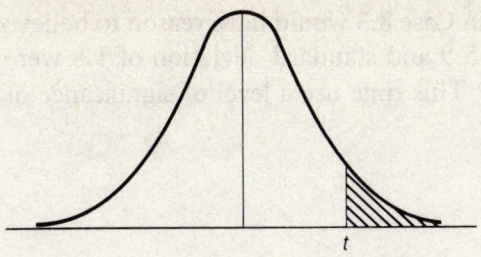

| $P$ | 0.10 | 0.05 | 0.025 | 0.01 | 0.005 |
|-----|------|------|-------|------|-------|
| $\nu$ | | | | | |
| 1 | | | | | |
| 2 | | | | | |
| 3 | | | | | |
| 4 | | | | | |
| 5 | | | | | |
| 6 | | | | | |
| 7 | | | | | |
| 8 | | | | | |
| 9 | | | | | |
| 10 | | | 2.228 | | |
| . | | | | | |
| . | | | | | |
| . | | | | | |
| $\infty$ | | | 1.960 | | |

the same as with large samples except that the *t* statistic now replaces the *Z* statistic. The number of degrees of freedom available is equal to $N-1$. This is illustrated in Example 8.1 using the same approach as the one used in Section 8.6.

In the case of testing the difference in mean values the procedure is less straightforward. We know from Section 6.4 that the *Z* transformation for large samples is:

$$Z = \frac{(\bar{X}_1 - \bar{X}_2) - (\mu_1 - \mu_2)}{\sqrt{s_1^2/N_1 + s_2^2/N_2}}$$

For small samples the relevant transformation is given by:

$$t = \frac{(\bar{X}_1 - \bar{X}_2) - (\mu_1 - \mu_2)}{\sqrt{(N_1 - 1)s_1^2 + (N_2 - 1)s_2^2}} \times \sqrt{\frac{N_1 N_2 (N_1 + N_2 - 2)}{(N_1 + N_2)}}$$

which has $\nu = N_1 + N_2 - 2$ degrees of freedom. The *t* statistic then replaces the *Z* statistic and the calculations proceed as in Section 8.7 and as illustrated in Example 8.2.

# Example 8.1

Do you think that the holiday maker referred to in Case 8.3 would have reason to believe the agent had been misleading if the average of 5.9 and standard deviation of 1.8 were for a 9 day holiday rather than a 30 day holiday? This time use a level of significance of 0.01.

We are given in Case 8.3:

$H_0$: $\mu = 7$

$H_1$: $\mu < 7$

From the above we know that $\bar{X} = 5.9$, $\sigma = 1.8$ and $N = 9$. The standard error $\sigma_{\bar{X}} = 1.8/\sqrt{9} = 0.6$. The relevant $t$ value for 8 degrees of freedom and significance level 0.01 is 2.82. The required confidence limit therefore is given by:

$$7 - 2.82 \times 0.6 = 5.31$$

We are therefore 99% confident that if $H_0$ is true the sample mean will be greater than 5.31 hours. This is shown in Fig. 8.5. The sample value is in fact 5.9 hours. Therefore, the holiday maker no longer has reason to believe that the agent has been misleading. The sample value of 5.9 hours is not significantly less than $\mu = 7$ hours at the 0.01 level of significance.

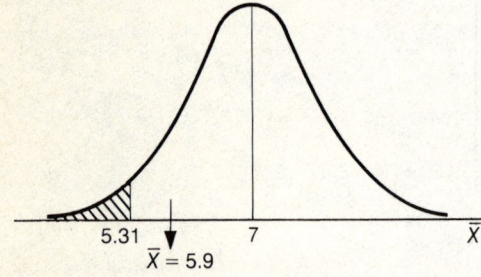

Figure 8.5   Sampling distribution for Example 8.1

# Example 8.2

Refer to Case 8.2. If the values of $N$ were changed to $N_1 = 17$ and $N_2 = 15$, determine whether the two samples have come from the same population.

The null and alternative hypotheses are given by:

$H_0$: $\mu_1 - \mu_2 = 0$

$H_1$: $\mu_1 - \mu_2 \neq 0$

The relevant $t$ statistic is given by:

$$t = \frac{(\bar{X}_1 - \bar{X}_2) - (\mu_1 - \mu_2)}{\sqrt{(N_1 - 1)s_1^2 + (N_2 - 1)s_2^2}} \times \sqrt{\frac{N_1 N_2 (N_1 + N_2 - 2)}{(N_1 + N_2)}}$$

$$= \frac{16.3 - 14.7}{\sqrt{16 \times 10.24 + 14 \times 20.25}} \times \sqrt{\frac{17 \times 15 \times 30}{32}}$$

$$= \frac{1.6 \times 15.46}{21.15}$$

$$= 1.17$$

From Fig. 8.6 we can see that the $t$ statistic for $\nu = 17 + 15 - 2 = 30$ degrees of freedom with a 0.02 level of significance for a two-tail test equals $\pm 2.46$. Since the calculated value of $t = 1.17$ falls within the 98% values for $t$ given in the table, we accept the null hypothesis and conclude that the two samples have come from the same population (see Exercise 8.2).

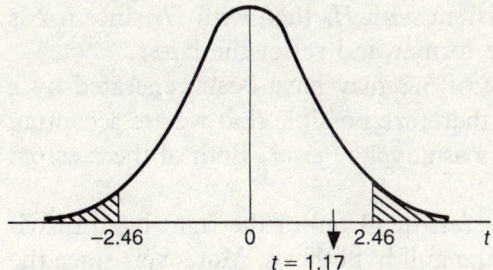

Figure 8.6   $t$ distribution for Example 8.2

## 8.9  Making decisions and making errors

In all the tests considered so far our task has been to choose between two competing hypotheses on the basis of available sample evidence. Since we can never be certain of reaching the correct conclusion, we need to discuss the kinds of errors it is possible to make. To do this we will modify Case 8.3.

Let us assume that there are now two travel agents making competing claims. The first claims an average daily amount of sunshine of 7 hours and the second claims an average of 5 hours, that is:

$H_0$:  $\mu = 7$
$H_1$:  $\mu = 5$

We further assume that daily sunshine is distributed normally as shown in Fig. 8.7. In order to choose between $H_0$ and $H_1$ we will introduce the following simple decision rule: if the sample value is closer to 7 accept $H_0$, but if it is closer to 5 accept $H_1$. This means that a value of 6 represents the cut off point which allows us to choose between the two hypotheses. Consider now the sample value of 5.9 hours given. With this information we would reject $H_0$ and accept $H_1$ since it is closer to 5 than to 7.

But notice that it is nevertheless possible for a value of 5.9 to be generated by a

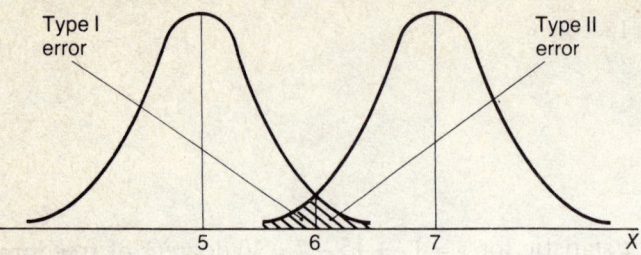

Figure 8.7   Type I and type II errors

distribution whose mean value is 7. It is therefore possible that we are rejecting $H_0$ when $H_0$ is true. This is clearly an error and we refer to this as a *type I error*.

But, let us now assume that the sample value is 6.2 hours instead of 5.9 hours. We would conclude that the evidence is more consistent with $H_0$ than with $H_1$ since 6.2 is closer to 7 than to 5, and we would accept the former and reject the latter.

Again, however, we need to see that a value of 6.2 may have been generated by a distribution whose mean value is 5 hours. It is therefore possible that we are accepting $H_0$ when $H_1$ is true. Such an error is referred to as a *type II error*. Both of these errors are shown in Table 8.3.

In Fig. 8.7 it can be seen that the area in the left-hand tail of the right-hand distribution is equivalent to the rejection area under the null hypothesis. Moreover, since the area is also the level of significance of the test, it follows that the level of significance of a test is equal to the probability of making a type I error.

From Fig. 8.7 we can also see the probability of making a type II error. This is given by the shaded area in the right-hand tail of the distribution on the left.

As presented in the diagram these two probabilities are equal, but this need not be the case. It is quite possible to choose a cut-off value of, say, 5.5 hours in which case the probability of making a type I error decreases and the probability of making a type II error increases.

If we now return to Case 8.3 we can see that we have now introduced a substantial modification. In this section our alternative hypothesis has been:

$$H_1: \mu = 5$$

Table 8.3   Correct and incorrect decisions

|                     | $H_0$ true           | $H_1$ true         |
|---------------------|----------------------|--------------------|
| Final decision      |                      |                    |
| Accept $H_0$        | Correct decision     | Type II error      |
| Accept $H_1$        | Type I error         | Correct decision   |

but our earlier discussion (Section 8.2) led to the alternative hypothesis:

$H_1$: $\mu < 7$

The difference is important. In practice we are rarely able to be as specific with the alternative hypothesis as we have been in our discussion of the two types of errors. We are, therefore, rarely able to obtain the sampling distribution for the alternative hypothesis and hence although we can specify the probability of making a type I error, we cannot specify the probability of making a type II error. In any practical situation we need to exercise care in our choice of significance level, because associated with our choice will be an unknown probability of making a type II error.

## Exercises

**8.1**  Work through Case 8.1 using the approach developed in Section 8.6.

**8.2**  Work through Case 8.2 using the approach developed in Section 8.7. Compare your conclusion with the one reached in Example 8.2.

**8.3**  It has been claimed that 50% of all families move at least once every 3 years. In a sample survey 218 families out of 400 moved at least once over a 3 year period. Does this evidence suggest that the proportion of families that move is more than 50%?

**8.4**  A survey conducted in a large city showed that 68 out of 100 housewives preferred washing powder A to washing powder B. In a similar survey carried out in a small village 213 out of 300 housewives made a similar choice. Is there a significant different between the two sets of preferences? Use a level of significance of 0.01.

**8.5**  An identical achievement test was given to random samples of size 50 at two different schools. Given that the results were:

$N_1 = 50$, $\overline{X}_1 = 89$, $s_1 = 4$
$N_2 = 50$, $\overline{X}_2 = 92$, $s_2 = 3$

test at a level of significance of 0.05 whether the difference between the two sample means is significant.

**8.6**  A random sample of 20 college students were tested using a newly constructed intelligence test. The mean for this sample was 124 and the standard deviation was 15.1. If it is known that the intelligence of college students throughout the country is normally distributed with a mean value of 121, is there reason to believe that the new test is biased upwards.

**8.7**  In two neighbouring constituencies by-elections were held on the same day. In an article written three days before election day a non-partisan newspaper claimed that the two Labour Party candidates would each poll the same proportion of votes. On the day the article appeared the results of two opinion polls were published showing that in the first constituency 35% of a sample of 400 voters intended voting Labour, while in the other constituency 45% of a sample of 600 voters intended voting Labour. Show that the results of the two opinion polls do not support the newspaper's claim.

**8.8**   The data below show average salary (£) earned by samples of graduates during their first year of employment ($N$ = the number of observations in each sample and $s$ = the standard deviation).

| Institution / Class of degree | University | | | Polytechnic | | |
|---|---|---|---|---|---|---|
| | Mean | $N$ | $s$ | Mean | $N$ | $s$ |
| First | 6500 | 30 | 725 | 6600 | 40 | 650 |
| Third | 6300 | 35 | 675 | 6000 | 35 | 625 |

(a)   Is there a significant difference in salary earned between:
(i)    university graduates with a first and polytechnic graduates with a first?
(ii)   university graduates with a first and university graduates with a third?
(iii)  polytechnic graduates with a first and polytechnic graduates with a third?
(b)   On the basis of your results what advice would you give to a person who is unsure whether to apply for a place at a university or a polytechnic?

**8.9**   Opponents of the Prime Minister in the UK have made the following claim: 'At least half the voters in the country now believe that the Prime Minister should resign.' In order to test this claim a sample of voters was selected from each of two parliamentary constituencies with each person being asked whether the Prime Minister should resign. Agreement was indicated by 106 out of 220 voters from the first constituency and by 95 out of 250 in the second.
(a)   Do the results in either constituency support the claim made above?
(b)   Is there a significant difference in the support for the Prime Minister between the two constituencies?
(c)   Briefly discuss the conclusions reached.

**8.10**   The daily sales of petrol (in gallons) for a particular garage over a 15 day period are given below:

| | | |
|---|---|---|
| 130 | 152 | 142 |
| 163 | 138 | 156 |
| 148 | 164 | 146 |
| 174 | 159 | 162 |
| 143 | 162 | 170 |

Does the daily average for this period differ significantly from the daily average of 170 gallons in the previous year? Use a significance level of 0.05. Briefly discuss your conclusion.

**8.11**  Use the information given in Case 8.2 in order to test at a 0.04 level of significance whether either sample mean differs significantly from the national average of 15.3%. Are your conclusions affected by changing the significance level from 0.04 to 0.02? Discuss.

**8.12**  Refer to the data in Table 7.1. Test each of the following propositions at a level of significance of 0.02.
(a)  Unemployment amongst City University graduates is less than the national average of 16.3%.
(b)  There is a significant change in the proportion unemployed amongst Leeds graduates between 1981 and 1982 (assume that $N$ in 1981 is the same as in 1982).
(c)  There is a significant difference in the proportions unemployed in 1982 at Bradford and York.

# 9 Tests of hypotheses— non-parametric tests

9.1 Related and unrelated samples
9.2 Mann–Whitney test using unrelated samples
9.3 Wilcoxon test using related samples

9.4 Comparing parametric and non-parametric tests
Exercises

In the previous chapter our analysis of hypothesis testing was based on two assumptions both of which now have to be relaxed.

The first assumption is that we have taken samples from a normal population so that our resulting sampling distribution is also normally distributed, therefore allowing us to use the $Z$ distribution (or $t$ distribution if the sampling distribution is approximately normally distributed) in order to choose between hypotheses.

We already know that if $N$ is sufficiently large a population not normally distributed will generate a normally distributed sampling distribution (see Section 6.2). But this is not so if $N$ is as small as say 10, in which situation an alternative procedure is required where no assumption is made concerning the distribution of the population variable. Such an approach is often referred to as *distribution free inference*.

The second assumption implicit in the previous chapter is that the variables of interest are measured on an interval basis where it is possible to measure both the direction and degree of difference between observations. We have seen in Section 1.6, however, that measurement is often possible at no better than on an ordinal basis where only the direction of difference between observations can be measured. Again, in such a situation, the tests introduced in Chapter 8 are not applicable and new tests have to be introduced.

When either the first or both of these assumptions are relaxed we move into the area of *non-parametric tests*. Many non-parametric tests are available for use by economists and in this chapter we illustrate their use by introducing two of the more commonly used ones, namely the Mann–Whitney test and the Wilcoxon test.

## 9.1 Related and unrelated samples

Consider the situation in which we wish to investigate empirically whether or not large companies are more profitable than small companies. One way of doing this is to take a sample of large firms and a sample of small firms and compare the profit performance of both groups. But the way in which the samples are chosen will determine the relationship between them, which in turn has implications for the final choice of testing procedure to use.

One way of taking the samples is to select them in such a way that they are unrelated to each other. This could be achieved by randomly selecting each large company from a population consisting of large companies and each small company from a population consisting of small companies. The kind of figures that might result from such an exercise are shown in columns 1 and 3 of Table 9.1 where profits are expressed as a percentage of net assets. Once the dependent variable (in this case profits) and the independent variable (in this case size) are chosen, the selection of one sample is unrelated to the selection of the other.

Alternatively, we could select the samples in such a way that they are related to each other. Let us extend our previous example of the relationship between size and profits. Suppose it is known that some industries are more profitable than others and that the more profitable ones are represented in the sample of large firms more than in the sample of small firms. If the large firms are found to be more profitable than the small firms, it is not clear whether this is because they are larger or because they belong to more profitable industries. We need to be able to isolate the effect of size by removing the effect of industry membership.

We can do this by selecting our samples in such a way that every large firm from a given industry is matched with a small firm from the same industry. By choosing matched pairs in this way we are ensuring that they are related to each other. The kind

Table 9.1 Ranking of firms by profits for samples of large and small firms

| Large firms | | Small firms | |
| Profits (%) | Rank | Profits (%) | Rank |
| --- | --- | --- | --- |
| 20.8 | 4 | 7.8 | 17 |
| 15.3 | 9 | 4.4 | 20 |
| 23.5 | 1 | 9.4 | 15 |
| 22.1 | 2 | 6.8 | 18 |
| 12.8 | 12 | 19.5 | 5 |
| 17.7 | 7 | 14.6 | 10 |
| 16.4 | 8 | 13.3 | 11 |
| 10.9 | 14 | 5.2 | 19 |
| 21.8 | 3 | 8.8 | 16 |
| 18.6 | 6 | 11.9 | 13 |
| | 66 | | 144 |

of figures that might result from such an exercise are shown in the first three columns of Table 9.2.

There is a second way in which we could select our samples such that they are related to each other. To illustrate this let us assume that we are testing the hypothesis that company profits vary with the business cycle in such a way that during times of expansion in the economy profits are high while during times of contraction they are low. Once we have defined our periods of expansion and contraction, we could select a sample of firms and for each firm in the sample calculate average profits for each of the two periods. To remove the effect of size on the results, we would need to choose only firms that have not changed in size during the period. The kind of figures that might result are shown in columns 1, 2 and 3 of Table 9.3. In this case the samples are related, since each pair of observations relate to the same firm at different points in time.

We therefore have a clear distinction between samples which are related and samples which are unrelated, and this forms the basis of our choice between the two non-parametric tests to be introduced in the rest of this chapter.

## 9.2  Mann–Whitney test using unrelated samples

The Mann–Whitney test can be used to investigate the data for two samples when two conditions are met. First, the underlying shape of the distribution from which the samples are taken is unknown. Second, the two samples must be unrelated. It can also be applied to situations where the data are measured on an ordinal basis, so that values can be arranged in rank order both within samples and across samples.

The basic idea behind the test is very simple and will be explained by making use of the data for the unrelated samples shown in Table 9.1. Let us assume the table shows the profit performance of each firm measured on an interval basis. After combining firms from both samples the rank of each firm has been assessed, with the most profitable firm being ranked 1 and the least profitable ranked 20. It there is a tie in the rank order of any two firms each is given a value equal to one half of the combined ranks that would have been given in the absence of a tie.

If there is no difference in the profitability of large firms compared with small firms, we would expect the sum of ranks in the first group to be about the same as the sum for the second group. Alternatively, if large firms are more profitable than small firms, we would expect the sum of ranks of the first group to be much smaller than the second. By calculating the sum of ranks of one group, the Mann–Whitney test allows us to determine the probability that this sum will arise by chance. If the probability is small we can reject the null hypothesis that profits and size are unrelated.

The test statistic involved is referred to as the $U$ statistic which can be applied to both samples. The required formulae are:

$$U = N_1 N_2 + \frac{N_1(N_1 + 1)}{2} - R_1$$

and

$$U = N_1N_2 + \frac{N_2(N_2 + 1)}{2} - R_2$$

where $N_1$ = the number of observations in the first sample
      $N_2$ = the number of observations in the second sample
      $R_1$ = the sum of ranks in the first sample
      $R_2$ = the sum of ranks in the second sample

Either of the two resulting values for $U$ can be used to reach a final decision, but in practice the Mann–Whitney test statistic (see Appendix E) is based on the smaller of the two values. We therefore take the smaller of the two calculated values for $U$ and compare it with the tabulated value. If the former is *less* than the latter we reject the null hypothesis of no relationship between company size and profits.

For the data in Table 9.1 we obtain

$$U = 10 \times 10 + \frac{10 \times 11}{2} - 66 = 89$$

and

$$U = 10 \times 10 + \frac{10 \times 11}{2} - 144 = 11$$

The tabulated value for $U$ given in Appendix E for $N_1 = 10$ and $N_2 = 10$ is 23. Since the calculated value of $U = 11$ (the smaller of the two calculated values) is less than the tabulated value of 23, we reject the null hypothesis of no difference and conclude that large firms are significantly more profitable than small firms.

Notice finally that the table for the Mann–Whitney test is based on a 0.05 level of significance for a two-tail test. In our example the alternative hypothesis contained the assumption that large firms were more profitable than small firms. We therefore have a one-tail test, so our results are significant at the 0.025 level of significance (see Exercises 9.2 and 9.5).


## 9.3   Wilcoxon test using related samples

The Wilcoxon test is used when samples are related in either of the two ways previously discussed in Section 9.1, i.e. the samples consist of matched pairs of observations or each member of a sample is measured on two separate occasions. As with the Mann–Whitney test no assumption is made about the populations generating the samples, but unlike the Mann–Whitney test measurement of variables is required on an interval basis. Although the test statistic $T$ is based on rank values which require ordinal measurement, these rank values are based on differences between pairs of observations and the calculation of these differences requires interval measurement of the original variables.

The rationale behind the test is quite straightforward. Assume we have two samples consisting of matched pairs of firms with both members of each pair selected from the same industry. We will also assume that we measure the profits of all firms in the samples as shown in columns 2 and 3 of Table 9.2 and obtain the difference $(d_i)$ between each pair as shown in column 4. If size has no effect on profitability we would expect that on average we would have about as many + signs as we have − signs in column 4, and that the larger (smaller) positive differences would tend to match the larger (smaller) negative differences.

Alternatively, if large size leads to higher profits we would expect a preponderance of + over − signs. Consequently if we rank the values of $d_i$ and calculate the sum of ranks with − signs we would expect a low value to result. Thus, if the final sum is *less* than the critical value in the table, the null hypothesis can be rejected and the alternative hypothesis accepted.

Let us now return to Table 9.2. The values of $d_i$ and the corresponding rank values are shown in columns 4 and 5. The rank values given in column 5 are obtained by taking the modulus of $d_i$ (i.e. the value of $d_i$ ignoring the sign) and giving the rank 1 to the smallest value for $d$ and 10 to the largest value. For convenience column 5 shows the sign associated with the corresponding difference in the previous column.

We now compare the sum of the positive ranks $(8 + 3 + 10 + 9 = 30)$ with the sum of the negative ranks $(5 + 7 + 6 + 1 + 2 + 4 = 25)$ ignoring the signs, and take the *smaller* value as our calculated value of $T$. This is shown in the final column where $T = 25$.

It is this value of $T = 25$ which has to be compared with the critical value of $T$ for the Wilcoxon test as given in Appendix F. The critical values depend on the value of $N$ and on the level of significance. The levels of significance given in Appendix F are for a two-tail test and have to be halved when used for a one-tail test. Thus, for $N = 10$ and a level of significance of 0.01 (assuming a one-tail test), the critical value of $T$ is 5. Since $T = 25$

Table 9.2   Calculations for Wilcoxon test using matched pairs

| Pair number | Profits of large firms (%) | Profits of small firms (%) | Difference $(d_i)$ | Rank of $d_i$ | Least sum ranks |
|---|---|---|---|---|---|
| 1 | 27.1 | 19.3 | 7.8 | (+)8 | |
| 2 | 13.9 | 18.5 | −4.6 | (−)5 | 5 |
| 3 | 10.2 | 16.4 | −6.2 | (−)7 | 7 |
| 4 | 17.9 | 15.9 | 2.0 | (+)3 | |
| 5 | 6.3 | 12.1 | −5.8 | (−)6 | 6 |
| 6 | 24.4 | 9.4 | 15.0 | (+)10 | |
| 7 | 8.4 | 8.5 | −0.1 | (−)1 | 1 |
| 8 | 7.7 | 7.9 | −0.2 | (−)2 | 2 |
| 9 | 14.3 | 4.4 | 9.9 | (+)9 | |
| 10 | 21.8 | 25.6 | −3.8 | (−)4 | 4 |
| | | | | | $T = 25$ |

Table 9.3  Calculations for Wilcoxon test using the same firms at different times

| Firm number | Average profits during expansion (%) | Average profits during recession (%) | Difference $(d_i)$ | Rank of $d_i$ | Least sum ranks |
|---|---|---|---|---|---|
| 1 | 21.3 | 17.4 | 3.9 | $(+)6$ | |
| 2 | 19.1 | 14.9 | 4.2 | $(+)7\frac{1}{2}$ | |
| 3 | 10.4 | 6.2 | 4.2 | $(+)7\frac{1}{2}$ | |
| 4 | 8.8 | 10.2 | $-1.4$ | $(-)3$ | 3 |
| 5 | 16.5 | 8.0 | 8.5 | $(+)9$ | |
| 6 | 5.9 | 6.4 | $-0.5$ | $(-)1$ | 1 |
| 7 | 24.8 | 15.8 | 9.0 | $(+)10$ | |
| 8 | 13.6 | 10.2 | 3.4 | $(+)5$ | |
| 9 | 12.8 | 13.6 | $-0.8$ | $(-)2$ | 2 |
| 10 | 7.2 | 5.0 | 2.2 | $(+)4$ | |
| | | | | | $T = 6$ |

is greater than the critical value of 5, we accept the null hypothesis and conclude that for the data given in Table 9.2, size and profits are not significantly related.

It will be recalled from Section 9.1 that the data in Table 9.3 are based on related samples where the profits of each firm are measured on two separate occasions in order to test the alternative hypothesis that profits are higher during periods of expansion than during periods of recession. From the values of $d_i$ given in column 4 we obtain the rank values of $d_i$ in column 5. Since the sum of the negative ranks $(3 + 1 + 2 = 6)$ is less than the sum of the positive ranks $(6 + 7\frac{1}{2} + 7\frac{1}{2} + 9 + 10 + 5 + 4 = 49)$, our calculated value of $T$ equals 6. From Appendix F we see that for a one-tail test with a level of significance of 0.025 and $N = 10$, the critical value for $T$ is 8. Since the calculated value of $T$ is less than the critical value, we reject the null hypothesis and accept the alternative hypothesis. Profits of firms are significantly higher during periods of expansion than during periods of recession.

Further applications of the Wilcoxon test can be found in Exercises 9.1, 9.3 and 9.4.

## 9.4  Comparing parametric and non-parametric tests

In this and the previous chapter we have introduced a range of significance tests and have discussed the various issues which determine which test is to be used in any given situation. In this section we will briefly discuss the ability of both parametric and non-parametric tests to make a correct choice between competing hypotheses.

The ability to make a correct choice between competing hypotheses is a rather loose definition of the power (or efficiency) of a test. In Section 8.9 we discussed the two possible types of error one can make when using a test of significance. A type I error was defined as rejecting $H_0$ when it is true and a type II error was defined as accepting $H_0$ when it is false. With these definitions we can formally define the power of a test as being the probability of rejecting $H_0$ when it is false, that is:

Power $= 1 - P$ (type II error)

Given this definition of the power of a test we can compare parametric and non-parametric tests. It can be shown that in general parametric tests are more powerful than non-parametric tests in the sense defined above. This is not suprising.

We have seen that in the two non-parametric tests discussed in this chapter, ordinal data are used at some stage of the testing procedure, and the use of ordinal data instead of interval data always involves a loss of information. This loss of information will increase the amount of sampling error thereby increasing the probability of making a type II error. Thus the power of a parametric test is in general greater than that of a non-parametric test. However, in situations where the population being sampled is not normally distributed and where very few observations are available measured at best on an ordinal basis, non-parametric tests are to be preferred.

## Exercises

**9.1** The average annual percentage rate of inflation over a five year period for a selection of Western and Third World countries is given below. Perform a Wilcoxon matched pairs test. Do your results suggest that inflation in the former group is less than in the latter?

| Western countries (%) | Third World countries (%) |
|---|---|
| 10.8 | 12.9 |
| 8.3 | 16.4 |
| 6.4 | 9.6 |
| 7.8 | 10.1 |
| 9.1 | 8.3 |
| 4.3 | 7.2 |
| 12.2 | 10.9 |
| 4.2 | 8.2 |

**9.2** Two samples of firms were randomly selected from the north and south of England. The management of each firm was assessed and given a score between 0 (poor management) and 100 (excellent management). The resulting scores are given below.

| Southern firm number | Score | Northern firm number | Score |
|---|---|---|---|
| 1 | 100 | 1 | 82 |
| 2 | 42 | 2 | 64 |
| 3 | 96 | 3 | 21 |
| 4 | 79 | 4 | 72 |
| 5 | 84 | 5 | 58 |
| 6 | 98 | 6 | 78 |
| 7 | 76 | 7 | 38 |
| | | 8 | 62 |
| | | 9 | 15 |

Is there any difference in the overall managerial abilities in the two regions?

**9.3** The weekly sales of eight sales people was measured immediately before and after attending a sales promotion course. The results are given below. Do the results suggest that the course was beneficial?

| Sales person | Weekly sales before course (£) | Weekly sales after course (£) |
|---|---|---|
| 1 | 520 | 550 |
| 2 | 380 | 460 |
| 3 | 940 | 710 |
| 4 | 720 | 760 |
| 5 | 510 | 600 |
| 6 | 470 | 360 |
| 7 | 840 | 860 |
| 8 | 790 | 810 |

**9.4** The head of each of seven families was asked to record his or her weekly expenditure on alcohol immediately before and after a budget in which tax on alcohol was increased. The results are given below. Test at a 0.01 level of significance whether the budget had any effect on alcohol consumption. Briefly discuss.

| Head of family number | Expenditure on alcohol before budget (£) | Expenditure on alcohol after budget (£) |
|---|---|---|
| 1 | 4.52 | 5.22 |
| 2 | 2.81 | 3.91 |

*Continued*

| Head of family number | Expenditure on alcohol before budget (£) | Expenditure on alcohol after budget (£) |
|:---:|:---:|:---:|
| 3 | 6.41 | 5.81 |
| 4 | 9.15 | 7.21 |
| 5 | 6.28 | 7.15 |
| 6 | 10.15 | 8.72 |
| 7 | 4.52 | 5.34 |

**9.5**  Two random samples of blacks and whites were asked to indicate their degree of opposition to apartheid on a scale from 1 to 20 with 1 indicating weak opposition and 20 indicating strong opposition. The results were as follows:

| Blacks | Whites |
|:---:|:---:|
| 19 | 15 |
| 15 | 14 |
| 12 | 12 |
| 10 | 18 |
| 17 | 8 |
| 16 | 16 |
| 17 | 13 |
| 9 | 6 |
|  | 4 |
|  | 11 |

Do these results indicate a difference of opinion between the two groups?

# 10 Correlation

10.1 Coefficient of correlation
10.2 Example
10.3 How good is our estimate?

10.4 Rank correlation
Exercises

It often happens in the social sciences that there is reason to believe that two variables $Y$ and $X$ are inter-related. In sociology, for example, we may assume that there is some degree of correlation between infant mortality ($Y$) and the general standard of health care ($X$) measured across countries. Similarly in psychology we may assume that an individual's intelligence ($Y$) is related to the intelligence of the parents ($X$). Or, in economics, we may consider that there is a relationship between an individual's level of expenditure ($Y$) and level of income ($X$). In each of these three situations we are looking at the possibility of the variables $X$ and $Y$ being correlated in some way with each other.

In order to pursue this matter empirically it is necessary to have access to an index or a measure which will allow us to measure the amount of correlation which exists. Although there are various ways of doing this we will concentrate mainly on introducing a measure which is referred to as the product moment coefficient of correlation or Pearson's $r$, or, more popularly, the *linear coefficient of correlation*, $r$. Towards the end of this chapter we will introduce a further measure of correlation known as Spearman's rank correlation coefficient.

## 10.1 Coefficient of correlation

The linear coefficient of correlation, $r$, is constructed in such a way that it has a maximum value of $+1$ and a minimum value of $-1$. Formally we can say that:

$$-1 \leqslant r \leqslant +1$$

There are two features of this property that are important when interpreting the value of $r$.

The first is that it provides an indication of the degree of relationship between the two variables concerned: since the values $\pm 1$ indicate the upper and lower values of $r$, we can say that the closer $r$ is to $+$ or $-1$ the greater is the degree of correlation between $X$ and $Y$. Also we can say that the absence of any relationship between $X$ and $Y$ is associated with a value of $r$ close to zero.

The second feature of the above property is that the sign of the coefficient indicates the nature of the relationship. A positive sign indicates a direct relationship in which the variables $X$ and $Y$ move in the same direction, that is increases (decreases) in $X$ are associated with increases (decreases) in $Y$. A negative sign indicates an indirect relationship in which variables $X$ and $Y$ move in opposite directions: an increase (decrease) in $X$ being associated with a decrease (increase) in $Y$.

These two features are illustrated in Fig. 10.1. In part (a) we have a scatter diagram where all paired observations of $X$ and $Y$ lie on a straight line. Because the slope of the line is positive we have a situation of perfect direct linear correlation. It is perfect because all observations lie exactly on the straight line giving a maximum value for $r$ of $+1$ and it is direct because the trend line is such that increases in $Y$ are accompanied by increases in $X$. In part (b) the observations are scattered around the superimposed straight line. Although the observations are not on the line itself they are very closely scattered around it, suggesting high correlation between the variables. Moreover the trend makes it clear that as $Y$ moves in one direction $X$ moves in the other. The correlation in part (b) is therefore of the order $r = -0.9$. In part (c) of Fig. 10.1 the loose scatter of points around a positively sloped line suggests a rather weak direct relationship of the order $r = 0.4$. In part (d) the observations are randomly scattered suggesting no association between $X$ and $Y$ and a consequent value of $r = 0$.

Before introducing the formula for $r$ there are two features which require further emphasis.

First we have so far considered only linear correlation. If we have reason to believe that there is a non-linear relation between $X$ and $Y$ as illustrated in part (e) of Fig. 10.1,

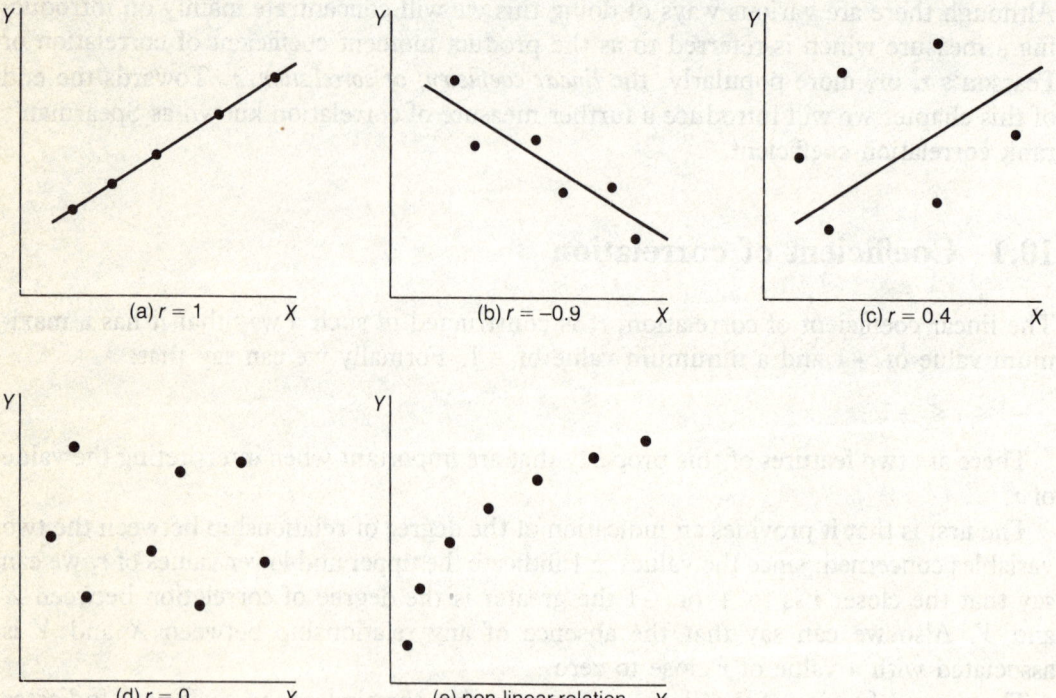

Figure 10.1   Differing degrees of correlation between $X$ and $Y$

it is not appropriate to apply the formula given below directly to the data (see Exercise 10.1).

Second, our previous reference to the association or correlation between $X$ and $Y$ in no way implies a causal relationship between them. There may be a causal relationship involved but the correlation coefficient does not address this issue. Indeed, it is quite possible for two variables to be causally related and yet have a low correlation coefficient, while two others, obviously unrelated causally, may have a high correlation coefficient.

Finally, we introduce the formula we will use in order to calculate $r$:

$$r = \frac{N\Sigma X_i Y_i - \Sigma X_i \Sigma Y_i}{\sqrt{[N\Sigma X_i^2 - (\Sigma X_i)^2][N\Sigma Y_i^2 - (\Sigma Y_i)^2]}}$$

The application of this formula is illustrated in the next section.

## 10.2  Example

The formula for the linear correlation coefficient $r$ has been applied to the data in Table 10.1. Column 1 shows average weekly household expenditure while column 2 shows

Table 10.1  Calculating $r$ for income and expenditure

| Consumer expenditure (£) $Y$ | Weekly income (£) $X$ | $XY$ | $Y^2$ | $X^2$ |
|---|---|---|---|---|
| 26 | 20 | 520 | 676 | 400 |
| 27 | 28 | 756 | 729 | 784 |
| 32 | 35 | 1 120 | 1 024 | 1 225 |
| 40 | 45 | 1 800 | 1 600 | 2 025 |
| 40 | 55 | 2 200 | 1 600 | 3 025 |
| 57 | 70 | 3 990 | 3 249 | 4 900 |
| 62 | 90 | 5 580 | 3 844 | 8 100 |
| 76 | 115 | 8 740 | 5 776 | 13 225 |
| 105 | 200 | 21 000 | 11 025 | 40 000 |
| 465 | 658 | 45 706 | 29 523 | 73 684 |

$$r = \frac{9 \times 45\,706 - 465 \times 658}{\sqrt{(9 \times 73\,684 - 658^2) \times (9 \times 29\,523 - 465^2)}}$$

$$= \frac{411\,354 - 305\,970}{\sqrt{(663\,156 - 43\,296) \times (265\,707 - 216\,225)}}$$

$$= \frac{105\,384}{\sqrt{230\,192 \times 49\,482}} = \frac{105\,384}{106\,725.3}$$

$$= 0.99$$

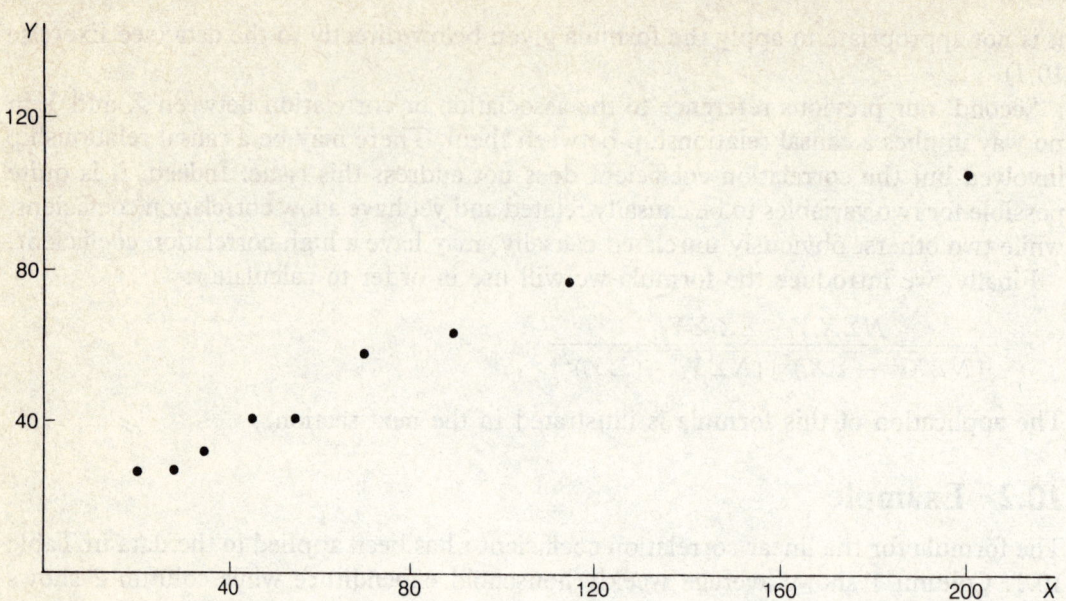

Figure 10.2    Scatter diagram for average weekly income ($X$) and average weekly expenditure ($Y$)

gross normal weekly income of households. The data have been taken from *FES*, 1979. The figures have been adapted for our purposes and have been rounded to the nearest pound. The scattergram for $X$ and $Y$ is shown in Fig. 10.2 from which it is evident that there is a very close direct relationship between the two variables. The calculations in Table 10.1 show $r = 0.99$ for the data given. This confirms what is evident from the scatter diagram, namely that there is a very high degree of correlation between household expenditure and weekly income.

## 10.3  How good is our estimate?

Let us assume that the data given in Table 10.1 relate to nine separate households, so that household 1 has a level of expenditure of £26 with weekly income of £20, household 2 has expenditure of £27 and income £28, etc. If we were to take another sample of nine different households, the values of $X$ and $Y$ would not be the same, and in general the resulting value for $r$ would be different from the one obtained in Section 10.2. A given value of $r$ obtained from sample data must therefore be seen as an estimate of the unknown population correlation coefficient and one which is subject to error. As with any other estimated coefficient it is therefore desirable to carry out a test of significance to see how good our estimate is.

Our starting point is to establish our null hypothesis in which it is assumed that the population correlation coefficient $\rho$ is zero, that is:

$H_0$: $\rho = 0$

If this is true $X$ and $Y$ are independent of each other, and if each is normally distributed, it can be shown that the resulting sampling distribution of $r$ is solely dependent on $N$, the number of observations in the sample.

Having established $H_0$, we can now establish the alternative hypothesis $H_1$. If we have a good *a priori* reason for indicating either a positive or a negative sign attached to $\rho$ we can establish a one-tail test; otherwise we shall assume a two-tail test. Let us assume that we choose a one-tail test given by:

$H_1$: $\rho > 0$

Finally, we need to choose the level of significance, which we assume to be 0.05.

With this information we can now perform a test of significance by making use of the table in Appendix C, which shows critical values of $r$ for given values of $N$ and given levels of significance assuming that $H_0$ as given above is true. For $N = 9$ and a significance level of 0.05 the value of $r$ in the table is 0.582, which means that if $\rho = 0$ we require a sample value of $r$ greater than 0.582 in order to reject the null hypothesis of no correlation. Since our value for $r$ is 0.99 we can reject the null hypothesis, since if $H_0$ were true there is very little chance of obtaining a value for $r$ of 0.99 based on only nine observations.

As indicated above the shape of the sampling distribution depends upon the value of $N$, and this is illustrated in Fig. 10.3. Part (a) of the diagram shows the sampling distribution for $N = 9$ and part (b) shows it for $N = 100$. Using a significance level of 0.05 for a one-tail test, Appendix C shows that the confidence limit in the former case is 0.582 and in the latter is 0.165. With a larger number of observations we are willing to accept a lower value for $r$ before rejecting $H_0$.

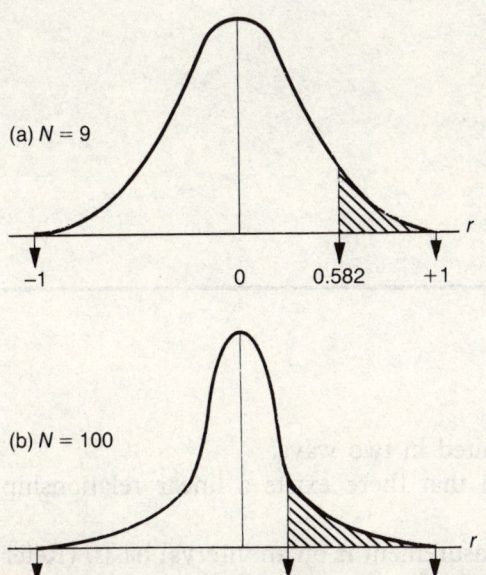

(a) $N = 9$

$-1$       0    0.582    $+1$    $r$

(b) $N = 100$

$-1$       0   0.165    $+1$    $r$

Figure 10.3   Critical values of $r$ for differing values of $N$

Our testing procedure so far has been based on a one-sided alternative hypothesis. However Appendix C can be used to perform a two-tail test at the 0.05 level of significance, in which case we need to refer to the column headed 0.025. Since this means that there is $2\frac{1}{2}\%$ of the area under the curve in each of the two tails, we have a combined rejection area of 5% as required. The calculations involved are illustrated in Example 10.1.

## Example 10.1 _____

Test the hypothesis that $\rho = 0$ for a sample of 25 observations which give a value for $r = 0.3$. Construct a two-tail test at the 0.05 level of significance.

Our two hypotheses are:

$H_0$: $\rho = 0$

$H_1$: $\rho \neq 0$

Figure 10.4 shows that our rejection region of 5% is distributed between the two tails with $2\frac{1}{2}\%$ in each tail. We therefore look in the table of critical values for $r$ (Appendix C) under the column headed 0.025 and the row labelled $N = 25$.

The value given by the table is 0.396.

If $H_0$ is true the presence of sampling error means that we can expect sample values of $r$ based on $N = 25$ to vary between $\pm 0.396$ before rejecting $H_0$ at the 0.05 level of significance. Since $r$ for our sample equals 0.3 we accept $H_0$ and reject $H_1$.

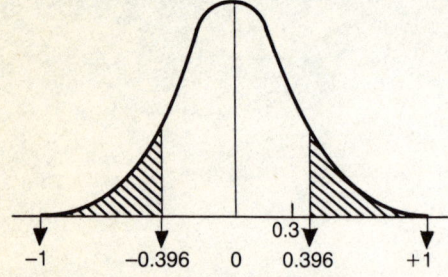

Figure 10.4   Critical regions for Example 10.1

## 10.4   Rank correlation

Our analysis of correlation so far has been limited in two ways.

First, it has been based on the assumption that there exists a linear relationship between the two variables of interest.

Second, it has been applied to data where measurement is on an interval basis. (Refer to Section 1.6 for a discussion of different kinds of measurement.)

It sometimes occurs, however, that one or both of these conditions is not met, in which case we need access to an alternative measure of correlation. Although there is a selection of such measures available, we will concentrate on the measure known as *Spearman's rank correlation coefficient* ($r_s$)

In order to calculate the value of $r_s$, observations for $X$ and $Y$ have to be arranged in terms of their rank order rather than their original values. The difference ($d_i$) between rank scores for each paired observation is calculated and the value of $r_s$ obtained from the formula:

$$r_s = 1 - [6\Sigma d_i^2 / N(N^2 - 1)]$$

The interpretation of $r_s$ is similar to the interpretation of $r$. Perfect direct rank order correlation gives a value of $r_s = 1$ (since $\Sigma d_i^2$ must be zero); perfect inverse rank order correlation gives a value of $r_s = -1$ (see Exercise 10.6); and rank independence between $X$ and $Y$ gives a value of $r_s = 0$.

A significance test for $r_s$ can be easily developed based on our previous analysis of hypothesis testing. It can be shown that for values of $N$ in excess of 10 the sampling distribution of $r_s$ is approximately normally distributed. And, since the standard error of $r_s$ ($\sigma_{r_s}$) can be shown to be equal to $1/\sqrt{(N-1)}$ we can introduce the $Z$ statistic:

$$Z = \frac{r_s - \rho_s}{1/\sqrt{(N-1)}}$$

based on the null hypothesis:

$$H_0: \rho_s = 0$$

where $\rho_s$ is the unknown population rank order correlation coefficient. The calculations involved are illustrated in Example 10.2.

# Example 10.2

The 12 companies given below have been selected from those given in Exercise 2.8. The rank order values given below (based on company sales) are derived from those given in Exercise 2.8. Calculate $r_s$ for these data. Is the resulting value significantly greater than 0 at the 0.02 level of significance?

|                  | Rank in 1980/1 ($Y$) | Rank in 1970/1 ($X$) | $d_i$ | $d_i^2$ |
|------------------|:---:|:---:|:---:|:---:|
| Dunlop           | 1  | 1 | 0  | 0  |
| Dalgety          | 9  | 2 | 7  | 49 |
| BICC             | 6  | 3 | 3  | 9  |
| Hawker Siddeley  | 5  | 4 | 1  | 1  |
| Bass Charrington | 4  | 5 | -1 | 1  |
| Woolworth        | 11 | 6 | 5  | 25 |

*Continued*

| | Rank in 1980/1 (Y) | Rank in 1970/1 (X) | $d_i$ | $d_i^2$ |
|---|---|---|---|---|
| Lonrho | 2 | 12 | −10 | 100 |
| Consolidated Gold | 8 | 10 | −2 | 4 |
| Metal Box | 7 | 9 | −2 | 4 |
| Brooke Bond Liebig | 12 | 8 | 4 | 16 |
| Burmah Oil | 3 | 7 | −4 | 16 |
| Beecham | 10 | 11 | −1 | 1 |
| | | | | 226 |

From the formula we know that:

$$r_s = 1 - [6\Sigma d_i^2/N(N^2 - 1)]$$
$$= 1 - [6 \times 226/12 \times 143]$$
$$= 1 - [1356/1716]$$
$$= 0.21$$

This value of $r_s = 0.21$ suggests that the rank correlation between $X$ and $Y$ is positive but not very strong. But is it significant? We establish:

$H_0$: $\rho_s = 0$

$H_1$: $\rho_s > 0$

and calculate the standard error of $r_s$ as follows:

$$\sigma_{r_s} = 1/\sqrt{(N-1)} = 1/3.32 = 0.30$$

Therefore the $Z$ statistic is given by:

$$Z = (r_s - \rho_s)/\sigma_{r_s}$$
$$= 0.21/0.3 = 0.7$$

The $Z$ value for a 0.02 level of significance for a one-tail test is 2.05. Since our calculated value of $Z = 0.7$ is less than the tabulated value of 2.05, we accept the null hypothesis and reject the alternative hypothesis. The rank order correlation between $X$ and $Y$ is not significantly greater than 0.

## Exercises

**10.1**

(a)  In a system of progressive taxation would you expect a linear or non-linear relation between after-tax income ($Y$) and before-tax income ($X$)? (A progressive tax system is one in which the proportion of income taxed increases as the level of income increases.)

(b) Confirm your answer to (a) by drawing the scatter of points for the data given below. Do you think it is valid to calculate the product moment correlation coefficient, $r$, for these data? Give reasons for your answer.

| Income after tax (£000) $Y$ | Income before tax (£000) $X$ |
|---|---|
| 11.5 | 19.9 |
| 7.2 | 9.6 |
| 5.7 | 7.2 |
| 4.8 | 5.9 |
| 4.0 | 4.8 |
| 3.3 | 4.0 |
| 2.8 | 3.3 |
| 2.3 | 2.6 |
| 1.9 | 2.1 |
| 1.5 | 1.7 |
| 1.3 | 1.3 |
| 0.9 | 0.9 |

**10.2** The following data show the height in cm $(X)$ and the weight in kg $(Y)$ of ten college students.

| $X$ | 160 | 180 | 175 | 170 | 165 | 172 | 190 | 175 | 160 | 180 |
|---|---|---|---|---|---|---|---|---|---|---|
| $Y$ | 56 | 84 | 73 | 75 | 64 | 70 | 95 | 75 | 57 | 78 |

(a)  Plot the scatter diagram.
(b)  Guess the value of Pearson's $r$.
(c)  Calculate $r$.

**10.3** The correlation between aptitude in mathematics and foreign languages based on tests designed to measure such aptitudes is found to be 0.4. How large a sample should be taken to be quite sure that the value of $r$ obtained would refute the claim that $\rho = 0$?

**10.4** The data below give the percentage of voters voting Conservative $(Y)$ and the percentage of voters classified as manual workers $(X)$ in each of ten constituencies in England.

| $Y$ | 27 | 39 | 22 | 10 | 14 | 38 | 32 | 7 | 22 | 16 |
|---|---|---|---|---|---|---|---|---|---|---|
| $X$ | 2 | 9 | 11 | 16 | 26 | 22 | 33 | 44 | 44 | 50 |

(a)  Calculate and interpret the value of $r$.
(b)  Is the value obtained significantly less than 0? Use a level of significance of 0.05. Illustrate your answer with a diagram.

**10.5**  The figures below show weekly income levels in twelve families where both spouses are gainfully employed.

| Family | Husband's income (£) | Wife's income (£) |
|--------|---------------------|-------------------|
| 1  | 107 | 87  |
| 2  | 134 | 159 |
| 3  | 120 | 132 |
| 4  | 142 | 132 |
| 5  | 139 | 128 |
| 6  | 98  | 87  |
| 7  | 105 | 100 |
| 8  | 185 | 167 |
| 9  | 224 | 198 |
| 10 | 176 | 165 |
| 11 | 137 | 132 |
| 12 | 84  | 74  |

(a)  Calculate $r$ and $r_s$ between husband's and wife's incomes and discuss your results. Which do you think is the better coefficient to use for this example? Give reasons for your answer.
(b)  Test the significance of $r$ and $r_s$.
(c)  Suggest a reason why this correlation is positive. Can you also suggest a reason why it might have been expected to be negative?

**10.6**  By choosing a set of five appropriate ordinal observations for $X$ and $Y$ use the formula for Spearman's rank order correlation coefficient to show that $r_s = -1$.

**10.7**  Select at random fifteen companies from those given in Exercise 2.8. Determine the rank order of $X$ and $Y$ within the sample chosen and calculate $r_s$. Is your coefficient significant? Compare your results with those given in Example 10.2.

**10.8**  The head of each of eight families was asked to record income ($Y$, £000) and the number of children in the family ($X$). The results were:

| $Y$ | 15 | 20 | 16 | 24 | 20 | 18 | 30 | 35 |
|-----|----|----|----|----|----|----|----|----|
| $X$ | 1  | 2  | 4  | 5  | 3  | 1  | 2  | 3  |

(a)   Graph the scatter of points of $X$ and $Y$
(b)   Calculate $r$ and test its significance. Discuss.

**10.9**   The data below show changes in the *Financial Times* 100 Share Index ($Y_i$) and the *Financial Times* 30 Share Index ($X_i$) for consecutive trading days in September 1986.

| $Y_i$ | $X_i$ |
|---|---|
| 19.7 | 18.7 |
| −31.6 | −27.4 |
| 13.7 | 13.0 |
| 3.8 | 4.4 |
| −13.8 | −10.5 |
| 16.7 | 13.7 |
| −7.1 | −10.9 |
| −6.6 | −7.4 |
| −27.5 | −22.2 |
| −7.3 | −3.9 |

Calculate $r$ for these data. Is the value obtained significantly different from zero? Discuss.

# 11 Bivariate linear regression

11.1 Basic regression model
11.2 Estimating regression coefficients
11.3 Example

11.4 Prediction
11.5 Standard error of estimates
Exercises

In our analysis of linear correlation in Chapter 10 we investigated the degree of correlation between two variables $X$ and $Y$. We will now take this further by developing the analysis of bivariate linear regression.

The relationship between the two can be seen in Fig. 10.1 which shows scatters of paired observations of $X$ and $Y$. In parts (a), (b) and (c) of the diagram each scatter of points can be seen in relation to a straight line trend. If the points are close to the line the correlation is high, and when they are more widely dispersed the correlation is low. The straight line in each case is referred to as the *bivariate linear regression line of Y on X*, and it allows us to further our analysis of the relationship between $X$ and $Y$ in two ways: first, by introducing a line of causation between $X$ and $Y$; second, by predicting the value of one variable given the value of the other.

For any scatter of points it is possible to obtain both an estimated correlation coefficient and an estimated regression line. In order to obtain the latter we must first explain in detail the basic features of the linear regression model. In doing so we will often use the word 'regression' but for our purposes this must be understood to mean *bivariate linear regression*.

## 11.1 Basic regression model

Let us assume we have two variables $X_i$ and $Y_i$ where $X_i$ = company profits and $Y_i$ = company investment in plant and machinery. We will further assume that $Y_i$ is dependent in some way upon $X_i$, that is:

$$Y_i = f(X_i) \quad \text{for} \quad i = 1, \ldots, N$$

By expressing our model in this way we have introduced a line of causation between the two variables: investment ($Y_i$) is dependent upon profits ($X_i$). For this reason we call $Y_i$ the *dependent* variable and $X_i$ the *independent* variable: $Y_i$ is dependent upon $X_i$ and

$X_i$ is independent of $Y_i$. If we were to show this graphically we would put $Y_i$ on the vertical axis and $X_i$ on the horizontal axis.

But to proceed further we need to say something about the nature of the relationship between $X_i$ and $Y_i$. In particular we need to know whether it is linear or non-linear. If we assume it is linear, we can introduce the equation for a straight line:

$$\hat{Y}_i = a + bX_i$$

This equation is shown in Fig. 11.1 along with an assumed scatter of points for $X_i$ and $Y_i$.

Notice from the diagram that the points are distributed around the regression line rather than lying exactly on it. If they were all on the regression line we would have an *exact* relationship between $X$ and $Y$ (see Exercise 11.1), which would mean that we would be able to determine exactly the level of investment for any given level of profits, i.e. the level of profits is the sole determinant of investment. This is obviously unrealistic since there are other factors apart from profits which determine company investment. For this reason the observations are scattered around the line and the relationship between $X_i$ and $Y_i$ is said to be *stochastic* in nature, where the level of profits is only one, albeit an important one, of the determinants of company investment.

We can develop this further by considering the first paired observation in Fig. 11.1 shown circled. The vertical distance $Y_1$ can be broken down into two parts, $\hat{Y}_1$ and $e_1$, as shown.

The first part, $\hat{Y}_1$, is the vertical distance between the horizontal axis and the regression line and is the value of $Y$ given by the regression line for a given value of $X$. It is

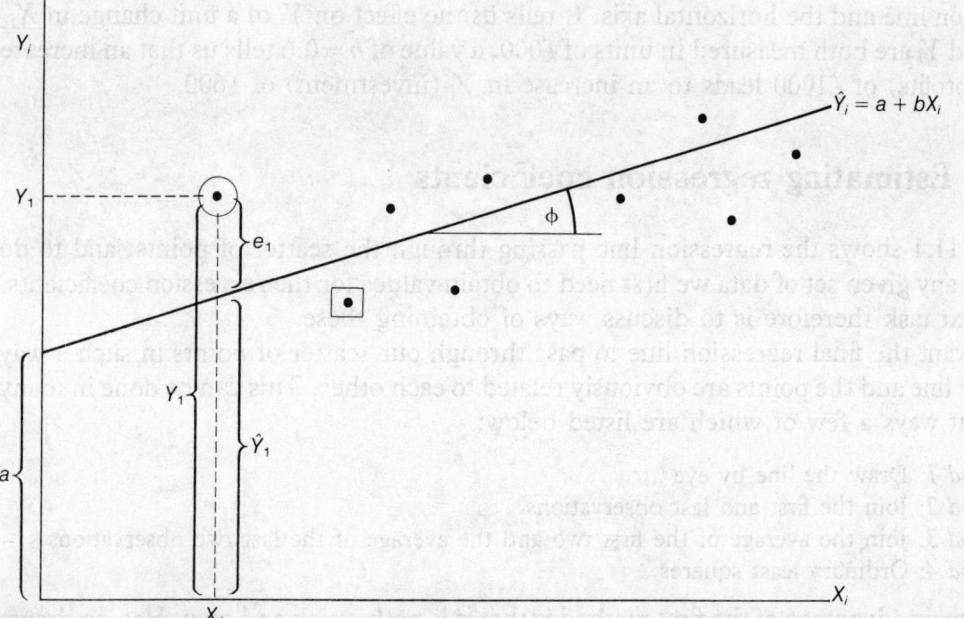

Figure 11.1 Regression line of $Y$ on $X$

called the *expected value of Y* because it is the value we can expect $Y$ to be if $X$ takes on the value $X_1$ and if $X$ is the only variable affecting $Y$.

The second part, $e_1$, is the vertical distance from the regression line in the observation and is called the *residual term*. It can be thought of as showing the effect of all other influences which determine the final value of $Y_1$, such as quality of management, effect of government policy, etc. For the first observation the value of $e_1$ is positive because it is above the line, but in other cases, such as the second observation shown in a square, it will be negative if it falls below the line.

It therefore follows from this that in general the actual value of $Y$ equals the expected value of $Y$ plus the residual:

$$Y_i = \hat{Y}_i + e_i$$

Also since:

$$\hat{Y}_i = a + bX_i$$

it follows that:

$$Y_i = a + bX_i + e_i$$

The coefficients $a$ and $b$ together fully define the regression relationship between $Y_i$ and $X_i$.

Coefficient $a$ is the *intercept term* and tells us the value of $Y_i$ when $X_i = 0$, that is it is the point where the regression line intercepts the vertical axis assuming that $X_i = 0$ and $Y_i = 0$ at the origin of the graph (see Exercise 11.2). The main function of the intercept term is to fix the position of the line.

Coefficient $b$ is the *slope coefficient* and is the tangent of the angle $\varphi$ between the regression line and the horizontal axis. It tells us the effect on $Y_i$ of a unit change in $X_i$. If $X_i$ and $Y_i$ are both measured in units of £000, a value of $b = 0.6$ tells us that an increase in $X_i$ (profits) of £1000 leads to an increase in $Y_i$ (investment) of £600.

## 11.2  Estimating regression coefficients

Figure 11.1 shows the regression line passing through the scatter of points, and to do this for any given set of data we first need to obtain values for the regression coefficients. Our next task therefore is to discuss ways of obtaining these.

We want the final regression line to pass through our scatter of points in such a way that the line and the points are obviously related to each other. This can be done in many different ways a few of which are listed below:

*Method 1*: Draw the line by eye
*Method 2*: Join the first and last observations
*Method 3*: Join the average of the first two and the average of the last two observations
*Method 4*: Ordinary least squares

The main advantage of the first method is that it is both quick and easy. Having drawn the line the values of $a$ and $b$ can be read from the diagram and the resulting equation written down. The main disadvantage of this approach is that it is not in any way objective, so that different people will in general get different results.

Method 2 is also very easy, since only two points are required. The straight line joining the first and last observations will provide a line of the form $\hat{Y}_i = a + bX_i$ and the resulting values of $a$ and $b$ can once again be obtained. However, the first and last observations may not be typical of the scatter in general, in which case the resulting values of $a$ and $b$ will be biased.

This is partly overcome by method 3 where we join the average of the first two and the average of the last two values of $X$ and $Y$. By doing this we help smoothe out the effects of atypical values of $X$ and $Y$. But there is a further limitation which applies to methods 2 and 3, namely that both omit much of the information contained in the entire scatter of points.

The final method, that of *ordinary least squares*, is the one we will concentrate on, because it is objective and uses all the information contained in the sample. It is also optimal in a way which will be defined below. From our previous discussion we know that:

$$e_i = Y_i - \hat{Y}_i$$

where $e_i$ is the residual term. If we square each residual and take the sum of squares across all observations, we obtain $\Sigma e_i^2$, which is the sum of squared residuals.

Now refer to the scatter of points shown in Fig. 11.2. The diagram shows three different regression lines and for each line we would obtain a different series of values for $e_i$. This means that the values of $\Sigma e_i^2$ that result (call them $\Sigma e_{1i}^2$, $\Sigma e_{2i}^2$ and $\Sigma e_{3i}^2$) will all be different. In principle there is an infinite number of lines which could be drawn through a given scatter of points and therefore an infinite number of different sums of squared residuals. Given this infinite number of regression lines, the ordinary least

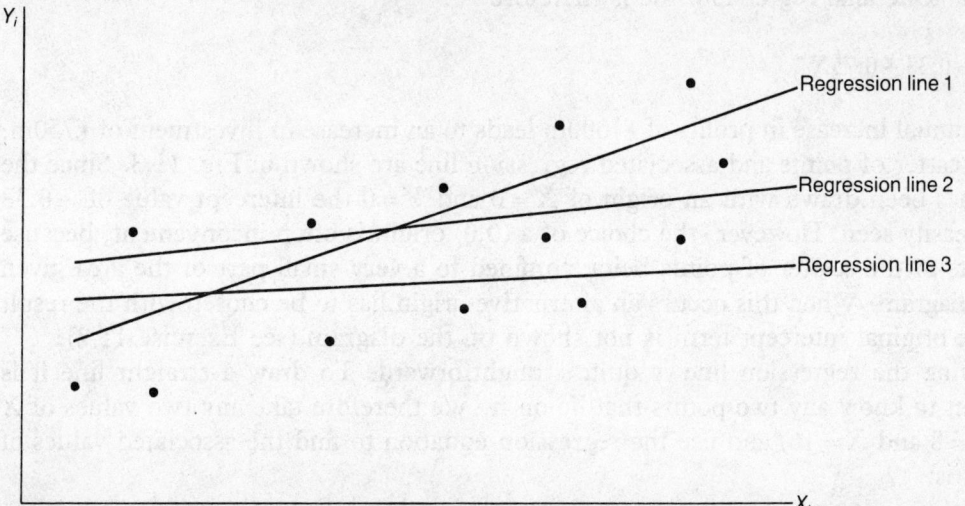

Figure 11.2  Obtaining ordinary least squares values of $a$ and $b$

squares principle chooses that line whose values of $a$ and $b$ are such that the resulting sum of squared residuals $(\Sigma e_i^2)$ is as small as possible.

We will not go into the mathematical details necessary to develop this principle in full. It is sufficient to say that applying the appropriate mathematical analysis results in the following formulae for $a$ and $b$:

$$a = \frac{(\Sigma Y_i)(\Sigma X_i^2) - (\Sigma X_i)(\Sigma X_i Y_i)}{N \Sigma X_i^2 - (\Sigma X_i)^2}$$

$$b = \frac{N \Sigma X_i Y_i - (\Sigma Y_i)(\Sigma X_i)}{N \Sigma X_i^2 - (\Sigma X_i)^2}$$

The resulting values of $a$ and $b$ allow us to draw the regression line which passes through the scatter of points in such a way that the resulting residuals provide a value for $\Sigma e_i^2$ which by definition is the smallest possible for the given scatter of points of $X_i$ and $Y_i$. The calculations involved are illustrated in Section 11.3. A comparison of results applying all four methods to the same set of data can be found in Exercise 11.3.

## 11.3   Example

We will illustrate the calculations involved by taking data for investment and profits from a government publication *Economic Trends Annual Supplement*, 1982. Investment is defined as gross fixed domestic capital formation and our profits variable is defined as undistributed company income, i.e. company income after dividends, interest and tax have been paid. The data are aggregate figures for all industrial and commerical companies in the UK for the period 1971–80 and are shown in Table 11.1. Applying the formulae given in Section 11.2 to the data in the table we get values of $a = -0.33$ and $b = 0.75$. Our final regression line is therefore

$$\hat{Y}_i = -0.33 + 0.75 X_i$$

Every annual increase in profits of £1000m leads to an increase in investment of £750m.

The scatter of points and associated regression line are shown in Fig. 11.3. Since the graph has been drawn with an origin of $X = 0$ and $Y = 0$ the intercept value of $-0.33$ can be easily seen. However, the choice of a $(0,0)$ origin is often inconvenient, because it results in the scatter of points being confined to a very small part of the area given to the diagram. When this occurs an alternative origin has to be chosen with the result that the original intercept term is not shown on the diagram (see Exercise 11.2).

Drawing the regression line is quite straightforward. To draw a straight line it is sufficient to know any two points that lie on it. We therefore take any two values of $X$ (say $X = 8$ and $X = 16$) and use the regression equation to find the associated values of $\hat{Y}$, that is:

$$X = 8, \quad \hat{Y} = -0.33 + 0.75 \times 8 = 5.67$$

Table 11.1  Calculating regression coefficients $a$ and $b$

|      | Investment $Y$ (£000m) | Profits $X$ (£000m) | $X^2$ | $XY$ | $Y^2$ |
|------|------|------|------|------|------|
| 1971 | 3.5  | 4.4  | 19.36  | 15.40  | 12.25  |
| 1972 | 3.9  | 5.8  | 33.64  | 22.62  | 15.21  |
| 1973 | 4.9  | 8.1  | 65.61  | 39.69  | 24.01  |
| 1974 | 6.0  | 9.0  | 81.00  | 54.00  | 36.00  |
| 1975 | 6.9  | 9.7  | 94.09  | 66.93  | 47.61  |
| 1976 | 8.1  | 13.7 | 187.69 | 110.97 | 65.61  |
| 1977 | 9.7  | 15.0 | 225.00 | 145.50 | 94.09  |
| 1978 | 11.9 | 16.8 | 282.24 | 199.92 | 141.61 |
| 1979 | 13.7 | 19.4 | 376.36 | 265.78 | 187.69 |
| 1980 | 15.6 | 14.2 | 201.64 | 221.52 | 243.36 |
|      | 84.2 | 116.1 | 1566.63 | 1142.33 | 867.44 |

$$a = \frac{(\Sigma Y)(\Sigma X^2) - (\Sigma X)(\Sigma XY)}{N\Sigma X^2 - (\Sigma X)^2}$$

$$= \frac{84.2 \times 1566.63 - 116.1 \times 1142.33}{10 \times 1566.63 - 116.1^2} = \frac{-714.27}{2187.09}$$

$$= -0.33$$

$$b = \frac{N\Sigma XY - (\Sigma X)(\Sigma Y)}{N\Sigma X^2 - (\Sigma X)^2}$$

$$= \frac{10 \times 1142.33 - 166.1 \times 84.2}{10 \times 1566.63 - 116.1^2} = \frac{1647.68}{2187.09}$$

$$= 0.75$$

$$\therefore \hat{Y}_i = -0.33 + 0.75X_i$$

and

$$X = 16, \quad \hat{Y} = -0.33 + 0.75 \times 16 = 11.67$$

If we join these two points, the resulting straight line is the regression line of $Y$ on $X$. This is shown in Fig. 11.3.

From the diagram it is clear that the observation for 1980 (shown in a circle) is somewhat out of line with the rest. If this happens when $N$ is small it can have a considerable effect on the resulting values of the regression coefficients. If we re-estimate the equation after omitting the relevant observation and compare the new results with the original results, we can get some idea of the effect of the atypical observation on our coefficients and bear this in mind when finally interpreting and discussing the results (see Exercise 11.4).

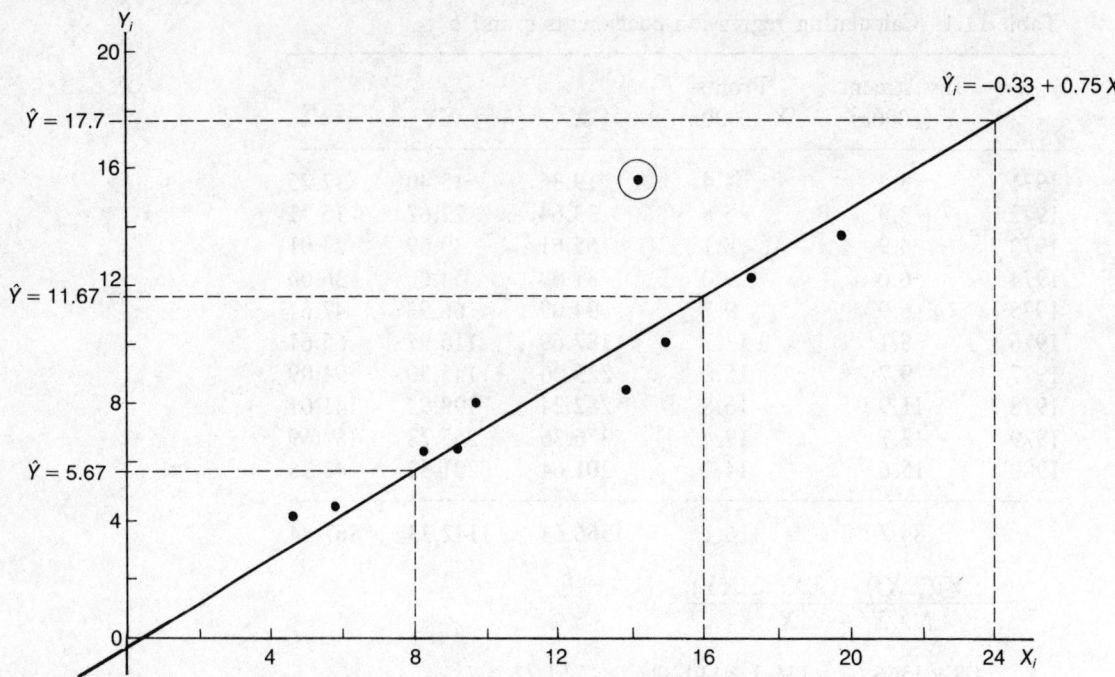

Figure 11.3   Scattergram and regression line for profits/investment example

## 11.4   Prediction

Our estimated regression line $\hat{Y}_i = -0.33 + 0.75X_i$ passes through the middle of our scatter of points and represents the average relationship between profits and investment. If we can reasonably assume that this average relationship will persist into the future, we can use the estimated equation to forecast future values of $Y$ for given values of $X$.

Let us assume that we wish to know the expected level of investment when profits reach a level of £24 000m. We can approach this in two ways.

The first approach uses the regression line shown in Fig. 11.3. We project forward our regression line until it is crossed by the vertical line passing through the value $X = 24$ and read from the diagram the resulting value of $\hat{Y}$, i.e. 17.7.

The second, and more accurate, approach makes use of the regression equation. By feeding the value of $X = 24$ into the equation, we obtain an expected value of $Y$ given by:

$$\hat{Y}_i = -0.33 + 0.75 \times 24 = 17.67$$

In a similar way we can obtain the forecast value of $Y$ for any future value of $X$.

In order to use the estimated relationship in this way we need to be confident that it will persist into the future. This, however, is not easy to determine. We have already seen that the last observation for $Y$ and $X$ in Table 11.1 is quite different from the rest, and we need to ask whether this represents an aberration following which the normal trend will return, or whether it is the beginning of a new trend. If it is the beginning of a new trend, the estimated equation cannot be used for predicting values of $Y$ with any degree of confidence (see Exercise 11.5).

## 11.5   Standard error of estimates

From our estimated regression line we can obtain values of $Y$ for given values of $X$. Each value obtained in this way is a point estimate of the average value of $Y$ for the associated value of $X$, and as such is subject to sampling error. In order to convert this point estimate into an interval estimate, we need a measure of the variation of the residuals about the estimated regression line. The situation is similar to estimating a mean: $\bar{X}$ is a point estimate of $\mu$, and an interval estimate can be obtained by the introduction of the standard error of the mean. In the same way each value of $\hat{Y}$ can be converted into an interval estimate by introducing the standard error of $\hat{Y}$ known as the *standard error of estimate*, $S_e$.

The formula for the standard error of estimate is:

$$S_e = \sqrt{\frac{\Sigma(Y_i - \hat{Y}_i)^2}{N-2}}$$

where   $Y_i$ = observed value of $Y$

$\hat{Y}_i$ = expected value of $Y$

$N$ = number of observations

From this we can see that, as with any standard deviation, we are measuring variation about a fixed point: in this case the fixed point is $\hat{Y}$. In order to estimate the regression line we need first to calculate the two parameters $a$ and $b$ so that we have $N-2$ degrees of freedom left in order to calculate $S_e$ as shown in the denominator.

Although this version of the formula makes clear what is being measured, it is possible to express it in the following form which is easier for the purpose of calculating $S_e$:

$$S_e = \sqrt{(\Sigma Y_i^2 - a\Sigma Y_i - b\Sigma X_i Y_i)/(N-2)}$$

Table 11.1 contains all the information required to calculate the value of $S_e$ for the example on profits and investment in Section 11.3:

$$S_e = \sqrt{[867.44 - (-0.33 \times 84.2) - (0.75 \times 1142.33)]/8}$$
$$= 2.2$$

Since our values of $X$ and $Y$ are expressed in units of £000m, our value of $S_e$ is to be interpreted in the same units, i.e. $S_e$ = £2200m.

If we now assume that our values of $X$ in the sample form one set of values obtained in a process of repeated sampling, and if we also assume that these values are normally distributed, we can calculate confidence limits for our estimated values of $\hat{Y}$. Our 95% confidence limits ($CL_{0.95}$) would be given by:

$$CL_{0.95} = \hat{Y}_i \pm 1.96 S_e$$

For samples where $N-2$ is less than 30 we would use the $t$ distribution.

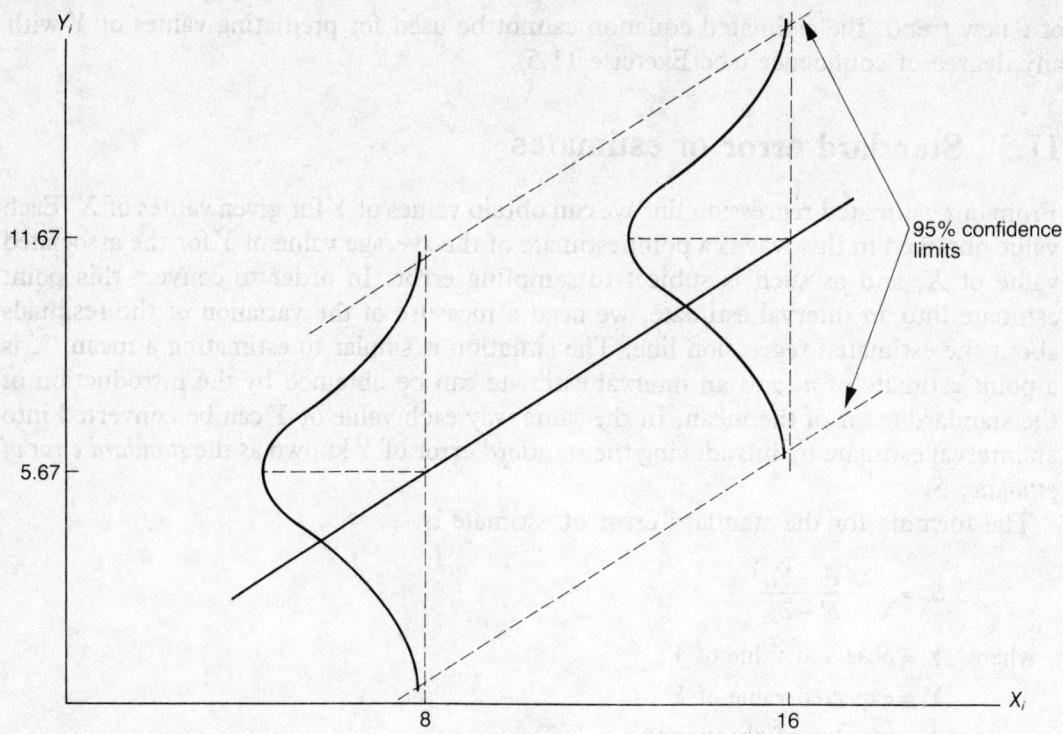

**Figure 11.4** Confidence limits for estimated regression line

In the above example where $N - 2 = 8$, our 95% confidence limits would be:

$$\text{CL}_{0.95} = \hat{Y}_i \pm 2.31 S_e$$
$$= \hat{Y}_i \pm 5.1$$

From this it follows that for any given value of $X$ we can be 95% confident that the true value of $Y$ falls in the range $\hat{Y} \pm 5.1$. This is shown in Fig. 11.4 (see also Exercises 11.8 and 11.9).

# Exercises

**11.1** In the right-angled triangle ABC $Y$ and $X$ are the angles in degrees as shown.

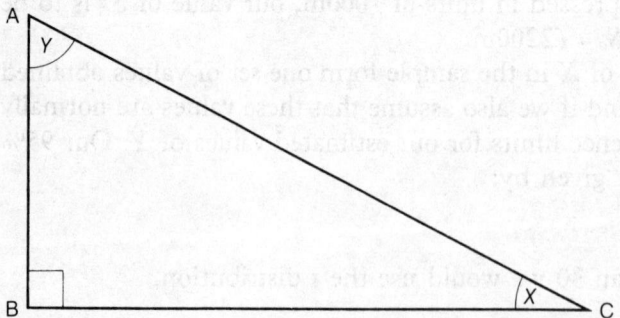

Choose ten different values of $Y$ and obtain the resulting values of $X$. Given that:

$$\hat{Y}_i = a + bX_i$$

(a) What values would you expect $a$ and $b$ to have?
(b) Confirm your answers by using the formulae for $a$ and $b$.
(c) Show diagrammatically that the relationship between $Y_i$ and $X_i$ is an exact relationship.

**11.2** Draw a diagram with $Y$ on the vertical axis (values ranging from 10 to 20) and $X$ on the horizontal axis (values ranging from 4 to 10). Make $X = 4$ and $Y = 10$ the origin. On your diagram draw the regression lines of:

(a) $\hat{Y}_i = 15 + 0.50X_i$
(b) $\hat{Y}_i = 18 - 0.81X_i$
(c) $\hat{Y}_i = 7 + 0.75X_i$

For each equation obtain the value of $Y$ where the line crosses the vertical axis. Why does the value differ from the intercept term given in the equation?

**11.3** Obtain values for $a$ and $b$ in the equation:

$$\hat{Y}_i = a + bX_i$$

applying methods 1, 2 and 3 (discussed in Section 11.2) to the data contained in Table 11.1. Discuss your results and compare them with those in Section 11.3 using method 4. Draw the scatter diagram showing all four regression lines.

**11.4** Estimate the regression line:

$$\hat{Y}_i = a + bX_i$$

for the period 1971–9 (i.e. omitting 1980) using data from Table 11.1. Compare your results with those given in the table. Discuss.

**11.5** Use the estimated equation from Exercise 11.4 in order to forecast $Y$ when $X = £24\,000m$. Compare your answer with the forecast value of $Y$ given in Section 11.4.

**11.6** Data are given below for the variables $Y_i$ (crop yield measured as tonnes per acre) and $X_i$ (rainfall measured in inches per time period)

| $Y_i$ | $X_i$ |
|-------|-------|
| 4     | 3     |
| 6     | 5     |
| 10    | 7     |
| 5     | 3     |
| 3     | 2     |
| 8     | 6     |
| 11    | 8     |

(a)   obtain the values of $a$ and $b$ in the equation

$\hat{Y}_i = a + bX_i$

(b)   Interpret the value of $b$

(c)   Use the equation to predict crop yield when rainfall equals 10 inches.

**11.7**   Estimate the bivariate linear regression of $Y$ on $X$ for the data given in Exercise 10.8.

**11.8**   Obtain the linear regression equation of $Y$ on $X$ for husband's income $(Y)$ and wife's income $(X)$ using the data given in Exercise 10.5. Find the expected value of $Y$ when $X = 100$. Calculate the standard error of estimate of $Y$ and hence find the 98% confidence limits for $Y$ when $X = 100$. Briefly discuss.

**11.9**   For the data in Table 11.1 show diagrammatically the estimated regression line and the 90% confidence limits for values of $Y$. Interpret the actual values of $Y$ for 1971 and 1980 in relation to your confidence limits.

**11.10**   Calculate $a$ and $b$ in the equation:

$Y_i = a + bX_i + e_i$

using the following data.

| Day number | Change in the FT 100 Share Index $(Y_i)$ | Change in the FT 30 Share Index $(X_i)$ |
|---|---|---|
| 1 | 11.6 | 10.8 |
| 2 | −5.0 | −2.7 |
| 3 | 2.9 | 4.6 |
| 4 | 9.6 | 9.7 |
| 5 | 4.5 | 4.1 |
| 6 | −18.2 | −14.7 |
| 7 | 6.8 | 7.4 |
| 8 | −9.9 | −13.2 |
| 9 | −27.0 | −19.7 |
| 10 | −27.9 | −27.3 |

Draw the resulting regression line and the scatter of points of $X$ and $Y$. How do your values of $a$ and $b$ compare with those you would expect to obtain if the values of $X$ and $Y$ on each day were the same? Briefly discuss.

# 12 Index numbers

The need often arises in economics to express movements in a group of variables by a single figure. For example, given the change in the prices of a large number of company shares, we may require a single figure to represent the movement of all share prices over a given period. Similarly, given the change in price and quantity of a large number of goods and services, we may require a single figure to represent the change in value of all goods and services produced in a given period. In each case the need can be met by constructing an *index number*.

The need expressed in the first example given above has given rise to the *Financial Times* Industrial Ordinary 30 Share Index, and the need expressed in the second example has resulted in the construction of index numbers designed to measure changes in Gross Domestic Product.

In this chapter we shall illustrate the different ways in which index numbers can be used, and discuss the different ways in which they can be constructed.

## 12.1 Making comparisons across units

Index numbers can be used to measure changes in a given variable across different units. The units concerned could be countries, firms, individuals or time.

Consider, for example, the data in column 2 of Table 12.1 showing Gross Domestic Product (GDP) in the UK valued at current prices. At its simplest, GDP is a measure of the total domestic economic activity of a country for a given period, and in the table data are presented in units of £000m per year. When presented in this form it is not easy to readily interpret changes in GDP over time. To do this we need to express the information in index number form.

We begin by choosing one of the years given as the base year, i.e. the year with which all others are compared. We will choose 1980 as the base year, though this choice is an arbitrary one, and as we shall see an alternative could easily have been chosen.

The base year is assigned a value of 100 and the values of GDP for all remaining years

Table 12.1   GDP (Gross Domestic Product) at current and constant prices

| Year | GDP at current prices (£000m) | Index numbers (1980 = 100) | Price index for GDP at current prices | GDP at constant prices (£000m) | Index of GDP at constant 1980 prices |
|------|------|------|------|------|------|
| 1975 | 106 | 46.1  | 50.0  | 212 | 92.2  |
| 1976 | 127 | 55.2  | 57.5  | 220 | 95.7  |
| 1977 | 146 | 63.5  | 65.5  | 223 | 97.0  |
| 1978 | 168 | 73.0  | 72.9  | 230 | 100.0 |
| 1979 | 197 | 85.7  | 83.5  | 236 | 102.6 |
| 1980 | 230 | 100.0 | 100.0 | 230 | 100.0 |
| 1981 | 254 | 110.4 | 111.5 | 228 | 99.1  |
| 1982 | 276 | 120.0 | 120.1 | 230 | 100.0 |
| 1983 | 301 | 130.9 | 126.2 | 239 | 103.9 |
| 1984 | 320 | 139.1 | 131.4 | 244 | 106.1 |

*UK National Accounts*, 1986

Note: Data in this table are valued at market prices

are expressed accordingly. For example the index number, $IN$, for 1975 is:

$$IN_{1975} = \frac{\text{GDP in 1975} \times 100.0}{\text{GDP in 1980}} = \frac{106 \times 100.0}{230} = 46.1$$

Following this procedure for each of the remaining years allows us to obtain the figures in column 3, which is a series of index numbers measuring GDP at current prices with 1980 as the base year.

With the original data expressed in this form changes in GDP over the period are much easier to interpret. For example, we can see straight away that GDP increased by 39.1% between 1980 and 1984. Also, in 1975 it was 46.1% of the total in 1980.

If comparison with 1975 instead of 1980 was required it would be easy to express the figures based on 1975 = 100 and interpret the results in the appropriate manner. It could be shown, for example, that if 1975 = 100, the value of GDP in 1976 was 19.8% higher than the year before (see Example 12.1 and Exercise 12.10).

In Table 12.1 the variable of interest is measured for one country across time, but index numbers can also be used to measure changes in a variable across units with time held constant.

Table 12.2 shows the price per tonne for a range of commodities in 1984. By choosing wheat as the base commodity and setting its price equal to 100, we can obtain the index number for oats as follows:

$$IN_{\text{oats}} = \frac{\text{Price of oats} \times 100.0}{\text{Price of wheat}} = \frac{123.44 \times 100.0}{114.96} = 107.4$$

Thus, in 1984 the price of oats was 7.4% higher than the price of wheat. By following

Table 12.2  Prices of selected commodities in 1984

| Commodity | Price per tonne 1984 (£) | Index numbers with wheat as base commodity |
|---|---|---|
| Wheat | 114.96 | 100.0 |
| Barley | 113.26 | 101.5 |
| Oats | 123.44 | 107.4 |
| Rye | 120.54 | 104.9 |

*UK National Accounts*, 1986

a similar procedure we can obtain the remaining index numbers shown in Table 12.2. From our argument in the previous paragraph, it follows that we could choose an alternative commodity as the base commodity and obtain the resulting index number values (see Example 12.2 and Exercise 12.11).

# Example 12.1

The data in column 2 of Table 12.1 can be expressed in index number form with 1975 = 100 as shown below.

| Year | GDP at current prices (£000m) | Index numbers (1975 = 100) |
|---|---|---|
| 1975 | 106 | 100.0 |
| 1976 | 127 | 119.8 |
| 1977 | 146 | 137.7 |
| 1978 | 168 | 158.5 |
| 1979 | 197 | 185.8 |
| 1980 | 230 | 217.0 |
| 1981 | 254 | 239.6 |
| 1982 | 276 | 260.4 |
| 1983 | 301 | 284.0 |
| 1984 | 320 | 301.9 |

For 1976 the index number is given by

$$IN_{1976} = \frac{\text{GDP in 1976} \times 100.0}{\text{GDP in 1975}} = \frac{127 \times 100}{106} = 119.8$$

Therefore GDP in 1976 was 19.8% higher than in 1975. The index number for each of the remaining years can be obtained by following a similar procedure.

## Example 12.2

Given the data in Table 12.2 we can take rye as the base commodity and obtain the resulting index numbers given below.

| Commodity | Price per tonne 1984 (£) | Index numbers with rye as base commodity |
|-----------|--------------------------|------------------------------------------|
| Wheat     | 114.96                   | 95.4                                     |
| Barley    | 113.26                   | 94.0                                     |
| Oats      | 123.44                   | 102.4                                    |
| Rye       | 120.54                   | 100.0                                    |

Thus the index number for wheat is:

$$IN_{wheat} = \frac{\text{Price of wheat} \times 100}{\text{Price of rye}} = \frac{114.96 \times 100.0}{120.54} = 95.4$$

so that the price of wheat per tonne in 1984 was 4.6% lower than the price of rye.

## 12.2   Price index numbers

The example introduced in Table 12.2 brings us to a particularly important kind of index number, a price index number. Such an index is important because it not only serves as a measure of the extent of inflation for different commodities, but it may also be used to remove the effect of inflation from a given set of figures.

Let us return to Table 12.1. We already know from column 3 that GDP at current prices increased by 10.4% between 1980 and 1981. Because the items included in GDP have been valued at current prices, the increase of 10.4% reflects a combination of a change in prices and a change in quantity produced during the year. Since any change resulting from inflation is a nominal rather than a real change it may be desirable to remove its effect.

We can do this by making use of the data in column 4 of Table 12.1 which shows the price index for all goods included in GDP. Thus the value of 120.1 in 1982 shows that prices increased by 20.1% between the base year 1980 and 1982. With the figures given in column 4 we can now remove the effect of inflation as follows:

$$\text{GDP 1975 (constant prices)} = \frac{(\text{GDP 1975 current prices}) \times (\text{price index 1980})}{(\text{price index 1975})}$$

$$= \frac{106 \times 100.0}{50.0} = 212$$

Thus the value of GDP in 1975, valued in terms of prices in 1980, was £212 000m. That is to say, GDP in 1975 would have totalled £212 000m if prices in that year had been the same as they were in 1980. A parallel interpretation follows for the remaining figures in column 5. Finally, column 6 shows the figures given in column 5 expressed in index number form:

$$IN_{1975}(\text{constant prices}) = \frac{(\text{GDP 1975 constant prices}) \times 100.0}{(\text{GDP 1980 constant prices})}$$

$$= \frac{212 \times 100.0}{230} = 92.2$$

Therefore, in 1975 GDP was 7.8% lower than it was in 1980 after the effect of inflation has been removed, compared with being 53.9% lower before the effect of inflation has been removed.

In order to obtain the constant price data given in columns 5 and 6, we needed access to the price index numbers given in column 4. How are these obtained?

To explain this we need to introduce the concept of a price relative. A *price relative* compares the price of a given item at two points in time. Thus, if $p_N$ and $p_0$ are prices in the current period $N$ and the base period 0, the price relative for the $i$th item is given by:

$$P_i = 100(p_N/p_0)$$

If we want an index for all items in an individual's budget or portfolio, we need to take some kind of average of all the price relatives. If we take the arithmetic mean of all the price relatives, we are implicitly assuming that all items are of equal importance. Alternatively, we could introduce a range of weights reflecting the relative imprtance of the different items.

Thus, our price index number reflecting the average change in the level of prices across all items is given by:

$$PIN = \Sigma P_i W_i / \Sigma W_i$$

where $W_i$ is the weight of the $i$th item and $P_i$ is the price relative of the $i$th item. Notice that if all items are equally important $W_i = 1$ for all $i$, and $PIN$ is the arithmetic mean of the price relatives of all items.

Since the values given to the weights have an important effect upon the result obtained, we must next consider where they come from. In practice they are obtained from the expenditure patterns of the individuals whose behaviour is being investigated. The more spent on a particular share in an investor's portfolio or the more spent on a particular commodity in a consumer's budget, the greater the weight the share or commodity is considered to have. So, we can express $W_i$ as the expenditure on item $i$ in the relevant period. Since expenditure on item $i$ is the product of price $(p)$ and quantity $(q)$:

$$W_i = pq \text{ in the relevant period}$$

We shall illustrate our discussion by making reference to Table 12.3 which shows the prices of selected shares on 1 January and 22 June 1984.

Table 12.3  Calculating price index numbers for selected shares

| Share | Share price 1/1/84 $p_0$ | Share price 22/6/84 $p_N$ | Price relative $P_i$ | Quantity $q'$ | Weight $W_i'$ | $P_iW_i'$ | Quantity $q''$ | Weight $W_i''$ | $P_iW_i''$ |
|---|---|---|---|---|---|---|---|---|---|
| Distillers | 244 | 300 | 123.0 | 5 | 1220 | 150 060 | 10 | 2440 | 300 120.0 |
| Hanson Trust | 172 | 214 | 124.4 | 5 | 860 | 106 984 | 7 | 1204 | 149 777.6 |
| BOC | 296 | 240 | 81.1 | 5 | 1480 | 120 028 | 1 | 296 | 24 005.6 |
| Boots | 180 | 170 | 94.4 | 5 | 900 | 84 960 | 2 | 360 | 33 984.0 |
| | | | | 20 | 4460 | 462 032 | 20 | 4300 | 507 887.2 |

*Observer*, 24 June 1984

Assume that two investors buy shares in the companies listed. Each buys 20 shares on 1 January 1984, the quantities bought ($q'$ and $q''$) being shown in columns 5 and 8. With this information we can obtain the weights for the first investor shown in column 6 ($W_i' = p_0q'$), and for the second investor shown in column 7 ($W_i'' = p_0q''$).

The price index numbers reflecting the average change in share prices for the different portfolios are as follows:

*Investor 1*:

$$PIN = \Sigma P_iW_i'/\Sigma W_i' = \frac{462\ 032}{4460} = 103.6$$

*Investor 2*:

$$PIN = \Sigma P_iW_i''/\Sigma W_i'' = \frac{507\ 887.2}{4300} = 118.1$$

Thus on average the price of shares held by investor 1 increased by 3.6%, while the price of shares held by investor 2 increased 18.1%. The main reason for the difference between these two figures is that investor 2 shows a much larger weight for the two shares whose price increased the most over the period, i.e. Distillers and Hanson Trust (see Exercises 12.4 and 12.9).

In our discussion so far we have defined the weight $W_i$, as being expenditure on item $i$ in the relevant period. But what do we mean by the relevant period? Do we take our weights from the base period (0) or the current period (N)?

If there is no change in the weights between the base period and the current period the choice does not matter, but if there is a change our choice of period affects the results obtained. In Sections 12.3 and 12.4 we shall see that the need to choose our weights from either the base period or the current period gives rise to two different kinds of price index numbers.

## 12.3  Laspeyre price index numbers

If we take our weights from the base period we can calculate an index number which is known as a *Laspeyre price index number*.

From the previous section we know that:

$$PIN = \Sigma P_i W_i / \Sigma W_i$$

and that for the base period 0:

$$W_i = p_0 q_0$$
$$\therefore PIN = \Sigma P_i (p_0 q_0) / \Sigma p_0 q_0$$

But:

$$P_i = 100(p_N / p_0)$$

$$\therefore PIN = \frac{\Sigma 100 p_N (p_0 q_0)}{p_0} / \Sigma p_0 q_0$$

$$= \frac{\Sigma p_N q_0}{\Sigma p_0 q_0} \times 100 \quad \text{or} \quad \frac{100 \Sigma p_N q_0}{\Sigma p_0 q_0}$$

Notice in this final form of the Laspeyre index number that as we move from denominator to numerator, quantities remain fixed in the base period and prices change from base period to current period. We therefore have an index number which measures the change in prices across items between the base period and the current period assuming that weights are as given in the base period. A Laspeyre price index number is therefore sometimes referred to as a *base period weighted index*.

We can now calculate a Laspeyre price index number for the share price data given in Table 12.3. The price data from that table have been presented again in columns 2 and 3 of Table 12.4 along with hypothetical quantities for each share in column 4.

We can therefore calculate $\Sigma p_N q_0$ (column 6) and $\Sigma p_0 q_0$ (column 7) and obtain our

Table 12.4  Calculating Laspeyre and Paasche price index numbers for selected shares

| Share | Share price 1/1/84 $p_0$ | Share price 22/6/84 $p_N$ | Quantity in base period $q_0$ | Quantity in current period $q_N$ | $p_N q_0$ | $p_0 q_0$ | $p_N q_N$ | $p_0 q_N$ |
|---|---|---|---|---|---|---|---|---|
| Distillers | 244 | 300 | 7 | 1 | 2100 | 1708 | 300 | 244 |
| Hanson Trust | 172 | 214 | 8 | 3 | 1712 | 1376 | 642 | 516 |
| BOC | 296 | 240 | 3 | 8 | 720 | 888 | 1920 | 2368 |
| Boots | 180 | 170 | 2 | 9 | 340 | 360 | 1530 | 1620 |
| | | | | | 4872 | 4532 | 4392 | 4748 |

Laspeyre index number from our formula:

$$\frac{100 \sum p_N q_0}{\sum p_0 q_0} = \frac{100 \times 4872}{4532} = 107.5$$

Thus taking weights as given in the base period, we conclude that the average price of the shares of the companies listed increased by 7.5% between 1 January and 22 June (see Exercises 12.2 and 12.7).

## 12.4 Paasche price index numbers

Instead of using base period weights when calculating index numbers, we could use current period weights instead. This results in the construction of *Paasche price index numbers* given by the expression:

$$\frac{100 \sum p_N q_N}{\sum p_0 q_N}$$

From the formula we can see that as we move from denominator to numerator, prices change from the base period to the current period but the weights, i.e. the quantities, remain fixed and equal to the values for the current period. We therefore have an index number which measures changes in prices over the period assuming that quantities remain fixed and equal to current period values.

We can calculate the Paasche price index number for the data in Table 12.4. From the formula given above we have:

$$\frac{100 \sum p_N q_N}{\sum p_0 q_N} = \frac{100 \times 4392}{4748} = 92.5$$

If the shares are given the weights of the current period, the result is that on average their prices fell by 7.5%.

This is in contrast to the Laspeyre price index number calculated in Section 12.3 which showed that the prices of the shares on average increased by 7.5%. The reason for the difference between these two results can be seen by comparing the weights in the two periods.

In the base period a large majority of shares was held in Distillers and Hanson Trust whose prices increased over the period, while in the current period a large majority was held in BOC and Boots whose prices decreased over the period. Consequently, the base weighted index records an increase and the current weighted index records a decrease (see Exercises 12.6 and 12.7).

## 12.5 Which weights?

In Sections 12.3 and 12.4 we used different weights in order to calculate different kinds of index numbers. We now need to consider if there is any reason for using weights in the base period in preference to weights in the current period or vice versa. In principle there is no way of choosing between them. The choice ultimately is determined by the questions asked by the researcher. In practice, however, Laspeyre indices are often preferred.

The reason for this is easily seen by referring to the formulae. To calculate a series of Laspeyre index numbers we require price and quantity information for the base period but only quantity information for each subsequent period. But to calculate a Paasche series both price and quantity data are required for every period in the series. Data collection is often expensive and if cost is an important factor in the research being conducted, base period weighted indices are often used in preference to indices weighted in the current period.

If data are available for the calculation of both Laspeyre and Paasche index numbers, we can combine the results by taking an average of the two. Thus we can calculate a compromise index number given by:

$$\frac{\text{Laspeyre } PIN + \text{Paasche } PIN}{2}$$

Alternatively we could calculate an index number called a *Fisher index number* which is a geometric average of the two given by:

$$\text{Fisher } PIN = \sqrt{(\text{Laspeyre } PIN)(\text{Paasche } PIN)}$$

See Exercise 12.9.

## 12.6 Disaggregation of indices

Sometimes it is possible to decompose an index number into separate components. To illustrate this we will refer once again to Table 12.1 where in column 3 we are given a series of index numbers for GDP valued at current prices. Each number given is a measure of the value of goods and services produced. Since value is equal to the product of price and quantity we are able to disaggregate the value indices into component price and quantity indices as follows:

$$\frac{\text{Value } IN}{100} = \frac{\Sigma p_N q_N}{\Sigma p_0 q_0}$$

Multiplying the right-hand side of the equation by $(\Sigma p_0 q_N / \Sigma p_0 q_N)$ gives:

$$\frac{\text{Value } IN}{100} = \frac{\Sigma p_N q_N}{\Sigma p_0 q_N} \times \frac{\Sigma p_0 q_N}{\Sigma p_0 q_0}$$

$$= \frac{\text{Paasche price index number}}{100} \times \frac{\text{Laspeyre quantity index number}}{100}$$

Our value index number has now been expressed as the product of a Paasche price index number and a Laspeyre quantity index number, the former being contained in column 4 of Table 12.1 and the latter being contained in column 6 of Table 12.1. Since the value index number is contained in column 3, we can say that:

$$\frac{\text{column 3}}{100} = \frac{\text{column 4}}{100} \times \frac{\text{column 6}}{100}$$

This can be confirmed for 1975 where:

$$\frac{46.1}{100} = \frac{50.0}{100} \times \frac{92.2}{100}$$

i.e. $0.461 = 0.5 \times 0.922$

See Exercises 12.3, 12.5 and 12.8.

# Exercises

**12.1** The data given below relate to the monthly averages of new registration of cars (measured in thousands) for the period 1968–78 in Great Britain.

| Year | New registration of cars |
|------|--------------------------|
| 1968 | 93.1  |
| 1969 | 82.3  |
| 1970 | 91.4  |
| 1971 | 108.5 |
| 1972 | 138.6 |
| 1973 | 137.1 |
| 1974 | 102.8 |
| 1975 | 97.2  |
| 1976 | 104.7 |
| 1977 | 107.1 |
| 1978 | 130.1 |

(a)  Use these figures to obtain index numbers based on 1968 = 100.
(b)  Using only the results obtained in (a) obtain index numbers based on 1973 = 100.
(c)  Using only the results obtained in (b) obtain index numbers based on 1978 = 100.
(d)  Use the figures given in the table to confirm your answers in (b) and (c).

**12.2** The various items listed below are the broad categories used in the construction of the retail price index for the UK.
(a)  Briefly discuss the changes in the patterns of the weights over the period. What effect are these changes likely to have on the calculation in (b)?
(b)  Calculate a Laspeyre and a Paasche price index number for the change in general retail prices over the period 1956 to 1962.

| | Price relative (Jan 1962 compared with Jan 1956) | Weight (Jan 1956) | Weight (Jan 1962) |
|---|---|---|---|
| Food | 110.7 | 350 | 319 |
| Alcoholic drink | 108.2 | 71 | 64 |
| Tobacco | 123.6 | 80 | 79 |
| Housing | 140.6 | 87 | 102 |
| Fuel and light | 130.6 | 55 | 62 |
| Durable household goods | 102.1 | 66 | 64 |
| Clothing and footwear | 106.6 | 106 | 98 |
| Transport and vehicles | 126.7 | 68 | 92 |
| Miscellaneous | 128.2 | 59 | 64 |
| Services | 130.1 | 58 | 56 |

**12.3** The figures below contain the prices and quantities of six commodities for each of three separate years:

| | 1970 | | 1975 | | 1980 | |
|---|---|---|---|---|---|---|
| Commodity | $p_0$ | $q_0$ | $p_1$ | $q_1$ | $p_2$ | $q_2$ |
| 1 | 35 | 4 | 39 | 5 | 50 | 7 |
| 2 | 12 | 8 | 14 | 10 | 15 | 19 |
| 3 | 3 | 12 | 5 | 18 | 8 | 20 |
| 4 | 21 | 3 | 22 | 4 | 29 | 5 |
| 5 | 41 | 8 | 44 | 10 | 51 | 11 |
| 6 | 73 | 2 | 75 | 2 | 80 | 3 |

(a) Calculate a Laspeyre price index number for 1975 and 1980 with 1970 as the base year.
(b) Calculate a Laspeyre price index number for 1980 with 1975 as the base year.
(c) Calculate a Laspeyre quantity index number for 1975 and 1980 with 1970 as the base year.
(d) Calculate a Laspeyre quantity index number for 1980 with 1975 as the base year.
(e) Calculate a Paasche price index number for 1975 and 1980 compared with 1970.
(f) Calculate a Paasche price index number for 1980 compared with 1975.
(g) Calculate a Paasche quantity index number for 1975 and 1980 compared with 1970.
(h) Calculate a Paasche quantity index number for 1980 compared with 1975.

**12.4** Briefly discuss the data below showing changes in the weights of selected items used in the construction of the UK index of retail prices.

| | All items | Food | Housing | Clothing & footwear | Transport & vehicles | Other |
|------|------|------|---------|---------------------|----------------------|-------|
| 1974 | 1000 | 253 | 124 | 91 | 135 | 397 |
| 1984 | 1000 | 201 | 149 | 70 | 158 | 422 |

*Annual Abstract of Statistics*, 1986

**12.5** The table below shows the price and number of shares held by an investor in six companies on 1 January and 22 June 1984.

| | 1 January 1984 | | 22 June 1984 | |
|--|----------------|--|--------------|--|
| | Price of share (p) | Number of shares held | Price of share (p) | Number of shares held |
| Associated Dairies | 150 | 5 | 164 | 8 |
| Imperial Group | 142 | 4 | 156 | 7 |
| Vickers | 137 | 6 | 162 | 8 |
| GKN | 177 | 5 | 172 | 3 |
| Boots | 180 | 6 | 170 | 4 |
| P and O | 168 | 3 | 220 | 6 |

(a)  Use these figures to calculate a Laspeyre quantity index number and a Paasche price index number.
(b)  Use the answers obtained in (a) to calculate the increase in the value of the investor's holding over the period. Explain and discuss.

**12.6**
(a)  What is an index number? Illustrate the ways in which index numbers can be used to measure changes in variables of interest in the social sciences.

| | Price per unit (p) | | Quantities per family | |
|------|------|------|------|------|
| Item | 1980 | 1983 | 1980 | 1983 |
| White bread | 40 | 50 | 6 | 2 |
| Brown bread | 44 | 46 | 1 | 5 |
| Coffee | 100 | 150 | 1 | 0 |
| Fruit juice | 40 | 42 | 0 | 3 |
| Meat | 150 | 300 | 2 | 1 |
| Cheese | 80 | 85 | 1 | 4 |

(b) Using the data at the foot of p. 158 calculate a base year weighted price index number and a current year weighted price index number measuring the average change in prices for all items. Discuss your results.

(c) What factors would you take into account when deciding whether any price index should be current year or base year weighted?

**12.7**

(a) Calculate a Paasche price index number for 1980 using the data given below. Briefly interpret your result.

| Item | Price per unit (p) 1979 | Price per unit (p) 1980 | Quantities 1979 | Quantities 1980 |
|------|------|------|------|------|
| A | 20 | 18 | 4 | 2 |
| B | 120 | 180 | 2 | 4 |
| C | 5 | 10 | 21 | 20 |
| D | 45 | 46 | 14 | 10 |
| E | 52 | 53 | 3 | 2 |
| F | 81 | 109 | 1 | 3 |
| G | 10 | 12 | 5 | 6 |

(b) By inspecting the data given say whether a Laspeyre price index number is likely to be higher or lower than the value calculated in (a). Give reasons for your answer. (You are not required to calculate the Laspeyre price index number.)

**12.8** The data given below are for imports of goods and services into the UK (M) at both current and constant prices for the period 1960-9.

| | M (£m) current prices | M (£m) constant (1963) prices |
|------|------|------|
| 1960 | 5554 | 5669 |
| 1961 | 5515 | 5628 |
| 1962 | 5604 | 5736 |
| 1963 | 5946 | 5946 |
| 1964 | 6711 | 6501 |
| 1965 | 6842 | 6545 |
| 1966 | 7095 | 6698 |
| 1967 | 7578 | 7099 |
| 1968 | 9048 | 7605 |
| 1969 | 9505 | 7784 |

(a) Calculate a Paasche price index number for each year.
(b) Calculate a Laspeyre quantity index number (1963 = 100) for each year.
(c) Use your results in (a) and (b) above to obtain an index number for each year (1963 = 100) showing changes in the value of imports of goods and services. Explain and discuss.
(d) Confirm the results obtained in (c) by expressing the current price figures given above in terms of 1963 = 100.

**12.9** An investor buys a total of twenty shares in the companies given below on 1 January 1984 and also on 22 June 1984.

| Company | 1 January 1984 | | 22 June 1984 | |
|---|---|---|---|---|
| | Price of share (p) | Number of shares bought | Price of share (p) | Number of shares bought |
| BOC | 296 | 10 | 240 | 1 |
| BICC | 254 | 6 | 225 | 2 |
| Distillers | 244 | 2 | 300 | 11 |
| P and O | 249 | 1 | 295 | 6 |
| Beecham | 305 | 1 | 305 | 0 |

(a) Calculate a base year weighted index number and a current year weighted index number which measure the average increase in the price of shares bought by the investor.
(b) Why are the answers obtained in (a) so different? Discuss.
(c) How would you use your results to obtain a single index number which measures the average increase in the price of the investor's shares? Discuss.

**12.10** Express the figures in column 2 of Table 12.1 in index number form with:
(a) 1977 = 100
(b) 1984 = 100

**12.11** Use the data in Table 12.2 to obtain index numbers for commodity prices in 1984 using oats as the base commodity.

# Appendix

# Appendix A   Standard normal distribution

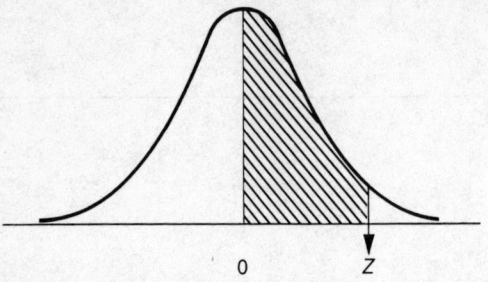

| Z | 0.00 | 0.01 | 0.02 | 0.03 | 0.04 | 0.05 | 0.06 | 0.07 | 0.08 | 0.09 |
|-----|-------|-------|-------|-------|-------|-------|-------|-------|-------|-------|
| 0.0 | .0000 | .0040 | .0080 | .0120 | .0160 | .0199 | .0239 | .0279 | .0319 | .0359 |
| 0.1 | .0398 | .0438 | .0478 | .0517 | .0557 | .0596 | .0636 | .0675 | .0714 | .0753 |
| 0.2 | .0793 | .0832 | .0871 | .0910 | .0948 | .0987 | .1026 | .1064 | .1103 | .1141 |
| 0.3 | .1179 | .1217 | .1255 | .1293 | .1331 | .1368 | .1406 | .1443 | .1480 | .1517 |
| 0.4 | .1554 | .1591 | .1628 | .1664 | .1700 | .1736 | .1772 | .1808 | .1844 | .1879 |
| 0.5 | .1915 | .1950 | .1985 | .2019 | .2054 | .2088 | .2123 | .2157 | .2190 | .2224 |
| 0.6 | .2257 | .2291 | .2324 | .2357 | .2389 | .2422 | .2454 | .2486 | .2517 | .2549 |
| 0.7 | .2580 | .2611 | .2642 | .2673 | .2703 | .2734 | .2764 | .2794 | .2823 | .2852 |
| 0.8 | .2881 | .2910 | .2939 | .2967 | .2995 | .3023 | .3051 | .3078 | .3106 | .3133 |
| 0.9 | .3159 | .3186 | .3212 | .3238 | .3264 | .3289 | .3315 | .3340 | .3365 | .3389 |
| 1.0 | .3413 | .3438 | .3461 | .3485 | .3508 | .3531 | .3554 | .3577 | .3599 | .3621 |
| 1.1 | .3643 | .3665 | .3686 | .3708 | .3729 | .3749 | .3770 | .3790 | .3810 | .3830 |
| 1.2 | .3849 | .3869 | .3888 | .3907 | .3925 | .3944 | .3962 | .3980 | .3997 | .4015 |
| 1.3 | .4032 | .4049 | .4066 | .4082 | .4099 | .4115 | .4131 | .4147 | .4162 | .4177 |
| 1.4 | .4192 | .4207 | .4222 | .4236 | .4251 | .4265 | .4279 | .4292 | .4306 | .4319 |
| 1.5 | .4332 | .4345 | .4357 | .4370 | .4382 | .4394 | .4406 | .4418 | .4429 | .4441 |
| 1.6 | .4452 | .4463 | .4474 | .4484 | .4495 | .4505 | .4515 | .4525 | .4535 | .4545 |
| 1.7 | .4554 | .4564 | .4573 | .4582 | .4591 | .4599 | .4608 | .4616 | .4625 | .4633 |
| 1.8 | .4641 | .4649 | .4656 | .4664 | .4671 | .4678 | .4686 | .4693 | .4699 | .4706 |
| 1.9 | .4713 | .4719 | .4726 | .4732 | .4738 | .4744 | .4750 | .4756 | .4761 | .4767 |
| 2.0 | .4772 | .4778 | .4783 | .4788 | .4793 | .4798 | .4803 | .4808 | .4812 | .4817 |
| 2.1 | .4821 | .4826 | .4830 | .4834 | .4838 | .4842 | .4846 | .4850 | .4854 | .4857 |
| 2.2 | .4861 | .4864 | .4868 | .4871 | .4875 | .4878 | .4881 | .4884 | .4887 | .4890 |
| 2.3 | .4893 | .4896 | .4898 | .4901 | .4904 | .4906 | .4909 | .4911 | .4913 | .4916 |
| 2.4 | .4918 | .4920 | .4922 | .4925 | .4927 | .4929 | .4931 | .4932 | .4934 | .4936 |
| 2.5 | .4938 | .4940 | .4941 | .4943 | .4945 | .4946 | .4948 | .4949 | .4951 | .4952 |
| 2.6 | .4953 | .4955 | .4956 | .4957 | .4959 | .4960 | .4961 | .4962 | .4963 | .4964 |
| 2.7 | .4965 | .4966 | .4967 | .4968 | .4969 | .4970 | .4971 | .4972 | .4973 | .4974 |
| 2.8 | .4974 | .4975 | .4976 | .4977 | .4977 | .4978 | .4979 | .4979 | .4980 | .4981 |
| 2.9 | .4981 | .4982 | .4982 | .4983 | .4984 | .4984 | .4985 | .4985 | .4986 | .4986 |
| 3.0 | .4987 | .4987 | .4987 | .4988 | .4988 | .4989 | .4889 | .4889 | .4990 | .4990 |

The value in the body of the table is the proportion of the area under the curve between $Z = 0$ and the value of $Z$ given by the first column and first row.

# Appendix B  *t* distribution

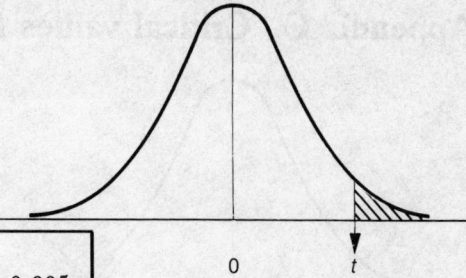

| P<br>ν | 0.10 | 0.05 | 0.025 | 0.01 | 0.005 |
|---|---|---|---|---|---|
| 1 | 3.078 | 6.314 | 12.706 | 31.821 | 63.657 |
| 2 | 1.886 | 2.920 | 4.303 | 6.965 | 9.925 |
| 3 | 1.638 | 2.353 | 3.182 | 4.541 | 5.841 |
| 4 | 1.533 | 2.132 | 2.776 | 3.747 | 4.604 |
| 5 | 1.476 | 2.015 | 2.571 | 3.365 | 4.032 |
| 6 | 1.440 | 1.943 | 2.447 | 3.143 | 3.707 |
| 7 | 1.415 | 1.895 | 2.365 | 2.998 | 3.499 |
| 8 | 1.397 | 1.860 | 2.306 | 2.896 | 3.355 |
| 9 | 1.383 | 1.833 | 2.262 | 2.821 | 3.250 |
| 10 | 1.372 | 1.812 | 2.228 | 2.764 | 3.169 |
| 11 | 1.363 | 1.796 | 2.201 | 2.718 | 3.106 |
| 12 | 1.356 | 1.782 | 2.179 | 2.681 | 3.055 |
| 13 | 1.350 | 1.771 | 2.160 | 2.650 | 3.012 |
| 14 | 1.345 | 1.761 | 2.145 | 2.624 | 2.977 |
| 15 | 1.341 | 1.753 | 2.131 | 2.602 | 2.947 |
| 16 | 1.337 | 1.746 | 2.120 | 2.583 | 2.921 |
| 17 | 1.333 | 1.740 | 2.110 | 2.567 | 2.898 |
| 18 | 1.330 | 1.734 | 2.101 | 2.552 | 2.878 |
| 19 | 1.328 | 1.729 | 2.093 | 2.539 | 2.861 |
| 20 | 1.325 | 1.725 | 2.086 | 2.528 | 2.845 |
| 21 | 1.323 | 1.721 | 2.080 | 2.518 | 2.831 |
| 22 | 1.321 | 1.717 | 2.074 | 2.508 | 2.819 |
| 23 | 1.319 | 1.714 | 2.069 | 2.500 | 2.807 |
| 24 | 1.318 | 1.711 | 2.064 | 2.492 | 2.797 |
| 25 | 1.316 | 1.708 | 2.060 | 2.485 | 2.787 |
| 26 | 1.315 | 1.706 | 2.056 | 2.479 | 2.779 |
| 27 | 1.314 | 1.703 | 2.052 | 2.473 | 2.771 |
| 28 | 1.313 | 1.701 | 2.048 | 2.467 | 2.763 |
| 29 | 1.311 | 1.699 | 2.045 | 2.462 | 2.756 |
| 30 | 1.310 | 1.697 | 2.042 | 2.457 | 2.750 |
| 40 | 1.303 | 1.684 | 2.021 | 2.423 | 2.704 |
| 60 | 1.296 | 1.671 | 2.000 | 2.390 | 2.660 |
| 120 | 1.289 | 1.658 | 1.980 | 2.358 | 2.617 |
| ∞ | 1.282 | 1.645 | 1.960 | 2.326 | 2.576 |

The first column gives degrees of freedom. The heading at the top
of each remaining column is the probability level for the shaded area
in the diagram.

# Appendix C   Critical values for linear correlation coefficient, *r*

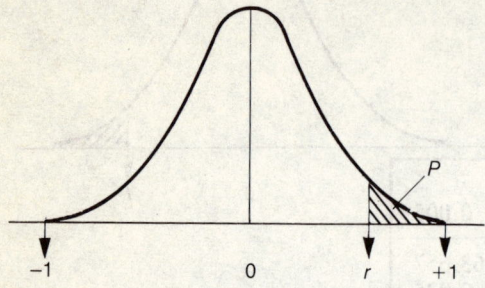

| N \ P | 0.05 | 0.025 | 0.005 |
|---|---|---|---|
| 5 | .805 | .878 | .959 |
| 6 | .729 | .811 | .917 |
| 7 | .669 | .754 | .875 |
| 8 | .621 | .707 | .834 |
| 9 | .582 | .666 | .798 |
| 10 | .549 | .632 | .765 |
| 11 | .521 | .602 | .735 |
| 12 | .497 | .576 | .708 |
| 13 | .476 | .553 | .684 |
| 14 | .457 | .532 | .661 |
| 15 | .441 | .514 | .641 |
| 16 | .426 | .497 | .623 |

| N \ P | 0.05 | 0.025 | 0.005 |
|---|---|---|---|
| 17 | .412 | .482 | .606 |
| 18 | .400 | .468 | .590 |
| 19 | .389 | .456 | .575 |
| 20 | .378 | .444 | .561 |
| 25 | .337 | .396 | .505 |
| 30 | .306 | .361 | .463 |
| 35 | .283 | .334 | .430 |
| 40 | .264 | .312 | .402 |
| 50 | .235 | .279 | .361 |
| 60 | .214 | .254 | .330 |
| 80 | .185 | .220 | .286 |
| 100 | .165 | .196 | .256 |

The values of *r* in the table are for a one-tail test based on the null hypothesis $\rho = 0$.

## Appendix D Critical values for Spearman's rank correlation coefficient, $r_s$

| N | Level of significance | | | N | Level of significance | |
|---|---|---|---|---|---|---|
| | 0.05 | 0.01 | | | 0.05 | 0.01 |
| 5 | 1.00 | — | | 18 | 0.48 | 0.61 |
| 6 | 0.89 | 1.00 | | 19 | 0.46 | 0.60 |
| 7 | 0.79 | 0.93 | | 20 | 0.45 | 0.58 |
| 8 | 0.74 | 0.88 | | | | |
| 9 | 0.68 | 0.83 | | 21 | 0.44 | 0.56 |
| 10 | 0.65 | 0.79 | | 22 | 0.43 | 0.55 |
| | | | | 23 | 0.42 | 0.54 |
| 11 | 0.61 | 0.77 | | 24 | 0.41 | 0.53 |
| 12 | 0.59 | 0.75 | | 25 | 0.40 | 0.52 |
| 13 | 0.56 | 0.71 | | | | |
| 14 | 0.54 | 0.69 | | 26 | 0.39 | 0.51 |
| 15 | 0.52 | 0.66 | | 27 | 0.38 | 0.50 |
| | | | | 28 | 0.38 | 0.49 |
| 16 | 0.51 | 0.64 | | 29 | 0.37 | 0.48 |
| 17 | 0.49 | 0.62 | | 30 | 0.36 | 0.47 |

The values of $r_s$ in the table are for a two-tail test based on the null hypothesis $\rho_s = 0$.

# Appendix E   Critical Values of $U$ for the Mann–Whitney test

| $N_1$ \ $N_2$ | 5 | 6 | 7 | 8 | 9 | 10 | 11 | 12 | 13 | 14 | 15 | 16 | 17 | 18 | 19 | 20 |
|---|---|---|---|---|---|---|---|---|---|---|---|---|---|---|---|---|
| 5 | 2 | 3 | 5 | 6 | 7 | 8 | 9 | 11 | 12 | 13 | 14 | 15 | 17 | 18 | 19 | 20 |
| 6 |  | 5 | 6 | 8 | 10 | 11 | 13 | 14 | 16 | 17 | 19 | 21 | 22 | 24 | 25 | 27 |
| 7 |  |  | 8 | 10 | 12 | 14 | 16 | 18 | 20 | 22 | 24 | 26 | 28 | 30 | 32 | 34 |
| 8 |  |  |  | 13 | 15 | 17 | 19 | 22 | 24 | 26 | 29 | 31 | 34 | 36 | 38 | 41 |
| 9 |  |  |  |  | 17 | 20 | 23 | 26 | 28 | 31 | 34 | 37 | 39 | 42 | 45 | 48 |
| 10 |  |  |  |  |  | 23 | 26 | 29 | 33 | 36 | 39 | 42 | 45 | 48 | 52 | 55 |
| 11 |  |  |  |  |  |  | 30 | 33 | 37 | 40 | 44 | 47 | 51 | 55 | 58 | 62 |
| 12 |  |  |  |  |  |  |  | 37 | 41 | 45 | 49 | 53 | 57 | 61 | 65 | 69 |
| 13 |  |  |  |  |  |  |  |  | 45 | 50 | 54 | 59 | 63 | 67 | 72 | 76 |
| 14 |  |  |  |  |  |  |  |  |  | 55 | 59 | 64 | 67 | 74 | 78 | 83 |
| 15 |  |  |  |  |  |  |  |  |  |  | 64 | 70 | 75 | 80 | 85 | 90 |
| 16 |  |  |  |  |  |  |  |  |  |  |  | 75 | 81 | 86 | 92 | 98 |
| 17 |  |  |  |  |  |  |  |  |  |  |  |  | 87 | 93 | 99 | 105 |
| 18 |  |  |  |  |  |  |  |  |  |  |  |  |  | 99 | 106 | 112 |
| 19 |  |  |  |  |  |  |  |  |  |  |  |  |  |  | 113 | 119 |
| 20 |  |  |  |  |  |  |  |  |  |  |  |  |  |  |  | 127 |

The critical values of $U$ in the table are for a two-tail test at the 5% level of significance.

# Appendix F   Critical values of $T$ for the Wilcoxon test

| $N$ \ Level of significance | 0.05 | 0.02 | 0.01 |
|---|---|---|---|
| 6 | 0 | — | — |
| 7 | 2 | 0 | — |
| 8 | 4 | 2 | 0 |
| 9 | 6 | 3 | 2 |
| 10 | 8 | 5 | 3 |
| 11 | 11 | 7 | 5 |
| 12 | 14 | 10 | 7 |
| 13 | 17 | 13 | 10 |
| 14 | 21 | 16 | 13 |
| 15 | 25 | 20 | 16 |

| $N$ \ Level of significance | 0.05 | 0.02 | 0.01 |
|---|---|---|---|
| 16 | 30 | 24 | 20 |
| 17 | 35 | 28 | 23 |
| 18 | 40 | 33 | 28 |
| 19 | 46 | 38 | 32 |
| 20 | 52 | 43 | 38 |
| 21 | 59 | 49 | 43 |
| 22 | 66 | 56 | 49 |
| 23 | 73 | 62 | 55 |
| 24 | 81 | 69 | 61 |
| 25 | 89 | 77 | 68 |

The critical values of $T$ in the table are for a two-tail test.

# Index